QUANTITY RECIPES

FROM MEALS FOR MANY*

MARION A. WOOD

KATHARINE W. HARRIS

*MEALS FOR MANY

(Cornell Extension Bulletin 477)

Now out of print

A publication of the
New York State College of Home Economics,
a unit of the State University of New York,
at Cornell University

FOREWORD

The recipes for 50 and basic guides for quantity food preparation here presented are planned to serve small institutions, schools, camps and community groups. The material is a revision of the recipe section of *Meals for Many,* Extension Bulletin 477, and replaces it.

CONTENTS

4

5

QUANTITY RECIPES
from MEALS FOR MANY

FOOD PREPARATION GUIDES

SELECTION AND INTERPRETATION OF QUANTITY RECIPES

Use standardized recipes which can be depended upon to give uniform results.

Know the size of the serving and the number you can get from the recipe.

Do not multiply a family-size recipe many times or break down a large quantity one too far. Mathematical errors may result or slight discrepancies in the original recipe be exaggerated to the extent of spoiling the product.

Enlarge or reduce a standardized quantity recipe as required before you use it or give it to a worker to use. Check the figures carefully, adjusting unusual fractions and making the necessary conversions. Change fractions of less than one-half to the next smaller whole unit of weight or measure, that is, express ¼ gallon as 1 quart or ⅝ pound as 10 ounces.

Use a simple recipe form and see that it includes everything that is needed. Be sure that:

(1) Ingredients are adequately described and listed in the order of their use

(2) Abbreviations are *not* used unless they are interpreted.

(3) Amounts are expressed in both measures and weights

(4) Steps in the recipe are numbered in order of performance and clearly worded with specific information as to:

    (a) Temperature and cooking time

    (b) Amount of mixtures to be put in pans or cooked at one time

    (c) Time at which product must be ready

    (d) How it is to be kept hot or cold if some time must elapse before serving

    (e) How it is to be cut or otherwise apportioned accurately

Determine the standard for each product to be prepared.

Plan the equipment needed and the organization of work.

Taste the finished product before it is served. Adjust seasonings as needed.

OVEN TEMPERATURES

Term	Temperature in degrees Farenheit
Slow	250 to 300
Very moderate	300 to 325
Moderate	325 to 375
Moderately hot	375 to 400
Hot	400 to 450
Very hot	450 to 500

EQUIVALENT MEASURES

1 pinch = $^1/_{16}$ teaspoon
1 tablespoon = 3 teaspoons
1 cup = 16 tablespoons
⅞ cup = 1 cup less 2 tablespoons
¾ cup = 12 tablespoons
⅔ cup = 10 tablespoons plus 2 teaspoons
½ cup = 8 tablespoons
⅓ cup = 5 tablespoons plus 1 teaspoon
¼ cup = 4 tablespoons
⅛ cup = 2 tablespoons

1 quart = { 4 cups or 2 pints
1 gallon = { 4 quarts or 16 cups
1 peck = 8 quarts
1 bushel = { 4 pecks or 32 quarts
1 pound = 16 ounces

AIDS TO ACCURATE MEASURING

Weight *is more accurate than is volume for the measurement of ingredients other than liquids;* but, if the ingredients are measured by volume, the use of suitable equipment and accepted procedures help to obtain good results. These are the following:

Use measures of standard capacity.

To measure fractions of a cup, use individual measures of ¼, ⅓, and ½ cup. Likewise, use measures of ¼, ½, and 1 teaspoon and a tablespoon for those amounts (figure 1c). Level the measures with the edge of a knife or spatula. Graduated quart measures and a graduated gallon measure should be among the equipment used in quantity cooking.

A   B   C

FIGURE 1.   WEIGHING AND MEASURING EQUIPMENT

A Balance scales for weigh-   B. Spring-balance scales   C. Measures:
ing small or large quan-   for quick weighing   Graduated: 1-gallon, 2-quart, 1-quart, 1-cup
tities   Individual: 1-cup, ½-cup, ⅓-cup, ¼-cup
                                                  1-tablespoon, 1-teaspoon,
                                                  ½-teaspoon, ¼-teaspoon

Sift flour just before using it. In measuring flour, it should be piled lightly into the measure with a scoop or spoon and the top leveled off with the edge of a spatula or knife; it should not be packed or leveled by shaking, neither should the measure be filled by dipping it into the flour. One pound of sifted flour, when accurately measured, makes 4 cups.

Pack fat tightly into the measure; fractions of cups of fat are best measured in individual cups of the capacity needed (figure 1c). One pound of butter measures 2 cups, while 1 pound of hydrogenated fat and lard measures from $2\frac{1}{3}$ to $2\frac{1}{2}$ cups.

Pack brown sugar tightly enough to hold the shape of the measure when turned out; any lumps should be softened before measuring, either by rolling them out or placing the lumpy sugar in a *slow* oven until just softened. One pound of brown sugar when packed measures about $2\frac{1}{4}$ cups.

TEMPERATURE OF INGREDIENTS

Ingredients for batters and doughs should be at room temperature at the time of mixing. Eggs, milk, and shortening should be removed from the refrigerator in sufficient time to bring them to room temperature before they are mixed.

INGREDIENTS

Baking Powders

A slow acting baking powder is best for large amounts of batters and doughs because the mixing and handling take somewhat longer than does the handling of small amounts. The recipes in this book use this type of baking powder. If quick-acting baking powders are used, the measure should be increased one-third.

Flour, Enriched

In recipes calling for white flour, enriched flour is recommended. Enriched flour is white flour containing specific amounts of iron, niacin, thiamine, and riboflavin. Many states require that all flour be enriched.

Flour, Soybean

Soybean flour may be used to replace small amounts of white flour to increase nutritive value. Baked products containing soybean flour keep moist longer. Because its composition and properties differ from those of ordinary flour, recipes adapted to its use result in more satisfactory products.

9

Sour Milk

Soda and sour milk or buttermilk may be substituted for sweet milk and some of the baking powder. An equal quantity of medium-sour milk or buttermilk may replace the sweet milk. For each cup of sour milk, ½ teaspoon of soda is added and only one-half the amount of baking powder called for in the recipe is used.

Dried Milk

Whole dry milk is the powdered form of whole milk from which only water has been removed. It may be used in place of whole fresh milk for cooking and for making milk beverages. Because of its fat content it must be stored carefully, usually under refrigeration.

Nonfat dry milk is the powdered form of skim milk, the water and fat having been removed from whole milk. Nonfat dry milk is used in place of skim milk and may be made the equivalent of whole milk by adding butter in proportions equal to the amount removed in processing (1½ ounces or 3 tablespoons for each quart of reliquified milk). However, the important factor in using nonfat dry milk is to increase the nutritive value of the diet. There are two ways to do this: 1) In recipes that call for whole milk you can use milk solids in addition to the whole milk, or 2) you can use milk solids instead of the whole milk but increase the proportions of the milk solids.

Most dry milk used is the nonfat kind. It should be stored in a cool dry place. It should not be exposed to air and should be tightly covered to prevent lumpiness and unpleasant changes in flavor.

Nonfat dry milk may be used in two ways: 1) You may reconstitute it with water for use as a beverage or in such dishes as soups, gravies, sauces, and custards or 2) you may mix the powder with the dry ingredients in baked products and use the water for reconstitution in place of the fluid milk called for in the recipe. One cup (4 ounces) of nonfat dry milk plus one quart of water equals about 1 quart of fluid skim milk. A higher proportion of nonfat dry milk (up to 6 ounces per quart) may be used to increase the nutritive value. For best results, use tested recipes.

To reconstitute or reliquify nonfat dry milk, sprinkle it on top of warm water and beat well with a rotary beater, wire whip, or power mixer. If you do not use it immediately, store it in the refrigerator. Since it scorches easily, cook reliquified dry milk over hot water, not over direct heat. The flavor of the reconstituted milk is improved if it can be prepared several hours before it is needed.

It is more accurate to weigh dry milk than to measure it. If you have to measure the dry milk, first stir with a spoon, then lift lightly into a measuring cup, leveling off the top. Recipes using dried milk are given in the list of references.

Dried Eggs

Dried whole eggs are eggs which have been removed from the shell and have then had most of the water removed. They have approximately the same nutritive value as shell eggs.

Dried eggs should be kept cool and dry. Dried eggs not packaged in air-tight cans should be stored in tightly covered containers. Store under refrigeration to prevent the development of off-flavors and a greyish tinge.

Use dried eggs only in thoroughly cooked dishes as baked breads, escalloped dishes, and baked desserts. They are unsatisfactory for use in egg-milk drinks, mayonnaise, omelets, scrambled eggs, cream puddings, or fillings, soft custards, ice creams, or cooked salad dressing.

It is more accurate to weigh dried eggs than to measure them. The following proportions are equivalent to shell eggs:

½ ounce (2 tablespoons firmly packed) dried egg + 2½ tablespoons water = 1 large whole egg

6 ounces (1½ cups firmly packed) dried egg + 2 cups water = 12 large eggs

Whole dried eggs may be used in recipes in 2 ways: 1) they may be reconstituted with the water or 2) they may be sifted with the dry ingredients and the water for reconstitution combined with the other liquid in batter and dough recipes.

To reconstitute dried eggs, sift the powder. Use cold or barely lukewarm water — never hot. Pour one-third of the water in a deep bowl, add the powder, and blend until smooth with a rotary beater, wire whip, or power mixer. Add remaining water and beat until well blended. Reconstituted eggs deteriorate as do fresh eggs removed from the shell and should be refrigerated. It is best to reconstitute only the amount to be used at one time.

Recipes using dried eggs are given in the list of references.

Frozen Eggs

Frozen eggs are available as whole eggs, egg yolks and egg whites. Frozen egg yolks contain added ingredients to increase their keeping qualities and to produce cakes of higher quality. These frozen products may be used in place of equal weights of fresh beaten whole eggs, egg yolks, or egg whites. These equivalents are given in the cake recipes in this bulletin. Thawed whites may be whipped in the same way as are fresh egg whites.

Frozen eggs should be thawed carefully. They may be thawed for from 18 to 24 hours in a refrigerator, or thawing may be hastened by setting the cans in a container of cool running water, but never in hot water or an oven. After thawing, the cans of eggs should be stirred thoroughly. Thawed eggs are very perishable. They should be used up quickly and should be refrigerated to prevent bacterial growth.

Chocolate and Cocoa

One 1-ounce square of chocolate is equal to 3 tablespoons of cocoa and 1 tablespoon of fat.

Fats

Fats differ somewhat in their shortening power. The following are approximately equal in shortening power to 1 pound (2 cups) of butter: 1 pound (2 cups) of margarine; ⅘ pound (about 2 cups) hydrogenated fat; ⅘ pound (about 2 cups) lard; ⅞ pound of chicken fat.

The desired flavor of the product and the cost should be considered in choosing the fat to be used.

COOKING MILK, CHEESE, AND EGGS

FIGURE 2. THE THICKENING OF SAUCES AND GRAVIES MADE EASY

The melted fat and the flour are first cooked together, then poured into the hot liquid and cooked until thickened. Stirring with a wire whip throughout prevents lumping; cooking over hot water prevents scorching

Milk needs special care in cooking, to prevent scorching. One method is to cook it in a hot-water bath; that is, in a double boiler or in a pan set in another pan of hot water (figure 2). A low temperature and the use of a heavy aluminum utensil will help to prevent scorching when milk is cooked over direct heat.

Cheese, when combined with other ingredients in a recipe, is usually ground, grated or chopped by hand or in an electric grinder, grater, or chopper. Cheese should be cooked at a low temperature because cooking at a high temperature for a long period results in a curdled product that may be stringy and tough.

Eggs should be cooked at a low or moderate temperature; a high

12

temperature toughens the product. When eggs are used to thicken liquids, the mixture is generally cooked over hot water kept just below the boiling point to prevent curdling or separation of the liquid.

When you make egg dishes such as scrambled eggs, baked custard, and custard sauce, you will get a better product if you divide the batches and cook them in small amounts.

To hard cook eggs on a range put only 2 or 3 dozen eggs in one container. Cover them with cold water, bring to simmering temperature, and cook over low heat for from 10 to 15 minutes. Drain off the hot water and cover the eggs with cold water. Remove the shells.

COOKING MACARONI, SPAGHETTI, AND NOODLES

Cook macaroni, spaghetti, and noodles in a large amount of water; then drain in a colander, rinse quickly with water, and place over hot water or in an oven to keep hot. With this method of cooking the product remains in separate pieces that are not gummy or pasty.

COOKING RICE

Rice, also, should remain in separate cooked grains. The newer type of rice which is called converted rice, keeps for long periods without danger of weevil infestation. Converted rice cooks so that each grain remains separate and stays in this condition whether you keep it warm for serving or refrigerated. It may be cooked in a steamer in just enough water to swell the rice. Wash the uncooked rice well. To each pound of rice add 1¼ quarts of water and 1 tablespoon of salt, cover and steam until tender, about 35 minutes. This makes about 2½ quarts of cooked rice.

Another new product on the market is quick-cooking or precooked rice which requires only about 1 minute's boiling and 10 minutes covered in a container.

PREPARING CREAMED AND ESCALLOPED DISHES

Many combinations are possible in creamed and escalloped dishes. A medium cream sauce is used in combination with foods that usually have been cooked previously to creaming and escalloping. Minced ham, cheddar cheese, herbs, and many other seasonings make possible countless flavor variations.

For creamed dishes the ingredients may be folded carefully into the cream sauce and combined as needed. To add interest and to facilitate serving foods that break up easily, such as asparagus spears, the food to be creamed may be arranged on the toast and the cream sauce poured

13

over all, or it may be added to each portion as served. Toast is only one base on which creamed foods may be served; there are a variety of items: toasted rolls; patty shells; squares of cornbread; baking powder biscuits; baked, mashed, or boiled potatoes; boiled noodles, rice, or macaroni (2½ pounds before cooking for 50 servings); fried (Chinese) noodles (2 pounds for 50 servings). The creamed mixture should be heated throughout before it is served. Heating over hot water as in a double boiler prevents scorching.

For escalloped dishes, foods are usually placed in baking pans or casseroles in layers with cream sauce usually ending with a layer of cream sauce. There are a variety of toppings. The following amounts are proportions for 50 servings: 1 quart of buttered or plain chopped bread; 1½ quarts of bread cubes; 2 quarts coarse cracker crumbs; 2 cups potato chips; 1½ cups cornflakes or other flake cereals; 1 cup soybean flakes; 3 to 4 quarts mashed white or sweet potatoes. Grated or chopped cheese may be mixed with soft bread crumbs for the topping. A moderate oven (350° F.) is used for baking for a length of time sufficient to heat the mixture throughout and to brown the top; the time varies from 20 to 30 minutes or longer depending on the temperature of the ingredients when the mixture is put into the oven.

A raw vegetable garnish added just before serving may consist of a tomato slice, a pepper ring, a parsley sprig or chopped parsley, chopped carrots or green pepper. A crisp bacon slice or chopped crisp bacon or salt pork may be used as a garnish with some escalloped dishes.

DEEP FAT FRYING[1]

Serving fried foods

Deep-fat fried foods are most commonly used where they are cooked to order, and are best when served right from the kettle. However, under certain conditions they may be used in cafeteria service where small quantities are fried throughout the meal. Fried foods may also be served where large numbers are fed at one time such as in dormitories or at banquets. However, it is important that these foods be kept hot under proper conditions. Usually this consists of frying the foods ahead of time, arranging the fried pieces, loosely stacked on brown paper in flat pans, and keeping them warm in a slow oven about 250° F.

Equipment

Equipment which provides thermostatic temperature control and a cool space, where the excess crumbs may collect without burning, produces superior fried foods. Such equipment should be easy to clean.

---

[1]Adapted from *Deep Frying Pointers*, Proctor & Gamble Research Bulletin.

Two smaller units are preferable to one larger frier because in the small units foods cook and brown more uniformly and less fat is required.

The frying fat

The fat for frying should have a smoking point above the temperature recommended for frying the particular food; fat should never be heated above 400° F. It should be bland so that it will impart no flavor of its own to the food. It should not absorb flavors readily or become rancid with continued use.

Care of fat and equipment

When you fry foods in deep fat, use small amounts of fat in the kettle — the kettle should be about one-half full — and add fresh fat as needed.

An accumulation of burnt food particles in the fat will cause the fat to spoil sooner than it would otherwise. Remove this accumulation each day by straining the fat through several thicknesses of cheesecloth. For a clearer fat, draw it off into a separate container and after it has cooled to below 212° F., sprinkle the surface with water. The water in settling to the bottom carries down the very fine particles of burnt food that have been suspended throughout the fat. The clear fat can then either be poured off the sludge of water and burnt particles, or the water and sediment can be drawn off from the bottom of the container through the outlet.

Frying kettles should be cleaned at least once a week. If they are used continually, daily cleaning is recommended. Scrub the cool kettles with a wire brush (fine wire) and plenty of hot water and a good detergent. (A trisodium phosphate solution, 2 ounces per gallon of water, may be used.) Rinse thoroughly with clear water and dry the kettle.

Complete replacement of the frying fat can be judged only by test-tasting the fried foods.

Steps in deep-fat frying

Prepare the foods for frying.

Foods such as meat cuts, fish fillets, chicken pieces, are usually dipped in a frying batter of seasoned milk-egg-flour and placed immediately into the hot fat or they may be dipped in a seasoned water-egg or milk-egg mixture and rolled in flour, crumbs, or cornmeal. Foods with a moist surface such as oysters are first dipped in crumbs, then in the egg mixture and again in crumbs. Croquette mixtures should be chilled before they are shaped and then rolled in crumbs.

15

Have foods free from surplus crumbs and moisture. Bring foods to room temperature before you fry them to avoid lowering the temperature of the fat too much. Fry pieces of similar size at the same time; in general, small pieces should be fried at a higher temperature than large pieces. Large pieces such as sliced egg plant should be fried in amounts to make only one layer deep.

Frying information is given in the Deep-Fat Frying Chart below. The frying times will vary depending on the size of the food pieces and the amount of food fried at one time. Large pieces require a longer frying time than small pieces. If the frying kettles are overloaded, the frying temperatures may drop so low that a much longer frying time will be necessary than that given in the chart, with the result that the foods become grease soaked and unappetizing. The person operating the kettle needs to determine the amount of food that may be added without causing a temperature drop of not over 40° F.

Deep-Fat Frying Chart*

Food	Temperature†	Time
French fried potatoes		
Complete frying (in one operation)	380–385° F.	7–8 minutes
Blanching	380–385° F.	5–6 minutes
Browning	380–385° F.	2–3 minutes
Fish		
Fillets	365–370° F.	3–5 minutes
Oysters, large	355–360° F.	2–4 minutes
Scallops	355–360° F.	3–5 minutes
Chicken		
Straight-through single frying	300–325° F.	14–16 minutes
Browned-off method for precooked chicken	350–375° F.	5–6 minutes
Cutlets and chops		
(1 inch thick)	345–350° F.	5–8 minutes
Croquettes	370–375° F.	2–3 minutes
French fried onions	340–345° F.	5–6 minutes
Fritters	370–375° F.	3–5 minutes
Vegetables: egg plant, cauliflower, asparagus	375–380° F.	5–7 minutes
Doughnuts		
Cake type	375–390° F.	1¼–2 minutes
Yeast raised	360–370° F.	1¼–2 minutes

*Adapted from *Deep Frying Pointers*, Proctor and Gamble Research Bulletin, and *Chicken Frying, Four Methods*, Poultry and Egg National Board.
†The frying fat should be heated to the above temperatures before the foods are added.
Note: Temperatures and times are based on average size batches of food.

OBTAINING UNIFORM SERVINGS

Use standard recipes and check the number of servings obtained. A few recording devices for checking servings are the following:

A multi-counter is a machine on which many items may be checked at the same time by means of levers; each time a lever is pressed a serving of a certain item is recorded, and the total may be noted at any time.

A check sheet has all items listed, to be checked by pencil as each is served.

Individual serving dishes, distinctive for each item, may be counted before serving; this method is not used in cafeterias where several items are offered on identical dishes.

Counting the number of servings of pies, cakes, sliced meat loaf, individual casseroles, bottled milk, rolls, and the like before the meal is served and deducting the number left, checks the number served. Such items as crackers and cookies may be apportioned according to their count to the pound.

Divide the food into servings before cooking whenever possible; some meats and some vegetables may be cut, divided, or counted into servings before they are cooked (figure 3); individual casseroles, containing standard amounts may be used for cooking and serving foods such as escalloped dishes, baked beans, meat pies (figure 3, B); some desserts may be prepared in individual portions such as tarts, cup cakes, dumplings, and custards.

Use standard pans for which the number of servings has been established; fill pans uniformly full (figure 3, B and F).

Meat or fish loaves or loaf cake may be baked in Pullman or sandwich loaf pans and sliced into a specific number of servings (figure 3, D).

Layer-cake tins and pie tins of standard diameter and depth yield standard servings of cake or pie.

FIGURE 3. STANDARDIZED SERVINGS

A. Apple rings cut before baking
B. Casseroles containing equal amounts
C. Creamed peas served with a half-cup ladle
D. Meat loaf cut into the desired number of slices
E. Mashed squash served with an ice-cream scoop
F. Meat pie in a standard baking pan and cut into standard servings
G. Buttered lima beans served with a slotted spoon
H. Utensils for cutting and servings
I. Cabbage wedges cut before cooking
J. Attractive plate arrangement showing standard servings

17

Baking pans, not too deep (figure 3, F), may be used to obtain equal portions of hot puddings, gelatin desserts, or cake.

Serving pans that hold a standardized number of servings may be used for cooking and serving such dishes as meat substitutes, escalloped or creamed dishes, omelets, and baked beans.

It is advantageous to equip a community kitchen with uniform pans for cooking various dishes, because food prepared in many sizes and kinds of dishes cannot easily be divided into uniform portions. The chairman of the food committee would then distribute containers from the community building to the persons who were to prepare specific dishes.

Cut or mark off the food into uniform servings whenever possible; the size varies according to conditions; for example, a rich dessert served at the end of meal may well be smaller in size than if it is to be sold as a separate dish (figure 3, F).

Weigh or measure sample servings of the desired amount; a roast-meat serving may be weighed in ounces, and a cooked-vegetable serving may be either weighed or measured.

Use standard serving equipment, such as ladles and spoons of known sizes, to obtain equal portions (figure 4 A and C). Ice-cream scoops (figure 4 D), when leveled, yield a specific number of servings, although such servings vary somewhat because scoops may be rounded by some persons, and packed by others. For example, 1 gallon of ice cream when dipped with a No. 10 scoop theoretically should yield 40 servings, or 10 servings to a quart; actually the average number obtained is about 25 to the gallon. A quart of salad mixture, such as potato or fruit salad, yields approximately 9 servings to a quart with a No. 12 scoop. The following gives approximate yields for several sizes of scoops:

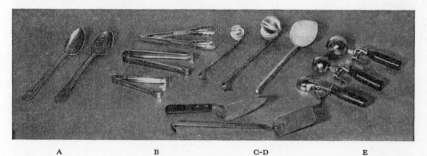

A	B	C-D	E

FIGURE 4.   SERVING EQUIPMENT

A. Solid spoon
   Perforated spoon for serving food drained from its juice

B. Big and little food tongs to help with cooking and serving
C. Different-sized ladles for measuring servings

D. Server for pieces of pie or cake.
   Turner for serving individual pieces of food

E. Ice cream dippers of different sizes for measuring servings

FIGURE 5.   PAPER CUPS

A. Baking cup cakes and
muffins in paper cups
saves washing the tins,
and keeps the food moist
for serving

B. Gelatin salads and desserts
molded in paper soufflé
cups may be unmolded by cutting down one side and across
the bottom

C. Small soufflé cups may be used
for jams, marmalades,
dressings, and relishes

Number of scoop (marked size)	Range in yield per quart
10	7 to 8
12	7 to 10
16	10 to 13
20	14 to 17
24	17 to 20
30	21 to 25

One gallon of a thickened mixture such as creamed foods, will yield from 20 to 25 servings when a half-cup ladle is used.

Paper ramekins or soufflé cups (figure 5) of specific capacity may be used to obtain standard servings; small ones, ¾- or 1-ounce capacity, are useful for jam, marmalade, relishes, and dressings; larger ones are suitable for molded gelatin salads or desserts. Their cost, however, adds to the food cost since they are used only once.

COOKERY DIRECTIONS AND RECIPES

The recipes have been planned to yield approximately 50 servings of average size. The size of the servings may be increased or decreased according to the group to be fed and to the income derived from the food. For a school lunch the size of serving given in these recipes may be too costly to sell at prices that the children can afford to pay, particularly when a complete lunch is offered at a minimum charge. For smaller children, half-size servings may be adequate. In camps and other places where second helpings are offered the recipes may need to be increased by one-third to one-half to provide for the additional servings.

The number of servings obtained from these recipes depends on the accuracy in measuring the ingredients, the care used in manipulation,

19

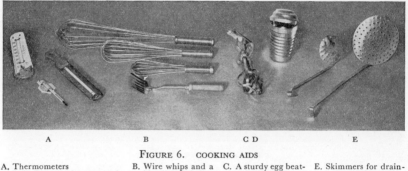

FIGURE 6. COOKING AIDS

A. Thermometers
Left: For oven-heat control
Center: For roasting meat to
a specific internal temperature
Right: For cooking candy and
cake icings to exact temperatures

B. Wire whips and a
blending fork for
stirring sauces,
gravies, and the like
to keep them from
lumping during
cooking

C. A sturdy egg beater has many uses in
quantity cookery

D. A swirl mixer for
mixing flour or
cornstarch pastes
without lumping

E. Skimmers for draining vegetables and
mixing tossed
salads

the final yield of the recipe, and the uniformity and size of the servings. Suggestions for obtaining uniform servings are given on page 16. Weighing and measuring equipment and other aids which are helpful in food preparation are shown in figures 1 and 6.

FIGURING THE COST OF RECIPES

The cost per serving should be figured frequently using current prices paid for the ingredients. This is important to the financial operation of the food service especially during times of rising and fluctuating prices.

To figure the cost per serving, total the cost of all ingredients used in a recipe and include any accompaniments served with it, such as a relish, sauce, or garnish; this total is divided by the number of servings. The following example shows the method:

MEAT LOAF PLUS RELISH

Yield: 50 to 64 slices

Ingredients	Cost per unit	Total cost
12 pounds ground pork and smoked ham	$0.55/pound	$6.60
1 quart bread, chopped	0.16/pound	0.06
8 eggs	0.50/dozen	0.34
2 cups milk	0.22/quart	0.11
1 tablespoon salt		0.01
½ teaspoon pepper		
2 quarts tomatoes	0.80/No. 10 can	0.54
4 pounds relish	0.20/pound	0.80
Total cost		$8.46

Cost per serving (50 slices) $0.169 ($8.46 ÷ 50)

Cost per serving (64 slices)   0.132 ($8.46 ÷ 64)

The cost per serving may be lowered by decreasing the size of the servings. The loaves in the example above would be cut into thinner slices. For dipped mixtures, a smaller ladle may be used.

Another means of decreasing the cost of a recipe is by extending the more expensive items with cheaper ones. Meat stew is used as an example:

MEAT AND VEGETABLE STEW

Yield: 50 servings

3 servings per pound of meat		*Price per unit*	*5 servings per pound of meat*	
15 pounds beef............	$9.00	$0.60/pound	10 pounds beef............	$6.00
1 cup onions..............	0.01	0.03/pound	1 cup onions..............	0.01
2 quarts carrots...........	0.12	0.03/pound	3 quarts carrots...........	0.18
2 quarts potatoes..........	0.08	0.02/pound	3 quarts potatoes..........	0.12
1 quart celery rings........	0.20	0.20/bunch	1½ quarts celery rings......	0.30
1½ quarts (2½ pounds) peas,		0.25/pound	2½ quarts (4 pounds) peas,	
frozen.................	0.63		frozen.................	1.00
Total cost.........	$10.04		Total cost........	$7.61
Cost per serving $0.20 ($10.04 ÷ 50)			*Cost per serving* $0.152 ($7.61 ÷ 50)	

The cost of left-over foods used in recipes should be included when figuring costs.

Average portion size and cost of portion, 1951, are given in the appendix.

SAUCE AND RELISH RECIPES

CREAM OR WHITE SAUCE

Yield: 1 gallon.

Thin	Medium-thin	Medium	Heavy
(for cream soup)	(sauce for vegetables)	(for creamed and escalloped dishes)	(for croquette base)

Ingredients

	Thin	Medium-thin	Medium	Heavy
Milk:	1 gallon	1 gallon	1 gallon	1 gallon
Fat:*	½ to 1 cup (4 to 8 ounces)	¾ to 1 cup (6 to 8 ounces)	1 to 2 cups (8 ounces to 1 pound)	1½ to 2 cups (12 ounces to 1 pound)
Flour:	1 cup (4 ounces)	1½ to 1¾ cups (6 to 7 ounces)	2 to 2½ cups (8 to 10 ounces)	3 to 4 cups (12 ounces to 1 pound)
Salt:	2 tablespoons	2 tablespoons	2 tablespoons	2 tablespoons

*In quantity cookery, the smaller amount of fat is used; half margarine and half bacon fat, beef drippings, or chicken fat give a less expensive sauce which is as palatable in many combinations as one in which butter is used.

Method 1*	Method 2
1. Heat the milk in the top of a double-boiler or in a hot-water bath.	1. Heat the milk as in method 1, retaining enough cold milk to mix with the flour.
2. Melt the fat, and stir in the flour.	2. Blend the flour with the cold milk to make a thin paste.
3. Add the fat-flour mixture to the hot milk and cook until thickened, stirring constantly with a wire whip (figure 2).	3. Add the flour paste to the hot milk and cook until thickened, stirring constantly with a wire whip (figure 2). Add the fat.†

4. Continue to cook the mixture over hot water until it is thickened; stir occasionally to prevent scum and lumps; season just before combining with other ingredients.

*Method 1 produces a mixture with no floating fat. Cream sauce should be thoroughly cooked to prevent a raw starch taste. Salting at the end of the cooking prevents curdling of the mixture. Greasing the utensil before putting in the milk helps to prevent the mixture from sticking.
†Fat may be omitted.

MEDIUM-THIN CREAM SAUCE

Nonfat dry milk solids (dry skim milk)

16 to 18 ounces (4 cups) dry milk solids

3¾ quarts warm water

1¼ cups (10 ounces) butter *or* fortified margarine

1½ to 1¾ cups (6 to 7 ounces) flour

2 tablespoons salt

1. Blend the dry milk solids with a small quantity of warm water, using a wire whip or electric beater. Add the remaining water and heat the mixture in a double-boiler. Proceed as for cream sauce made with fluid milk.

Evaporated milk

2 quarts evaporated milk

2 quarts water

¾ to 1 cup (6 to 7 ounces) butter *or* fortified margarine

1½ to 1¾ cups (6 to 7 ounces) flour

2 tablespoons salt

1. Combine the evaporated milk and water; proceed as for cream sauce made with fluid milk.

Variations

To 1 gallon of cream sauce, add:

Cheese sauce	1½ quarts (1½ pounds) of chopped cheese.
Egg sauce	1 dozen hard-cooked eggs, chopped.
Mushroom sauce	1¼ pounds of mushrooms, sliced and browned in fat.
Parsley sauce	1½ to 2 cups of chopped parsley.
Pimiento and/or green-pepper sauce	1½ to 2 cups of chopped pimiento and/or green pepper.

22

BEEF GRAVY*

Yield: 1 gallon

Size of serving: ¼ cup

1 gallon beef stock†
1½ cups beef drippings
2 to 2½ cups flour
½ tablespoon gravy coloring
1 teaspoon celery salt
Salt and pepper to taste

1. Heat the stock.

2. Melt the fat and stir in the flour. Cook together over low heat for 2 or 3 minutes. Add this to the hot stock and cook until thickened, stirring constantly with a wire whip. Add the seasonings.

*The method for making pan gravy is given in directions for making gravy, Method 1, page 00.
†Commercial beef concentrate may be used for making the stock or for adding color and flavor to it. Vegetable water may be used to dilute the concentrate.

Variations

Cream gravy: Use milk in place of the stock.

Mushroom gravy: To 1 gallon of gravy, add 1¼ pounds of sliced mushrooms, ¼ cup chopped onion, browned together in fat.

Vegetable gravy: To 1 gallon of gravy, add cooked vegetables: 2 cups peas; 2 cups carrots, diced fine; 1½ cups celery, diced fine.

NOTE: Gravy appropriate to the meat should be served, that is: pork gravy with pork; lamb gravy with lamb; chicken gravy with chicken.

BEET RELISH

Yield: 50 servings

Size of serving: 1½ tablespoons

3 cups beets, cooked, chopped
3 cups cabbage, chopped fine
1 cup horseradish
1½ cups sugar
2½ teaspoons salt
¾ teaspoon pepper
Pinch cayenne pepper
Vinegar to cover

1. Mix the ingredients in the order given; let the mixture stand for at least 1 hour. Drain before serving.

CRANBERRY AND APPLE RELISH

Yield: 50 servings

Size of serving: 1½ tablespoons

3 quarts (3 pounds) cranberries, raw

1. Wash the cranberries and drain them.

3 quarts apples, raw, quartered
4½ cups sugar

2. Grind or chop the cranberries and apples; mix with the sugar and let the mixture stand for from 3 to 4 hours before serving.

CRANBERRY AND ORANGE RELISH

Yield: 50 servings

Size of serving: 1½ tablespoons

4 quarts (4 pounds) cranberries, raw

1. Wash and drain the cranberries.

5 oranges
8 cups sugar

2. Grind the cranberries and whole oranges; add the sugar and let the mixture stand for from 3 to 4 hours before serving.

CRANBERRY SAUCE

Yield: 4 quarts   Size of serving: 1/4 cup

4 quarts (4 pounds) cranberries

1. Wash the cranberries.

5 to 7 cups sugar

4 to 5 cups water

2. Bring the sugar and water to the boiling point; add the cranberries and cook just below the boiling point until they appear transparent. Cool the sauce.

CRANBERRY JELLY

Use 1½ additional cups of sugar and strain while hot.

WHOLE-FRUIT CRANBERRY SAUCE

Yield: 4 quarts   Size of serving: 1/4 cup

4 quarts (4 pounds) cranberries

1. Wash the cranberries.

6½ cups sugar

2 quarts water

2. Boil the sugar and water for 5 minutes. Add the cranberries and boil without stirring until the skins pop. When they cease to pop, remove the sauce from the heat. Allow it to remain in the utensil undisturbed until cool.

HORSERADISH SAUCE

Yield: 50 servings   Size of serving: 1 tablespoon

1½ cups horseradish

1. Mix the horseradish, vinegar, and salt.

½ cup vinegar

2 teaspons salt

2 cups cream, heavy

2. Whip the cream and add the sugar; fold the horseradish mixture into it.

1 to 2 tablespoons sugar, confectioner's

MINT SAUCE

(To serve with lamb)

Yield: 1 quart   Size of serving: 1 tablespoon

1 quart vinegar*

½ cup sugar, confectioner's

2 cups mint leaves, chopped fine

1. Add the sugar to the hot vinegar and pour this over the mint. Let this mixture stand for 30 minutes over very low heat.

*Dilute the vinegar if it is too strong.

MINT CURRANT SAUCE

Yield: 1½ quarts   Size of serving: 1½ tablespoons

1½ quarts currant jelly

1. Beat together.

1 cup mint leaves, chopped fine

¾ cup ground orange rind

MOCK HOLLANDAISE SAUCE

Yield: 2½ quarts   Size of serving: 2½ tablespoons

2 quarts water *or* vegetable liquid

1 cup butter *or* fortified margarine

½ to 1 cup flour

¾ to 1 cup (9 to 12) egg yolks

½ cup butter *or* fortified margarine

¾ to 1 cup lemon juice

1 tablespoon salt

⅛ teaspoon pepper

½ teaspoon paprika

1. Heat the liquid.

2. Melt the butter and stir in the flour. Add this to the hot liquid, stirring constantly with a wire whip. Keep mixture below the boiling point and cook until thickened.

3. Beat the egg yolks slightly; add to the hot milk. Keep the mixture in hot (not boiling) water until ready to serve.

4. Add the butter, lemon juice, and seasonings very gradually until all have been added. *Serve at once.*

RAISIN SAUCE

Yield: 2 quarts   Size of serving: 2 tablespoons

7 cups water*

½ cup cornstarch

1 cup cold water

1 cup sugar, brown

2½ cups (1 pound) raisins, seeded

3 tablespoons lemon juice

¼ teaspoon salt

1. Heat the water to the boiling point.

2. Mix the cornstarch and cold water; add this to the hot water and cook until thickened, stirring constantly with a wire whip. Remove the mixture from the heat.

3. Add the sugar, raisins, lemon juice, and salt.

*Half ham stock and half water may be used in place of all water; then omit the salt.

TOMATO RELISH

Yield: 50 servings   Size of serving: 2 tablespoons

2 quarts tomatoes, cut fine and drained

2 cups onions, chopped fine

2 cups celery, chopped fine

1 cup green peppers, chopped

1½ cups sugar

2½ tablespoons salt

4 teaspoons white mustard seed

2 cups vinegar

1. Mix all together.

Yield: 1 gallon

Size of serving: ¼ cup

3¼ quarts (1 can No. 10) tomato juice*

1 quart meat stock
4 bay leaves
2 teaspoons cloves, whole
1 tablespoon peppercorns
3 tablespoons sugar
1 or 2 garlic cloves

1. Tie the spices in a cheesecloth bag and heat them with the tomatoes, stock, and sugar; boil for 5 minutes. Remove the spice bag.

1 cup fat
2 cups flour
2 tablespoons salt
2 tablespoons Worcestershire sauce

2. Melt the fat and stir in the flour; add this to the hot tomatoes and cook until thickened, stirring constantly with a wire whip. Add the salt and Worcestershire sauce. Add further seasoning as needed.

*Tomato puree or tomato flakes may be used in place of the tomato juice. Tomato puree may be diluted with water in proportions of 2/3 puree and 1/3 water. Follow directions on the package for reconstituting tomato flakes.

Variation

Spanish sauce
Yield: 5 quarts

1½ cups green peppers, chopped
1 cup onions, chopped
½ pound mushrooms,* chopped
⅓ cup fat
1½ cups pimientos

1. Cook the peppers, onions, and mushrooms with the fat until tender. Add them and the pimientos to 1 gallon of tomato sauce.

*Diced celery may be used in place of the mushrooms.

SOUPS
STOCK SOUPS

Soups stock is an important item when foods in quantity are being prepared because it furnishes the base for soups and sauces and makes enough gravy to serve with oven roasts. To be palatable, the stock must be made with enough meat and fat in proportion to bone to give a good flavor. If it is not a rich brown color, it can be made so with commercial coloring, or by browning onions in their skins with a small amount of fat. A little water, meat, or vegetable stock is added to the browned onions and the liquid is cooked until it is dark brown. Burnt-sugar sirup in small quantities also may be used to add color.

Commercial beef and chicken concentrates may be used for making clear stock soups and soups calling for meat stock as a base. Directions for using these concentrates are given on the containers.

Soup stock spoils quickly, therefore, if it is not be used immediately, it should be cooled. Pour small amounts into containers and place in a sink with cold running water or in ice water. When cooled, the stock should be covered and placed in the refrigerator. The fat which solidifies on the top forms a seal that helps to prevent spoilage; this should not be removed until the stock is used.

For clear soups, stock may be dipped from the top after it has been allowed to stand. The bottom part of the stock that contains sediment may be made into gravy. The accumulation of meat juices from roasts may be used for gravy or soup stock.

The cost for a serving of soups is determined by figuring the total cost of the ingredients and dividing by the number of servings. If the soup is made from stock, its cost should be included; the price varies according to the cost of the meat and bones used for stock. Standard ladles (figure 2, E) and serving dishes help to obtain uniform servings.

The meat used in making soup stock may be used in several ways. It may be added to the soup itself or used in a variety of other dishes such as sandwich fillings, hash, croquettes.

SOUP STOCK RECIPE

Yield: from 3 to 3½ gallons

10 pounds soup bones (shank or knuckle preferred)	1. Soak the bones and meat in cold, salted water for 1 hour.
6 pounds meat and trimmings*	2. Simmer the mixture for from 5 to 6 hours.
4 gallons water	3. Strain the stock from the bones and cool it quickly.
5 tablespoons salt	
½ pound onions, cut in pieces	4. Remove the fat just before using the stock.
½ pound carrots, cut in pieces	
¼ pound celery tops	

*Left-over cooked-meat scraps and bones from roasts and other meat dishes may be used, adding an extra quart of water for each pound of the cooked scraps. Fat may be used in addition to meat and bones in making stock; when the fat has solidified on the top of the stock, it may be removed and used as drippings.

CREAM SOUPS

Cream soups have as a base a thin cream sauce; chicken or veal stock may be substituted for part of the milk, and chicken fat may be substituted for butter or other fat. Evaporated milk, light cream, or top milk used with chicken or veal stock gives a rich sauce. If the milk base and the vegetable mixture are combined in small amounts and salted just before serving, there is less danger of curdling.

Variations

Cream-soup: Asparagus, broccoli, carrot, celery, chicken, corn, mushroom, onion, pea, potato, salmon, spinach, tomato.

27

GARNISHES AND ACCOMPANIMENTS FOR SOUPS

Garnishes for soup stocks		Accompaniments
Alphabets	Egg-custard cubes	Celery
Grated carrots	Lemon slices	Cheese straws
Chopped parsley	Okra	Crackers, butter, cheese, or toasted
Diced fresh tomatoes	Whipped cream	Croutons
Raw celery rings	Sour cream	Melba toast
Green-pepper strips or		Nuts
cubes		Olives
	Garnishes for cream soups	Radishes
Croutons	Crisp diced bacon or	Raw-carrot strips
Diced green pepper	salt pork	or curls
Paprika	Popcorn	Small sandwiches
Sprigs of (or chopped)	Toasted shredded almonds	Toast or bread sticks
parsley	Grated cheese	
Diced pimiento		
Chopped chives		

RECIPES

The yield is approximately 3 gallons for all soup recipes.

CHICKEN GUMBO

See variation of shrimp or crabmeat gumbo, page 32.

Clam Chowder

Clams may be purchased in the shell, frozen by the quart or gallon, or canned. Look the raw clams over carefully for pieces of shell; steam or simmer clams in their own juice for about 1½ hours. If there are hard parts, cut them out and cook for a longer time. Drain them and save the juice. Chop or grind them for making chowder.

PHILADELPHIA OR MANHATTAN CLAM CHOWDER

Yield: 50 servings Size of serving: 1 measuring cup

2½ quarts (5 to 6 dozen medium) clams and juice
or
4 cans, No. 2, clams, chopped

1. Strain the juice through a cheesecloth. Combine the chopped clams, strained juice and stock, and heat them.

1¼ gallons meat stock

½ pound bacon or salt pork
1½ cups onions, chopped

2. Chop the bacon or pork and brown it lightly with the onions; add them to the clams and stock.

3 cups celery, diced
1½ cups carrots, diced

3. Cook the celery and carrots and add them to the soup.

2½ quarts tomatoes
1 cup corn
1 cup peas, cooked

4. Add the remaining ingredients and heat.

28

2 to 3 tablespoons salt
¼ teaspoon pepper
1 tablespoon paprika
¾ teaspoon thyme
1 teaspoon celery salt

NEW ENGLAND CLAM CHOWDER

Yield: 50 servings

Size of serving: 1 measuring cup

2 quarts (4 to 5 dozens medium) clams and juice

or

3 cans, No. 2, clams, chopped

2 quarts potatoes, diced (about 4 pounds before peeling)

¼ pound bacon or salt pork

2 tablespoons onions, chopped

2½ gallons (10 quarts) cream sauce
  10 quarts milk
  1 cup butter, fortified margarine *or* bacon fat
  1½ cups flour

Salt and pepper to taste

1. Strain the juice through a cheesecloth.

2. Boil the potatoes until tender in 1 quart of water plus 1 tablespoon of salt. Do not drain off the water.

3. Chop the bacon or pork and brown it lightly with the onions.

4. Make the cream sauce.

5. Combine all the ingredients, season to taste, and heat.

CORN CHOWDER

Yield: 50 servings

Size of serving: 1 measuring cup

2 quarts, potatoes, diced (about 4 pounds before peeling)

1½ cups onions, chopped (3 to 4 onions)

2 gallons milk

2 bay leaves

½ to ¾ pound bacon *or* salt pork, diced

1 cup flour

3¼ quarts (1 can, No. 10) corn, cream style *or* whole kernel

¼ cup pimientos, chopped

¼ cup salt

½ teaspoon pepper

Garnish with:
  ⅓ cup parsley, chopped and the crisp diced bacon *or* pork

1. Boil the potatoes and onions until tender in 1 quart of water plus 1 tablespoon of salt. Do not drain off the water.

2. Heat the milk and bay leaves together. Remove the bay leaves.

3. Fry the bacon or pork until crisp. Drain off the fat and stir the flour into it. Add this to the hot milk and cook until slightly thickened stirring constantly with a wire whip.

4. Add the potatoes, onions, corn, pimientos, and seasonings to the soup.

29

CREAM OF ASPARAGUS SOUP

Yield: 50 servings

Size of serving: 1 measuring cup

2 gallons (8 quarts) stock, chicken *or* veal

1. Heat the stock.

3 quarts (1 can, No. 10) asparagus, canned

2. Sieve the asparagus and add it and the asparagus liquid to the stock.

2 cups butter *or* fortified margarine

3¾ cups flour

3. Melt the fat and stir in the flour; add this mixture to the hot stock and cook until thickened, stirring constantly with a wire whip.

5 cups (5 14½-ounce cans) evaporated milk

4. Add the milk to the thickened stock.

3 to 4 tablespoons salt

¼ teaspoon pepper

1 can, No. 2, asparagus tips

5. Add the seasonings; add further seasonings as needed. Garnish with the asparagus tips, cut into 1-inch lengths.

CREAM OF CHICKEN SOUP

Yield: 50 servings

Size of serving: 1 measuring cup

2¼ gallons (9 quarts) chicken stock from 12 pounds of fowl

2 cups onions, chopped

2 cups celery diced, or celery tops from 4 bunches

1. Heat the stock with the onions and celery; boil it for 5 minutes; strain or skim out the vegetables.

¾ cup chicken fat, butter, *or* fortified margarine

1¼ cups flour

2. Melt the fat and stir in the flour; add this to the hot stock and cook until slightly thickened, stirring constantly with a wire whip.

1 cup rice

3. Cook the rice and add it to the stock.

2 quarts milk

1 pint heavy cream, *or* evaporated milk

4 tablespoons salt

⅛ teaspoon pepper

2 cups chicken, diced

4. Add the milk and cream or evaporated milk, chicken, and seasonings to the soup just before serving.

NOTE: The remaining chicken meat may be used for salad or other chicken dishes.

CREAM OF MUSHROOM SOUP

Yield: 50 servings

Size of serving: 1 measuring cup

2 gallons milk

2 quarts chicken stock

1 cup chicken fat, butter, *or* fortified margarine

2 cups flour

1. Heat the milk and stock. Melt the fat and stir in the flour; add this to the hot liquid and cook until thickened, stirring constantly with a wire whip.

1½ pounds or 4 cans, No. 1, mushrooms

1½ cups onions

½ cup butter *or* fortified margarine

1 quart top milk, light cream, *or* evaporated milk

3 to 4 tablespoons salt

¼ teaspoon pepper

2. Wash the mushrooms and chop them; brown with the onions in the fat. Add them to the thickened stock. Just before serving, add the cream or evaporated milk and seasonings. Taste for further seasoning.

CREAM OF TOMATO SOUP

Yield: 50 servings

Size of serving: 1 measuring cup

6½ quarts (2 cans, No. 10) tomato juice

1 cup onions, quartered (about 3 onions)

6 bay leaves

1. Heat the tomato juice, onion, and bay leaves to boiling. Remove the onion and bay leaves.

1½ cups butter *or* fortified margarine

2¼ cups flour

2 tablespoons salt

½ to 1 cup sugar

2. Melt the fat and stir in the flour; add this to the hot tomato juice and cook until thickened, stirring constantly with a wire whip. Add the sugar and salt.

6 quarts milk, *cold*

3. Pour in the *cold* milk and stir. Heat the mixture to boiling.

CREOLE SOUP

Yield: 50 servings

Size of serving: 1 measuring cup

½ pound macaroni or spaghetti

1. Cook the macaroni or spaghetti in 2 quarts water with 1 tablespoon salt; drain it and rinse it with water.

2 cups green peppers, sliced thin

1 cup onions, chopped

1 quart meat stock

2. Cook the peppers and onions in the meat stock.

2 gallons meat stock, heated

3¼ quarts (1 can, No. 10) tomatoes

4 to 5 tablespoons salt

¼ teaspoon pepper

2 or 3 bay leaves

3. Combine the meat stock, tomatoes, green peppers, onions, macaroni, and seasonings, and heat the mixture. Remove the bay leaves before serving. Add further seasoning as needed.

FISH GUMBO

See variation of shrimp or crabmeat gumbo, page 32.

MINESTRONE SOUP

Yield: 50 servings

Size of serving: 1 measuring cup

1 cup beans, navy

1. Soak the beans overnight; cook them until tender.

2½ pounds bacon or ham, diced

3 cups onions, chopped

2. Brown the meat and onions lightly.

1½ quarts (½ can, No. 10) tomatoes

3 cups celery

1 quart cabbage, coarsely shredded

3. Add the tomatoes, celery, and cooked beans to the meat and cook until the celery is tender and the mixture is somewhat thick.

5 cups green vegetables mixed (peas, lima beans, green beans, asparagus tips, and/or others)

4. Cook the vegetables in salted water until just tender.

2¼ gallons (9 quarts) meat stock

Salt and pepper to taste

5. Heat the stock and add the other ingredients to it. Season to taste. Heat the soup.

31

MOCK TURTLE SOUP

Yield: 50 servings

Size of serving: 1 measuring cup

2 gallons meat stock

1. Heat the stock.

2½ quarts tomato juice
1½ tablespoons whole cloves
1 tablespoon peppercorns

2. Heat the tomato juice with the spices; boil for 5 minutes. Strain this into the stock.

1 cup bacon fat or beef drippings
2 cups flour

3. Melt the fat and stir in the flour; add this to the hot stock and cook until thickened, stirring constantly with a wire whip.

1 quart carrots, cooked
2½ cups onions, cooked
2 cups meat, cooked
8 eggs, hard-cooked
⅓ cup lemon juice
Salt and pepper to taste

4. Chop fine the carrots, onions, meat, and eggs. Add them, the lemon juice, and the seasonings to the thickened stock just before serving.

NAVY-BEAN SOUP

See variation of split-pea soup, page 33.

OYSTER STEW*

Yield: 50 servings

Size of serving: 1 measuring cup

3 quarts oysters, fresh
¾ cup butter or fortified margarine

1. Examine the oysters carefully for pieces of shell. Heat oysters in one-half of the butter until their edges curl slightly.

2¼ gallons (9 quarts) milk
2 tablespoons salt
½ teaspoon paprika

2. Heat the milk and add the seasonings; add the oysters and remaining butter just before serving.

*When making oyster stew in quantity, combine oysters and milk as needed.

SHRIMP OR CRABMEAT GUMBO

Yield: 50 servings

Size of serving: 1 measuring cup

2 gallons chicken stock
2 cups green peppers, chopped
1 can No. 2, okra, sliced
3 cups onions, chopped
2½ quarts tomatoes
1½ tablespoons salt
½ teaspoon pepper

1. Cook together the stock, peppers, okra, tomatoes, onions, salt, and pepper.

¾ cup butter or fortified margarine
1½ cups flour

2. Melt the fat, stir in the flour; add this to the hot mixture and cook until thickened stirring constantly.

1¼ pounds shrimp or crabmeat flaked

3. Add the flaked fish.

½ pound (1 cup) rice

4. Cook the rice in 2 quarts boiling water with 1½ teaspoons salt. Rinse the rice and add it to the soup just before serving.

Variations

Chicken gumbo: Use cooked, diced chicken in place of the fish.

Fish gumbo: Use flaked cooked fish in place of the shrimp.

SPLIT-PEA SOUP

Yield: 50 servings | Size of serving: 1 measuring cup

3 pounds (7 cups) split peas, dried

½ bunch leeks *or* 1 cup onions

1½ pounds salt pork, bacon ends, *or* ham bone

Celery leaves from 2 bunches

½ cup parsley

1. Wash the peas, cover with water and soak them overnight; boil or steam them in the water in which they were soaked with the leeks, pork, celery, and parsley. Strain the mixture. Measure the yield and add enough stock to make 5 quarts of mixture. Grind or cut the pork and use it as a garnish.

5½ cups tomato puree

1½ gallons (6 quarts) ham or beef stock

2. Combine the tomato puree, stock, and strained peas; heat the mixture.

½ cup bacon fat

1 cup flour

3. Melt the fat and stir in the flour; add this to the hot mixture and cook it until slightly thickened, stirring constantly with a wire whip.

3 cups light cream, top milk, *or* evaporated milk

½ cup butter, fortified margarine *or* bacon fat

Salt to taste

4. Just before serving, add the cream or evaporated milk. The amount of salt should be checked carefully if salty ham stock is used. Add the butter and browned pork cubes for a garnish.

Variation

Navy-bean soup: Use 3 pounds (7 cups) of dried navy beans in place of the spit peas.

NOTE: 2 cups of chopped raw carrots may be used as a garnish for either split pea or navy-bean soup.

TOMATO BOUILLON

Yield: 50 servings | Size of serving: 1 measuring cup

5½ quarts tomato juice

1½ tablespoons peppercorns

2 or 3 bay leaves

½ teaspoon cloves, whole

1 cup onions, cut up

1. Heat the tomato juice with the spices and seasonings; boil for 5 minutes and strain.

⅓ cup sugar

4 tablespoons salt

¼ teaspoon pepper

1¾ gallons (7 quarts) meat stock, heated

2. Combine the stock with the tomato juice. Garnish with unsweetened whipped cream, chopped parsley, sliced olives, or thin slices of lemon.

Variation

Tomato soup: Thicken the stock and tomato-juice mixture with 1 cup of butter or fortified margarine, melted, mixed with 1½ cups of flour.

VEGETABLE SOUP

Yield: 50 servings

Size of serving: 1 measuring cup

2 gallons meat stock

2 or 3 bay leaves

1. Heat the stock with the bay leaves; boil for 5 minutes; remove the bay leaves.

3 cups carrots, diced

3 cups celery, diced

2 cups onions, chopped

½ cup rice

2. Cook the carrots, celery, onions, and rice; add them to the stock.

2 quarts (⅔ can, No. 10) tomatoes

2 cups (1 can, No. 2) peas, cooked

2 tablespoons salt

¼ teaspoon pepper

3. Add the tomatoes, peas, and seasonings to the stock; add further seasoning as needed.

VEGETABLE SOUP

(without meat stock)

Yield: 50 servings

Size of serving: 1 measuring cup

2 quarts carrots, chopped (about 4 pounds before peeling)

1 quart turnips, chopped (about 4 pounds before peeling)

2 quarts potatoes, chopped (about 4 pounds before peeling)

4 quarts (1 can, No. 10, and 1 can, No. 2½) tomatoes

1¾ gallons water

1. Add the carrots, turnips, potatoes, and tomatoes to the water, cover, and boil until the vegetables are nearly tender.

2 quarts (2½ pounds) onions, chopped (about 3 pounds onions)

1½ cups salt pork or bacon fat

2. Brown the onions in the fat.

2 quarts (1 pound) cabbage, chopped or shredded

½ cup salt

3. Add the onions, cabbage, and salt and cook 15 minutes longer. Add further seasoning as needed.

NOTE: Vegetables such as celery, canned peas and corn may be substituted for other vegetables.

MEATS AND POULTRY

The use of large amounts of some of the more costly ingredients in the recipes that follow may make them too expensive to use in some situations. Many of the meat recipes have been extended with potatoes or other vegetables, cereals, or bread crumbs to make the meat flavor go farther. Commercial meat and chicken concentrates may be used to extend further the flavor in gravy and sauces. The use of monosodium glutamate may also increase the flavor of meat and poultry dishes. Tomato concentrates (puree, paste, or flakes) may be used in place of canned tomatoes in many of the meat extended dishes.

Frozen meat in general, is cut ready to cook before it is packaged and frozen. Roasts of various sizes and ground, cubed or diced meat may be purchased ready to cook. In quantity cookery, meat is generally defrosted before cooking. Thawing in the refrigerator is recommended because there is less loss of juices and bacterial growth is retarded. Small units thaw more quickly than do large ones. Other means of thawing and thawing times are as follows:

Time for thawing a three-pound package of meat by different methods.*

Method	Time†
	Hours
In refrigerator....................................	24 or longer
In room..	10 to 12
In room in front of fan............................	5 to 6
In warming oven (73° C. or 163° F.)................	3 to 4
In running water (in waterproof package)	3 to 4

*Taken from *Preserving Foods by Freezing.* Circular 249 Agricultural Experiment Station, Kansas State College of Agriculture and Applied Science, Manhattan, Kansas.
†The time given is only an approximation as it will vary with shape of package, especially thickness, with composition of meat, exact thawing temperature, and other factors.

Meat patties, cube steaks, cutlets, and chops may be cooked in the frozen state. Patties, one-inch thick, require about twice the cooking time of unfrozen ones, that is, from 30 to 35 minutes.

STANDARDIZING SERVINGS

Meats purchased in slices, such as round steak, veal cutlets, or fish fillets, may be cut into the desired number of uniform servings per pound before cooking. Ground meat for meat cakes may be weighed into pound portions and then divided. A metal ring or ice-cream dipper holding a known weight may be used to shape the patty and to standardize the size. Meat cakes of standard size may also be obtained by packing a known weight into loaf pans, turning the loaves out, slicing them evenly, and patting each slice into a cake. Chops and sausages vary in size, and therefore the number per pound and the cost vary accordingly. Bacon and Canadian bacon, bologna, and other cooked meat loaves may be sliced to different thicknesses to give the desired number of slices to a pound; if purchased sliced, the number of slices to a pound may be counted and the cost per slice determined. Example: 1 pound of Canadian bacon equals 16 slices at $1.12 a pound, or 7 cents a slice; 1 pound of sausages equals 9 sausages at 48 cents a pound, or 5⅓ cents each.

FIGURE 7.   CARVING A HAM

1. Remove any skin and excess fat
2. Place the ham, fat side down, on the cutting board
3. Using a small sharp boning knife, cut around the aitchbone at the butt (large) end, keeping close to the bone which spreads out under the surface
4. Slice off a thin piece of meat from this butt end.
5. Pull and cut the aitchbone free from the leg bone. These bones can be separated easily if the ham is well cooked
6. Cut slices from this boned butt end until the meat is even with the end of the leg bone
7. Stand the ham on the sliced surface of this butt end, with the thick side toward the right. Hold the ham by the shank bone with the left hand
8. Beginning at the top, cut down along the right side of the bone, close to it, removing the entire side of the ham. Place this piece on the carving board with the cut surface down (lower left). Slice across the grain; these will be the more attractive slices (lower right)
9. Remove the bone from the remaining piece of ham by cutting close to the bone on either side with a short, pointed knife. Place this piece on the carving board with the cut surface down. Hold it firmly and slice across the grain. For a small ham or for a leg of lamb, leave this section on the bone and slice it diagonally to the bone

Notes
1. Use a clean cloth for holding the pieces while slicing them
2. The boneless pieces may be sliced on a meat-slicing machine after the cooked hams have been out of the oven for about 30 minutes or are cold
3. A ham or a leg of lamb may be partially boned, leaving only the lower part of the shank bone. The meat should then be firmly tied with string before cooking. It may be sliced across the entire leg and the larger slices cut in half
4. A method for carving a ham or leg of lamb at the table is given in the pamphlet, *Meat Carving Made Easy*, which may be obtained free of charge from the National Livestock and Meat Board, 407 S. Dearborn St., Chicago
A leg of lamb may be carved by the same method

CARVING MEAT AND POULTRY

The aim in carving meat is to get as many attractive servings as possible. To insure this, a sharp knife with a thin, pliable steel blade that will hold a keen edge is needed. The meat should not be overdone; otherwise it will fall apart in the slicing. A roast may be sliced more easily if it has stood out of the oven for about 30 minutes in a warm place. Place the meat on a board when carving large roasts. Stack the slices firmly together and keep them moist by pouring a little pan gravy over them and covering them with a damp towel. To keep sliced meat warm for serving, place the pan in a slightly larger pan containing a little hot water and set them over low heat. A clean damp towel, pieces of damp cheesecloth, or aluminum foil placed over the sliced meat will prevent drying out.

The method of carving a ham is shown in figure 7.

36

Photograph from Poultry and Egg National Board

FIGURE 8.   CARVING POULTRY; STEPS 1 AND 2

1. Place the bird on one side, with the neck toward the carver
2. A good-sized piece of breast meat may be left attached to the wing, for the wing joint is actually well within the breast. If the bird has been trussed so that the wing forms a triangle, the blade of the knife is inserted parallel to the second joint of the wing for the first cut

A

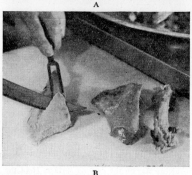

B

**FIGURE 9.   CARVING POULTRY;
STEPS 3 AND 4**

3. To remove the thigh and drumstick, place the knife between the thigh and the body and cut through the skin, drawing the knife from the back toward the carver. Press the leg outward and bend it back, separating it from the body at the hip joint. Cut through the remaining skin
4. The leg (thigh and drumstick) may be carved by either of two methods:

A. To obtain three pieces of dark meat from the thigh of a bird with a relatively small amount of meat in proportion to bone, cut a triangular piece from the inner side of the joint; this is done by making a cut through the muscle of the thigh to the joint and a similar cut through the muscle of the drumstick to the joint. Then separate the thigh from the drumstick by cutting the ligaments just over the round bone on the thigh side

B. For a bird with a large amount of meat in proportion to bone, several slices of dark meat may be obtained. Separate the thigh and drumstick as above: the drumstick may be served whole or slices may be cut from the large muscle. From the thigh, remove the two large muscles, one from each side of the bone, and slice each into from three to five slices, depending on the size of the thigh. The knife is held at a 45-degree angle for slicing. The meat is easier to carve if the skin is removed

Photographs from Poultry and Egg National Board

37

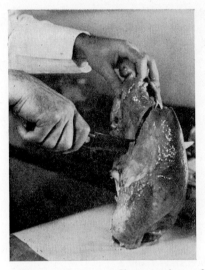

FIGURE 10. CARVING POULTRY; STEP 5

5. To separate the breast from the back, set the carcass upright and resting on the front tips of the breast with the back toward the carver. Make a straight-line cut through the "points" made by the ribs coming together from back and front, and the wing joint. The back and ribs thus cut off are not used

Photograph from Poultry and Egg National Board

For poultry, usually one piece of white meat and one of dark are used for each serving, with the slices of breast from ⅛ to ¼ inch thick. The method of carving depends somewhat on the size of the bird; a large bird yields more sliceable meat than does a small one. The steps in carving poultry are illustrated in figures 8 to 11 inclusive.

Photographs from Poultry and Egg National Board

FIGURE 11. CARVING POULTRY; STEPS 6 AND 7

6. Set the breast flat on the carving surface, with the keel bone up. Loosen the breast muscle by slipping the knife between the keel bone and the meat. The white meat is then eased and lifted away from each side, in a whole piece

7. To slice the white meat, lay the breast section skin-side-up flat on the carving surface. Hold the knife at a 45-degree angle while slicing

To Carve a Pork Loin

1. Purchase loins with the backbone separated from the ribs. Separation is made by sawing across the ribs close to the vertebrae. After the loin is cooked, the backbone can be removed by cutting between it and the rib ends.

2. Place the roast on a board with the rib side facing the carver. Use the rib bones as a guide in slicing.

3. Cut close against both sides of each rib. Alternately, cut one slice with a bone and one without to produce slices temptingly thin. In a small loin, each slice may contain a rib; in a large loin, it is possible to cut two boneless slices between the ribs.

The bones may be pulled out with pliers before the meat is carved.

MEAT COOKERY*

Moderate to low temperatures for both oven and top of range cooking are recommended for all meats.

The oven may be used instead of the top of the range or the broiler for such meats as bacon, chops, meat patties, sausage, and liver. With the temperature controls properly adjusted for slow cooking, stews and pot roasts also may be cooked in the oven.

Connective tissue may be broken up by grinding, cubing, scoring, or pounding to make less tender cuts more tender and to shorten the cooking time. The acids of fruits and vegetables also tenderize meat; the meat may be cooked with tomatoes or it may be placed in a mixture of vinegar or lemon juice and oil for several hours before cooking.

There are two basic methods of meat cookery. *Dry heat* methods are generally used for tender cuts and *moist heat* methods for the less tender cuts, and for pork chops, veal chops, and veal cutlets. Dry heat methods are: roasting, broiling, griddle-broiling (pan-broiling) and for certain cuts, frying. No water is used in any of these methods. Moist heat methods are: braising and simmering. In braising a small amount of water is used. Sometimes the steam formed provides sufficient moisture for braising. Pot-roasting and fricasseeing are other cookery terms for braising. Simmering consists of cooking at a temperature slightly under boiling (180° F.) in liquid to cover the meat.

Cooking losses (shrinkage) are due to: 1) evaporation or the loss of water and other volatile substances from the surface of the meat as it cooks 2) pan drippings or the loss of fat, water, salts, and extractives which accumulate in the utensil as the meat cooks.

---

*Information on meat cuts to be used for the various methods of cooking may be found in: *Cooking Meat in Quantity*. National Livestock and Meat Board, Department of Home Economics, Chicago 5, Illinois.

The amount of shrinkage during cooking affects the number of meat servings obtainable and therefore the cost of the meat as served; it also affects the appearance and palatability. Two of the most important factors affecting shrinkage are: 1) the cooking temperature and 2) the degree of doneness. Low cooking temperatures for all methods of cooking

Meat* and Poultry Roasting Chart

Meat	Approximate weight	Oven temperature	Interior temperature when done as tested with meat thermometer	Approximate total time†
	Pounds	*Degrees F.*	*Degrees F.*	*Hours*
Beef				
Standing rib				
7-rib	23	300° F.	125° F. (rare)	4
			140° F. (medium)	4½
			150° F. (well done)	5
Rolled rib				
7-rib	16–18	300° F.	150° F. (well done)	6
Chuck rib	5–8	300° F.	150° F. to 170° F.	2½ to 3½
Veal				
Leg	16	300 ° F.	170° F. (well done)	6
Rolled shoulder	20 (3 roasts)	300° F.	170° F. (well done)	5
Lamb				
Leg	6½ to 7½	300° F.	180° F. (well done)	3 to 4
Rolled shoulder	29 (5 roasts)	300° F.	180° F. (well done)	5
Pork, fresh				
Loin, bone-in	11 to 15	350° F.	185° F. (well done)	3 to 3½ ‡
Leg, boned	10 to 12	350° F.	185° F. (well done)	4 to 5§
Leg, bone-in	10 to 12	350° F.	185° F. (well done)	6‖
Ham, smoked				
Tenderized	10 to 14	325° F.	160° F. (well done)	3 to 3½
Precooked	10 to 14.	325° F.	130° F. (well done)	2 to 2½
Chicken, not stuffed	4 to 6	325° F.	Difficult to use meat thermometer	2 to 3
Turkey, stuffed¶	8 to 15	325–350° F.	Difficult to use meat thermometer	3 to 4
	15 to 20	325–350° F.	Difficult to use meat thermometer	4 to 5
	Over 20	325–350° F.	Difficult to use meat thermometer	5 to 6

*Adapted from *Cooking Meat in Quantity* National Livestock and Meat Board, Chicago, Ill.
†Cooking time cannot be determined accurately since it varies with the thickness and surface area of the meat, and with the proportion of bone, fat, and connective tissue. The thinner the piece of meat, the larger the surface area exposed, and the more bone and fat contained in it, the shorter the cooking time.
‡15 to 18 minutes per pound of meat.
§20 to 25 minutes per pound of meat.
‖30 to 35 minutes per pound of meat.
¶Allow from 30 to 60 minutes less total roasting time for unstuffed birds.

not only produce more palatable meat, but also more servings. Meat continues to shrink when cooked beyond the proper stage of doneness for the kind of meat.

Dry-heat Methods

Roasting

The meat browns gradually when low and constant temperatures are used throughout the cooking. Meat cooked to the proper degree of doneness is juicier, more flavorful, is more easily sliced, and yields more servings (less shrinkage) than meat which is overcooked for even a short period (figure 12). The use of a meat thermometer is the only accurate method of obtaining the correct degree of doneness of roasted meat. Directions for using a meat thermometer are given with figure 13. Another factor affecting shrinkage is oven load; there will be less evaporation when the oven is used to capacity.

The length of time for roasting, gaged according to minutes per pound, cannot be considered an accurate means of determining doneness. Approximate ranges are given in the chart on page 40, and may be used as a guide in determining total cooking time. Because of the many variables affecting the cooking time it is advisable to allow maximum time, removing the meat from the heat when just done and keeping it covered in a warm place until time for slicing it.

The variables affecting the roasting time are:

1. The oven temperature. Temperatures given in the chart produce the best quality product. However, it may be necessary sometimes to use a somewhat higher temperature because of limitations of time and oven space.

FIGURE 12. PROPER MEAT ROASTING

Comparison of pork loins roasted at different oven temperatures. Each loin weighed 4 pounds and was roasted until the meat thermometer registered an internal temperature of 185°F. Note the difference in the amount and color of drippings.

Basis of comparisons	Roasted at	
	350°F.	450°F.
Amount of shrinkage	13 ounces	1 pound 5 ounces
Percentage of loss	20 per cent	33 per cent

41

FIGURE 13. A MEAT THERMOMETER

Recording the internal temperature with this type of thermometer is the only reliable means of roasting meat to the desired stage of doneness. The thermometer is inserted into the muscle so that the bulb is at the center of the roast. The roast is done when the thermometer registers the desired internal temperature according to the kind of meat, as given in the temperature chart. The temperature will rise about 10 degrees after the roast is removed from the oven

2. The size and shape of the cut. In general the larger the cut the longer will be the total cooking time. A flat roast, however, will cook in less time than a chunky one of the same weight.

3. The style of the cut. Boned roasts (solid meat) take longer than roasts with bones left in.

4. The quality of the meat. The higher the grade or quality, or the heavier the fat covering and the marbling, the faster the roast will cook because melting fat is a better conductor of heat than lean meat.

5. The degree of doneness desired in beef roasts. Aluminum skewers placed in the roast, about two per pound of meat, shorten the roasting time.

DIRECTIONS FOR ROASTING

Method 1 (not seared)	Method 2 (seared)
1. Preheat the oven to 300° F. (350° F. for pork).	1. Preheat the oven to 450° F. (475° F. for pork).
2.	Place in a lightly greased pan with fat surface up.*
3. Place the meat in the oven and cook it at the above temperatures until the correct internal temperature is reached, as tested with a meat thermometer (figure 13).	3. Sear the meat for 15 to 20 minutes; reduce the temperature to 300° F. (350° F. for pork) and cook the meat until tender, as tested with a meat thermometer.

*A rolled roast should be placed on a rack and turned every half hour so that it cooks evenly.
NOTE: Roasts of meat, except pork, may be partially cooked, chilled, and sliced and the slices stacked in serving pans. Stock is added and the slices reheated in a moderate oven (350° F.) or in a steamer.

DIRECTIONS FOR MAKING GRAVY

Proportions:

2 cups of fat drippings (any excess should be removed from pan)	2 cups of flour
	1 gallon of meat stock

Method 1	Method 2

1. Blend the flour and hot fat and stir while cooking until the mixture becomes a rich brown.

2. Add the hot meat stock and cook until thickened, stirring constantly with a wire whip (figure 6).	2. Heat the meat stock; add the fat-flour mixture and cook until thickened, stirring constantly with a wire whip.

3. Season the gravy with salt and pepper.

NOTE: The flour may be lightly browned in the oven before blending with the fat. When this is done an additional ½ cup of flour is required. Milk may be substituted for all or part of the stock.

Broiling

The edging of fat on chops and steak should be slashed in several places to prevent the meat from curling. Cuts may be dipped in salad oil or the broiler rack may be greased to prevent sticking.

Meats broiled at a moderately low temperature, 350° F., throughout the cooking are uniformly cooked, and are tender and attractive in appearance; they shrink less and there will be less smoking than if broiled at a high temperature. The temperature may be increased at the end of the cooking period if a browner meat is desired. Broiled cuts may be kept hot for a short period by placing them on a rack in a pan and holding them in a slow oven.

DIRECTIONS FOR BROILING

Method 1 (broiler)	Method 2 (pan-broiling)
1. Preheat the broiler.	1. Preheat the griddle or pan.
2. Arrange the cuts on the broiler pan or rack in a pan.	2. Grease the griddle or pan lightly and arrange the cuts on it.
3. Place the broiler about 3 inches below the flame.	3. Brown the meat on both sides; then continue cooking at a reduced temperature.
4. Cook the meat on one side until nicely browned, season and turn it (5 minutes on a side if the cut is about ¾ inch thick)	4. Season the meat and hold as in method 1.

or

Broil the meat for a shorter time and finish cooking in an oven at 350° F.

5. Brush the meat with melted fat, season, and place it in a slow oven until time to serve (not more than 10 minutes).

Moist-heat Methods

Braising (pot-roasting)

Braising produces a meat dish that is richly browned, tender and juicy, with a developed flavor and aroma. Braising may be done in the

43

oven or on top of the range. The meat may or may not be dredged with seasoned flour. If it is floured, then brown it in a small quantity of fat; if not floured, it usually can be browned in its own fat. It is then covered and cooked at a low temperature either in its own juice (the steam that is formed may be sufficient) or in a small quantity of liquid (water, meat stock, sour cream, tomato juice, etc.)

DIRECTIONS* FOR BRAISING

Methods 1 (top of range)†	Method 2 (oven)
1. Use a heavy iron or alumnium kettle; add a small quantity of fat, if needed, and heat the kettle very hot.	1. Preheat the oven to 450° F.
2. Brown the floured or unfloured meat in the hot kettle on all sides, turning frequently.‡	2. Place the floured or unfloured meat in a heavy roasting pan. Brown for 30 minutes or until well browned.
3. Add a small quantity of water (just enough to cover the bottom of the kettle).	3. Add a small quantity of water.
4. Cover the kettle tightly, and reduce the heat to simmering temperature (185° F.)	4. Reduce the heat to 300° F. (The meat may be browned on top of the range and transferred to the oven which has been preheated to 300° F.) Cover the pan.

5. Continue to add small quantities of water as needed.

6. Cook until the meat is tender and the internal temperature of the pot roast reaches 185° F.

Simmering

Meat cooked in water shrinks less when cooked below the boiling point or at a simmering temperature. (The bubbles do not burst through the surface of the water in simmering.) Simmering results in softening the connective tissue without dissolving it. When connective tissue is dissolved the meat is dry and falls apart in the slicing.

Cooking large cuts: Cover with water, add seasoning, cover the kettle closely, bring to a simmering temperature (185° F.) and cook at that temperature until tender. If the meat is to be served cold, let it cool to room temperature, then chill in the stock in which it was cooked.

High grade commercially cured meats (tenderized) do not require soaking previous to cooking. Directions for cooking tenderized hams are given on page 51.

---

*Sliced onions and diced carrots may be added during the cooking for flavor.
†May be done in a steam-jacketed kettle.
‡For a pot roast of meat, place it fat side up on a rack after it is browned.

Stewing: In making a stew, the meat should be simmered in just enough water to cover the meat and in a utensil with a tight-fitting cover; a heavy utensil lessens the danger of scorching. Stewing may be done on top of the range or in the oven. For a brown stew, dredge the meat with flour and brown it over direct heat or in a hot oven with a small quantity of fat. A recipe for brown stew is given on page 56.

Recipes

The size of serving in many of these meat recipes is either ⅔ cup or ¾ cup. Two gallons of mixture yield about 50 servings, each a ⅔-cup size.

AUSTRIAN RAVIOLA

Yield: 50 to 55 servings   Size of serving: ¾ cup

2 pounds bacon, diced

1. Fry the bacon until golden brown; remove it from the pan.

5½ cups onions, sliced (about 2 pounds onions)
2 cups green peppers, chopped
6 pounds beef, raw, ground
⅓ cup salt
½ teaspoon pepper

2. Pour the bacon fat into baking pans, then put in the vegetables, meat, and seasonings. Brown the mixture in a hot oven (400° F.) or on top of the range. Reduce the heat to a simmering temperature (350° F. or moderate oven) and let the mixture cook for about 1 hour, stirring frequently.

1¾ pounds (7 to 9 cups) macaroni

3. Cook the macaroni in 1¾ gallons boiling water with 3 tablespoons salt; drain it in a colander, and rinse it with water.

1½ quarts (½ can, No. 10) tomatoes
1 quart tomato soup, condensed

4. Add the tomatoes and soup to the meat mixture, then add this to the macaroni; add further seasoning as needed. Heat the mixture.

3 quarts peas (5 pounds frozen *or* 1 can, No. 10)

5. Cook the frozen peas or heat the canned ones; drain and add them and the cooked bacon just before serving.

BEEF AND VEGETABLES À LA KING

Yield: 50 to 55 servings   Size of serving: ⅔ cup

3 pounds beef, raw, ground
½ cup onions, chopped

1. Brown the meat and onions in a hot oven (400° F.) or on top of the range.

3½ cups flour

2. Add the flour to the hot meat and fat and stir until well blended.

1½ gallons meat stock,* hot

3. Add the hot stock to the meat and cook until thickened stirring constantly.

2½ cups, celery, diced fine, cooked
2½ cups peas, cooked (1 pound frozen *or* 1 can, No. 2)
2½ cups carrots, diced, cooked

4. Add the cooked celery, peas, and carrots to the sauce, folding them in carefully.

---

*Commercial beef concentrate may be used to make the stock.

1¼ pounds mushrooms, sliced
¼ cup beef drippings
¼ cup salt
¾ cup catsup
2 tablespoons Worcestershire
sauce

5. Cook the mushrooms in the fat and add to the meat-vegetable mixture.

6. Add the salt, catsup, and Worcestershire sauce. Add further seasoning as needed.

Serve on:

Boiled noodles (2 pounds before cooking) *or,* other base (see page 14)

7. Cook the noodles in 2 gallons boiling water with ¼ cup salt; drain them in a colander, and rinse with water; reheat them in the oven.

CREOLE BEEF SPAGHETTI

Yield: From 50 to 55 servings

Size of serving: ¾ cup

2 pounds spaghetti
5 pounds beef,* raw, ground
1 quart onions, chopped (about 1½ pounds onions)
3 cups green peppers, chopped

1. Break spaghetti into 2-inch lengths and cook it in 2 gallons boiling water with ¼ cup salt; drain it in a colander and rinse it with water.

5 quarts (1½ cans, No 10) tomatoes

2. Brown the beef, onions, and peppers in a greased pan in a hot oven (400° F.), stirring frequently. Add the tomatoes and simmer them in a moderate oven (350° F.) or on top of the range for about 1 hour.

½ cup bacon fat
¾ cup flour
½ cup salt
½ teaspoon pepper
3 tablespoons sugar

3. Melt the fat and stir in the flour; add this to the hot mixture and cook until thickened, stirring constantly. Add the seasonings. Combine the meat sauce and the spaghetti and bake the mixture in a moderate oven (350° F.) for about 30 minutes.

1½ pounds (1½ quarts) cheese, chopped (may be omitted)

4. Add the cheese just before serving or sprinkle it over the individual servings.

*To extend the meat further, decrease the beef to 2 pounds; then increase the spaghetti to 2¾ pounds and the tomatoes to 6 quarts.

Variations

Creole liver spaghetti: Use sliced liver in place of the beef. Dredge it with seasoned flour; brown it with the onions, peppers, and bacon fat in a hot oven (400° F.) Dice it into ½-inch pieces. Add the tomatoes and proceed as above.

Meat balls and spaghetti: Serve 2 meat balls with each serving of spaghetti.

7½ pounds beef, raw, ground
1½ pounds (4 quarts) bread, soft, chopped
3½ cups water
5 tablespoons salt
1 teaspoon pepper
6 eggs

1. Combine the meat, bread, water, salt, pepper, and eggs. Using a No. 20 scoop, divide the mixture into equal portions; shape these into balls, roll them in flour and place them in baking pans. Brown them in a hot oven (400° F.). Cover them with meat stock and bake in a moderate oven (350° F.) for about 30 minutes.

CHILI CON CARNE

Yield: From 50 to 55 servings

Size of serving: ¾ cup

9 pounds beef, raw, ground
2 pounds pork,* fresh, raw, ground
1½ cups onions, chopped
1 cup beef drippings or other fat

1. Brown the meat and onions with the fat on top of the range or in a hot oven (400° F.).

3 quarts kidney beans (1 can, No. 10† or 1¾ pounds [4 cups] dried)
5 quarts (1½ cans, No. 10) tomatoes
2½ tablespoons chili powder
5 tablespoons salt
½ teaspoon pepper
3 tablespoons sugar

2. If dried beans are used, wash, and soak them over-night. Cook them in the water in which they were soaked; drain and add them to the browned meat. Add the tomatoes and seasonings and let the mixture simmer on top of the range or in a moderate oven (350° F.) for an hour. If not thick enough, thicken with a cornstarch-water paste.

½ pound crackers, broken

3. Add the crackers just before serving.

*Salt pork, fried until crisp, may be used in place of the fresh pork.
†If canned beans are used, add them to the mixture just long enough before serving to heat them through.

Variations

Omit the crackers. A larger yield is obtained with the following variations:

Chili con carne with macaroni or spaghetti: Cook 2 pounds of macaroni or spaghetti in 2 gallons of water and ¼ cup of salt. Drain it in a colander and rinse it with water. Combine it with the meat sauce and heat throughout.

Chili con carne with rice: Cook 3 pounds (6½ cups) of rice in 3 gallons of water and ⅓ cup of salt. Drain it in a colander and rinse it with water; reheat it in an oven. Serve a No. 16 scoop of rice with a ladle of meat sauce over it.

CHOP SUEY

Yield: 50 to 55 servings

Size of serving: ⅔ cup on a No. 16 scoop of rice

4½ pounds* beef and fresh pork, raw, cut into ½-inch cubes
3¼ quarts meat stock†

1. Cook the meat in the stock until tender.

1¼ cups (6½ ounces) cornstarch
1½ cups water

2. Mix the cornstarch and water; add this to the hot stock and cook until thickened, stirring constantly.

4 quarts (4 pounds) celery rings
1¼ quarts onions, sliced (about 2 pounds of onions)
1 cup soybean sauce
3 tablespoons salt
½ teaspoon pepper

3. Cook the celery and onions until just tender; add them, the soybean sauce and seasonings to the meat mixture.

2½ quarts sprouted soybeans or

4. Add the soybean sprouts or cooked soybeans.

*More meat may be used.
†Commercial beef concentrate may be used to make the meat stock.

47

1 can, No. 10, soybeans or 1½
pounds soybeans, dried‡

Serve on:

Boiled rice (2½ pounds [5⅓
cups] before cooking) or
fried noodles (2 pounds [4
quarts])

Heat the mixture.

5. Cook the rice in 2½ gallons boiling water with
5 tablespoons salt; drain it in a colander and
rinse with water. Keep hot in a slow oven until
ready for serving.

‡If dried soybeans are used, wash, cover with 3 quarts water and soak over night. Cook the
beans in the water in which they were soaked for from 2½ to 3 hours or until tender. Drain.

BREAD DRESSING

Yield: 50 servings

Size of serving: 1 No. 16 scoop

8 quarts (3¼ pounds) bread,
soft, chopped

2 cups beef drippings or suet,
finely chopped

1. Mix the bread and fat together.

1½ cups onions, chopped
⅓ cup butter or drippings
¼ teaspoon pepper
4 teaspoons sage or poultry
seasoning
2½ tablespoons salt
Hot stock to moisten

2. Cook the onions with the fat and add them to
the chopped bread. Mix in the seasonings; moisten slightly with the stock. Bake in greased pans
or use as stuffing in meat or poultry.

CREAMED DRIED BEEF

Yield: 50 to 55 servings

Size of serving: ⅔ cup on 1 slice toast

3 pounds dried beef, cut into
small pieces

1. Freshen the beef with hot water if too salty;
drain well.

1 cup butter or fortified margarine

2. Melt the fat and brown the beef in it.

1 cup flour

3. Add the flour and let this brown slightly.

2 gallons cream sauce
2 gallons milk
2½ cups fat
5 cups flour

4. Make the cream sauce; add the dried beef to
it. Add salt as needed. Paprika may be sprinkled
over the top.

Serve on:

50 slices bread, toasted, or
50 small baked or boiled potatoes
or 50 squares cornbread

ESCALLOPED DRIED BEEF AND EGGS

Yield: 50 to 55 servings

Size of serving: ¾ cup

2½ pounds dried beef

1. Cut the beef into medium-size pieces; freshen
it with hot water if it is too salty.

1 cup butter or fortified margarine

2. Melt the fat and cook the dried beef in it.

4 dozen eggs, hard-cooked

3. To hard cook the eggs, cover them with cold
water, bring to simmering temperature and cook

48

over low heat for 10 to 15 minutes. **Drain off the hot water and cover them with cold water. Remove the shells.**

6 quarts cream sauce
  6 quarts milk
  2 cups butter *or* fortified margarine
  4 cups flour

4. Make the cream sauce; add the dried beef. Add salt as needed.

5. Cut the hard-cooked eggs into quarters and arrange in baking pans. Cover these with the creamed dried beef.

Topping:
1½ quarts bread cubes *or* other topping (see page 14)

6. Put the bread cubes over the top. Bake in a moderate oven (350° F.) for from 20 to 25 minutes until the mixture is heated throughout and the top is browned.

ESCALLOPED DRIED BEEF AND MACARONI

Yield: 50 servings
3½ pounds macaroni

Size of serving: ¾ cup

1. Cook the macaroni in 3½ gallons of boiling water with ½ cup salt. Drain it into a colander and rinse it with water.

1 gallon cream sauce
  1 gallon milk
  1 cup butter *or* fortified margarine
  2½ cups flour
2 pounds dried beef
¾ cup butter *or* fortified margarine

2. Make the cream sauce.

3. Follow the same procedure as for *escalloped dried beef and eggs.*

BARBECUED FRANKFURTERS

Yield: 50 servings
100 frankfurters

Size of serving: 2 frankfurters and sauce

1. Split the frankfurters and place them in flat pans.

Barbecue sauce
1½ cups onions, minced
4 teaspoons white pepper
½ cup sugar
3 tablespoons dry mustard
3 tablespoons paprika
2 cups vinegar
4 cups catsup
6 cups water
⅓ cup Worcestershire sauce
1½ tablespoons Tabasco sauce
½ cup butter *or* fortified margarine
½ cup flour

2. Heat all the ingredients of the sauce together.

3. Melt the butter and stir in the flour. Add this to the hot sauce and cook until thickened. Pour the sauce over the frankfurters and simmer them on a range or bake them in an oven at 350° F. for from 20 to 30 minutes until heated throughout.

CREOLE FRANKFURTERS

Yield: 50 to 55 servings

Size of serving: 2/3 cup on a No. 16 scoop of rice

7½ pounds frankfurters

3 cups onions, chopped

1¼ pounds mushrooms, sliced *or* 3 8-ounce cans

1 cup butter *or* fortified margarine

1¾ cups flour

3 quarts water

1½ tablespoons salt

1 teaspoon pepper

2 bay leaves

2 cups green peppers, chopped

1 cup parsley, chopped

Serve on:

Boiled rice (2½ pounds [5⅓ cups] before cooking)

1. Cut the frankfurters into 2-inch rounds.

2. Cook the onions and mushrooms in the butter; stir the flour into this; add the water gradually and cook until thickened, stirring constantly.

3. Add the salt, pepper, bay leaves, green peppers, parsley, and frankfurters to the thickened mixture. Let simmer for 10 minutes. Remove the bay leaves.

4. Cook the rice in 2½ gallons boiling water with ⅓ cup salt. Drain it in a colander and rinse with water. Keep warm in a slow oven until served.

ESCALLOPED HAM AND EGGS

Yield: 50 to 55 servings

Size of serving: ¾ cup

3½ pounds ham, cooked, cut into ½-inch cubes

5 dozen eggs, hard-cooked

1 4-ounce can pimientos, cut into pieces

1 gallon cream sauce
  1 gallon milk
  1¼ cups butter *or* fortified margarine
  2½ cups flour
  2 tablespoons salt

Topping:

1½ quarts bread cubes *or* other topping (see page 14)

Garnish with:

⅓ cup parsley, chopped

1. Prepare the ham, eggs, and pimientos. To hard cook the eggs, cover them with cold water, bring to simmering temperature and cook over low heat for 10 to 15 minutes. Drain off the hot water and cover them with cold water. Remove the shells.

2. Make the cream sauce; add the ham and pimientos, folding them in carefully.

3. Put a layer of creamed ham in greased baking pans; slice the eggs and put a layer over the creamed mixture. Cover these with another layer of creamed ham.

4. Put bread cubes over the top; bake in a moderate oven (350° F.) for from 20 to 25 minues until mixture is heated throughout.

Variations

Escalloped ham, eggs, and asparagus:
Escalloped ham, eggs, and green beans:
Escalloped ham, eggs, and green peas:

Use only 2 dozen hard-cooked eggs and add 2 quarts of cooked asparagus cuts, green beans, or peas.

HAM À LA KING

See variation of chicken a la king, page 74.

BAKED HAM
(For carving directions see page 36.)

Yield: 12-pound ham — 30 to 36 servings   Size of serving: 3 to 3½ ounces
15-pound ham — 38 to 45 servings

12 to 15 pounds tenderized ham
            or
10 to 12 pounds canned or fully cooked
    ham
1 to 2 cups mild vinegar, cider, pineapple
    juice or spiced fruit syrup*
1½ to 2 cups sugar, brown
2 tablespoons whole cloves**

For tenderized hams

1. Place the hams in baking pans. Bake them in a moderate oven (325° F.) for about 3 hours, or until they are tender but not overcooked and reach an internal temperature of 150° F.

2. Add the liquid, sugar, and cloves as above. Raise the temperature to a hot oven (400° F.) and bake for from 15 to 30 minutes, or until the internal temperature reaches 160° F.

For canned or fully cooked hams

1. Place the hams in baking pans; add the liquid, sugar, and cloves as given above. Bake in a moderate oven (325° F.) for about 2 hours or until internal temperature reaches 130° F.

*From spiced peaches, watermelon, pears, or sweet pickles.
**Remove the cloves before carving.

HAM SAUSAGE *OR* BOLOGNA WITH CREAMED PEAS

Yield: 50 to 55 servings   Size of serving: ⅔ cup of creamed peas in a ham curl

5 quarts cream sauce
    5 quarts milk
    1½ cups butter *or* fortified
        margarine
    2½ cups flour
4½ quarts peas (7½ pounds frozen or 1½ cans, No. 10)
Salt to taste
3 tablespoons sugar
2½ to 3 pounds ham sausage or
    bologna slices*

1. Make the cream sauce.

2. Cook or heat the peas; drain. Add them and the seasonings to the cream sauce.

3. Remove the casings from the meat; place the slices in a lightly greased pan and broil them in a hot oven (450° F.) or run them under a broiler until the slices curl. Serve the creamed peas over the curls.

*More meat will be needed for thicker slices.

51

Ham sausage or bologna with creamed asparagus cuts: Use frozen or canned asparagus.

Ham sausage or bologna with creamed mixed vegetables: (see recipe page 116)

Ham sausage or bologna with hot potato salad: (see recipe page 133)

HAMBURGER DEEP-DISH PIE

Yield: 50 servings

Size of serving: 1 portion (3 × 2¾ inches)

2½ quarts carrots, diced (about 5 pounds before peeling)

3 pounds small onions (about 3½ pounds before peeling)

2¼ quarts potatoes, diced (about 4 pounds before peeling)

1. Boil the vegetables, saving the water for making the gravy.

8 pounds beef,* raw, ground

5 cups flour

1½ gallons vegetable liquid and water†

⅓ cup salt

Gravy coloring

2. Brown the meat in a hot oven (400° F.). Add the flour to the meat and fat and stir until well blended. Add the vegetable liquid and water and cook until thickened, stirring constantly. Add the salt and gravy coloring.

5 cups peas, cooked (2 pounds frozen or 2 cans, No. 2)

3. Add the peas and other vegetables to the meat mixture. Put into baking pans and heat throughout.

Drop-batter crust

8 eggs (1½ cups)

1 quart milk

1 tablespoon salt

1½ teaspoons sugar

1. Beat the eggs and milk; add the salt and sugar.

1 pound (1 quart) flour, all-purpose

3 tablespoons baking powder

2. Sift together the flour and baking powder; add to the egg-milk mixture and beat well.

½ cup shortening, melted

3. Add the melted shortening last. Cover the *hot* meat and vegetable mixture with the batter. Bake in a hot oven (400° F.) for about 18 minutes or until crust is done. Cut into squares for serving.

*Other raw meats may be used. Five pounds of chopped or diced cooked meat may be used in place of raw meat.
†Diluted commercial beef concentrate may be used to add flavor.

Variation

Meat upside-down cake: A biscuit crust may be used in place of the drop crust. Serve this with tomato sauce, gravy or vegetable gravy.

HAMBURGER GRAVY ON POTATOES

Yield: 50 to 55 servings

Size of serving: 2/3 cup on 1 serving of potato

8 pounds beef, raw, ground

1. Brown the beef in a hot oven (400° F.) for about 1 hour.

5 cups flour

2. Add the flour to the hot meat and fat and stir until well blended.

2 gallons water, hot
1/3 cup salt
Gravy coloring

3. Add the hot water slowly and cook until thickened, stirring constantly. Add the salt and gravy coloring as needed.

Serve on:
Mashed, boiled, *or* baked
  potatoes

NOTE: A small quantity of chopped onions, 2 to 3 medium size, may be added for flavor while the meat is browning.

Variation

Hamburger gravy on rice or noodles: Cook 2½ pounds (5⅓ cups) of rice or 2½ pounds noodles.

HAMBURGER SPANISH RICE

Yield: 50 to 55 servings

Size of serving: 3/4 cup

4 pounds beef, raw, ground
2 cups onions, chopped

1. Brown the beef with the onions in a hot oven (400° F.) or on top of a range.

2½ pounds (5¼ cups) rice

2. Cook the rice in 2½ gallons of boiling water and ¼ cup of salt. Drain it in a colander and rinse it with water.

1 cup green peppers, chopped
2 cans, No. 10, tomato soup, condensed
1 15-ounce can pimientos, cut up

3. Combine the meat, vegetables, tomato soup, and rice. Heat the mixture over hot water or place it in baking pans and bake it in a moderate oven (350° F.) for 20 to 30 minutes until it is heated throughout.

CORNED BEEF HASH

Yield: 50 to 55 servings

Size of serving: 3/4 cup

9 pounds corned beef, cooked or canned
9 pounds (6½ quarts) potatoes, cooked (about 12 pounds before peeling)

1. Chop the corned beef and potatoes together.

1 cup onions, chopped
½ cup meat drippings *or* other fat

2. Brown the onions lightly and add them to the meat-potato mixture.

1½ quarts meat stock*

Garnish with:
1/3 cup parsley, chopped, *or* 1 can pimiento strips

3. Add the meat stock. Place the mixture in baking pans. Bake in a moderate oven (350° F.) for from 30 to 45 minutes until the mixture is heated throughout.

*Commercial meat concentrate may be used to make the meat stock.

SOUTHERN HASH

Yield: From 50 to 55 servings   Size of serving: ¾ cup

8 pounds (8 quarts) meat,*
cooked, diced, chopped, or
coarsely ground

7 quarts potatoes, cooked,
chopped (about 12 pounds
before peeling)

2 cups green peppers, cut into   1. Cook the peppers and onions with the fat.
strips

2½ cups onions, sliced

½ cup drippings, fortified margarine *or* butter

1 cup (1 7-ounce can) pimientos,   2. Season the tomatoes well and combine them
cut into strips   with the meat, potatoes, and vegetables. Add a

2½ quarts (¾ can, No. 10)   small quantity of meat stock, if needed to
tomatoes   moisten. Put the mixture in greased baking pans,

Salt and pepper to taste   garnish with potato and pimiento strips. Bake

Meat stock to moisten   in a moderate oven (350° F.) for from 30 to 45

Cooked potato strips and   minutes.
pimiento strips to garnish

*Less meat and more potatoes may be used for a cheaper dish.

BAKED LIVER

Yield: 50 to 55 servings   Size of serving: 3- to 4-ounce slice

12 pounds liver, sliced, beef *or*   1. Trim the liver and remove the skin; dredge
lamb   with seasoned flour.

1½ cups flour
1½ tablespoons salt
½ teaspoon pepper

2½ cups bacon fat   2. Put the fat and onion in baking pans. Add

½ cup onions, minced (may be   the floured liver and bake in a hot oven (400° F.)
omitted)   for from 20 to 30 minutes.

LIVER CREOLE SPAGHETTI

See variation of creole beef spaghetti, page 46.

LIVER DUMPLINGS

Yield: 50 servings   Size of serving: 2 dumplings and ¼ cup sauce

5 pounds (3¾ quarts) beef or   1. Mix thoroughly all the ingredients except the
lamb liver, cooked, ground   stock and water. Chill. For shaping the dump-

1½ pounds fat salt pork *or*   lings use a No. 20 scoop that has been dipped
bacon, cooked, ground   in melted margarine; roll the dumplings in flour.

½ cup onions, chopped fine
1 cup parsley, chopped
1 dozen eggs, slightly beaten
1½ quarts bread crumbs, soft

2½ tablespoons salt
½ teaspoon pepper
5 quarts meat stock*
1½ quarts water

2. Heat the stock and water to boiling; drop the dumplings into the boiling stock; reduce the heat and simmer for about 10 minutes or until cooked throughout.

Serve with:
4 quarts tomato sauce *or* brown
   gravy

*Commercial beef concentrate may be used to make the meat stock.

MEAT AND NOODLES

Yield: 50 to 55 servings   Size of serving: ⅔ cup

2½ pounds noodles

1. Cook the noodles in 2½ gallons of boiling water with ½ cup of salt; drain them in a colander and rinse with water.

5 pounds beef,* raw, ground or
   diced
⅓ cup onions, chopped
¼ cup beef drippings
3½ quarts meat stock

2. Brown the beef and onions with the fat in a baking pan in a hot oven (400° F.) or on top of a range, stirring frequently. Add the stock and simmer the mixture for 30 minutes, or until the meat is tender.

½ cup beef drippings or butter
1 cup flour
Salt and pepper to taste
½ cup chili sauce

3. Melt the fat and stir in the flour; add this to the hot stock and cook until thickened, stirring constantly. Add the seasonings. Combine the noodles, meat, and sauce, or serve the meat mixture as a sauce over the noodles. Add further seasoning as needed.

*Other raw ground meats may be used. Three pounds of ground or diced cooked meats may be used in place of the raw meat.

MEAT AND POTATO PUFF

Yield: 50 to 55 servings   Size of serving: ⅔ cup and ¼ cup sauce *or* gravy

4 pounds (3 quarts) meat, cooked,
   chopped
15 to 20 pounds potatoes after
   peeling (7 quarts mashed) (20
   to 24 pounds before peeling)
2½ to 3½ quarts milk, hot
3½ tablespoons salt
¼ cup butter *or* fortified margarine

1. Cook the potatoes, mash them immediately. Add the salt, butter, and then the hot milk gradually.

1 cup onions, chopped
1½ cups bacon fat *or* drippings

2. Cook the onions with the fat.

1 cup parsley, chopped
3 cups gravy *or* cream sauce

3. Combine the meat, potatoes, onions, parsley, and gravy, mixing thoroughly. Add seasonings as needed.

1½ dozen eggs, beaten

4. Add the beaten eggs; pile the mixture lightly

into greased baking pans; bake in a moderate oven (350° F.) for 1 hour until the mixture is set in the center and the top is lightly browned. Test for doneness by inserting a knife blade into the center of the puff; knife will come out clean when the puff is done.

Serve with:
4 quarts tomato sauce *or* brown gravy

MEAT AND RICE BALLS

Yield: 50 to 55 servings   Size of serving: 2 balls

8 pounds beef,* raw, ground
3 tablespoons salt
3½ cups cold water
2 pounds (4¼ cups) rice, uncooked

2 quarts tomatoes
2 quarts hot water

1. Combine the meat, salt, cold water and uncooked rice, combining thoroughly. Using a No. 20 scoop divide the mixture into uniform portions. Shape these like a frankfurter roll and place in baking pans.

2. Cover the balls with the tomatoes and water. Bake them in a moderate oven (325° F.) for from 1½ to 2 hours, or until the rice is cooked. Add water during cooking to keep the balls completely covered.

*Other ground meat as lamb, veal, or pork may be used.

MEAT AND VEGETABLE STEW I

Yield: 50 to 55 servings   Size of serving: ¾ cup

15 pounds meat,* cut in 1-inch cubes
1 cup onions, chopped

1. Add the onions to the meat. For light stew, simmer the mixture in water. For brown stew, brown the mixture in a hot oven (400° F.), add water to cover and simmer in a slow oven (300° F.) until tender.

2 quarts carrots, diced or cut in chunks (about 4 pounds before peeling)
2 quarts potatoes, diced or cut in chunks (about 4 pounds before peeling)
1 quart celery rings
2½ cups flour
2½ cups cold water
5 tablespoons salt
½ teaspoon pepper

2. Cook the vegetables separately or cook them with the meat, adding them to the meat when it is partially done.

3. Make a paste of the flour and cold water; add this to the hot liquid and cook until thickened, stirring constantly but carefully. Use enough of the paste to make a medium-heavy gravy. Combine the meat mixture and the vegetables.

1½ quarts peas (2½ pounds frozen or 3 cans No. 2)

4. Cook or heat the peas; add them to the stew just before serving; they may be sprinkled over the top. Add further seasoning as needed.

Garnish with:

⅓ cup parsley, chopped

*Beef: chuck, brisket, shank, plate, short ribs
Lamb: chuck, breast
Veal: shoulder, chuck, breast

MEAT AND VEGETABLE STEW II

Reduce the meat to 10 pounds, and increase the vegetables by one-half.

Variations

Meat pie: place the hot mixture in baking pans and cover with baking powder biscuits.

Biscuits	
3 pounds (3 quarts) flour, all-purpose	1. Mix and sift the dry ingredients.
3 ounces (½ cup) baking powder	
2 teaspoons salt	
11 ounces (1½ cups) vegetable fat ,	2. Rub in the fat and add the milk, handling lightly; knead the dough on a lightly floured board for a few seconds until smooth. Roll the dough ½-inch thick and cut into 2½-inch rounds. Place the biscuits on top of the hot meat mixture and bake in a hot oven (425° F.), or the biscuits may be baked separately and placed on the hot mixture just before serving.
4½ to 5 cups milk	

Shepherd's pie: Use lamb cut into cubes for the meat. Cover the mixture with a mashed potato crust.

Mashed potato crust	
8 pounds potatoes, after peeling	1. Cook and mash the potatoes. Add the milk and seasonings. Dip the hot meat mixture into baking pans. Cover this with the mashed potatoes using a pastry tube. Brush with melted butter if desired and brown in a hot oven (425° F.) or under the broiler.
1½ to 2 quarts hot milk	
2 tablespoons salt	
¼ cup melted butter *or* fortified margarine	

Garnish with:

⅓ cup parsley, chopped

MEAT BALLS AND SPAGHETTI

See variation of creole beef spaghetti, page 46.

SAVORY MEAT BALLS

Yield: 50 servings   Size of serving: 2 meatballs

12 pounds beef, raw, ground	1. Mix together the beef, pork, eggs, milk, bread crumbs, salt, and pepper. Measure the mixture with a No. 16 ice cream scoop forming each scoopful into a ball. Roll the balls in flour. Brown them in an oven at 400° F. Reduce the heat to 350° F.
4 pounds pork, raw, ground	
12 eggs	
2 quarts milk	
2½ pounds (6 quarts) soft bread crumbs	
5 tablespoons salt	
1 teaspoon pepper	
1 quart apples, diced (3 to 4 medium apples)	2. Combine the apples, onions, celery, peppers, and tomatoes. Place this mixture over the meat balls and bake about 1 hour. Baste the meat balls occasionally with the juice and diced vegetable.
2 quarts onions, sliced (about 3 pounds onions)	
1 quart celery, diced	
1½ cups green peppers, chopped	
3¼ quarts (1 can No. 10) tomatoes	

MEAT* BISCUIT ROLL

Yield: 50 servings

Size of serving: 1 roll (3½-inch diameter) and
¼ cup of gravy or sauce

7 pounds (5 to 6 quarts) beef,*
cooked, chopped or ground
¼ cup onions, minced
¼ cup butter, fortified margarine, or drippings
5 cups thick cream sauce or
brown gravy
    5 cups milk or meat stock
    ¾ cup fat
    1¼ cups flour
Salt and pepper to taste.

1. Cook the onions with the fat; combine the
meat, onions, and sauce, and season to taste;
heat the mixture.

Biscuits

5 pounds (5 quarts) flour, all-
purpose
5 ounces (¾ cup) baking powder
4 teaspoons salt
1 pound (2½ cups) vegetable
fat
8 to 8½ cups milk

1. Mix and sift the dry ingredients.

2. Rub in the fat; combine all with the milk,
handling lightly; knead the dough on a lightly
floured board for a few seconds until smooth.
Divide the mixture into parts; roll into rectangles
from ⅛ to ¼ inch thick. Spread them with the
meat mixture and roll up as for a jelly roll. Cut
in slices about ¾ inch thick, and place them in
lightly greased pans. Bake in a hot oven (425° F.)

Serve with:

4 quarts tomato or mushroom
sauce or brown gravy

*Other cooked meats as veal, lamb, liver, pork, or combinations of them may be used.

Variations

Tunafish biscuit roll:

1 quart celery rings
¾ cup butter or fortified margarine

1. Cook the celery until just tender.

1½ quarts peas (2½ pounds
frozen or 3 cans, No. 2)

2. If the peas are frozen, cook them; drain.

¾ cup pimientos, chopped
6 13-ounce cans tunafish*
6 eggs, slightly beaten

3. Combine all the ingredients. Proceed as for
beef biscuit roll. Serve with a cream sauce to
which peas have been added.

*The amount of fish may be reduced by one-half. Then use one quart of additional vegetables.

Salmon biscuit roll: Use 5 1-pound cans of salmon in place of the tunafish.

CREOLE MEAT

Yield: 50 to 55 servings

Size of serving: ⅔ cup on a slice of toast

10 pounds (7½ quarts) meat,
cooked, cubed

½ cup onions, chopped	1. Cook the onions and peppers in the fat.
½ cup green peppers, chopped	
¾ cup butter *or* fortified margarine	
1½ quarts (½ can, No. 10) tomatoes	2. Heat the tomatoes and stock together.
2 quarts meat stock*	
¾ cup bacon fat	3. Melt the fat and stir in the flour; add this to the hot tomato-stock mixture and cook until thickened stirring constantly with a wire whip.
1½ cups flour	
3 tablespoons lemon juice	4. Add the lemon juice, horseradish, meat, onions, peppers. Heat throughout.
3 tablespoons horseradish	
Salt and pepper to taste	

Serve on:

50 slices bread, toasted, *or* other
 base (see page 14)

NOTE: Mushrooms may be added; use ¼ pound and cook them with the onions and peppers.

*Commercial beef concentrate may be used to make the meat stock.

MEAT CROQUETTES

Yield: 50 to 55 servings   Size of serving: 2 croquettes and ¼ cup of gravy *or* sauce

7 pounds (5½ quarts) meat, cooked, chopped, *or* ground	1. Combine the meat, rice, and eggs.
3⅓ quarts cooked rice *or* mashed potato	
6 eggs, slightly beaten	
⅓ cup onion, minced	2. Cook the onions and peppers in the fat. Add these, the parsley and pimiento to the meat-rice mixture. Combine all the ingredients using enough cream sauce or gravy to bind them together. Add seasonings as needed. Using a No. 20 scoop as a measure, shape the mixture into croquettes.
⅓ cup green pepper, minced	
1 cup butter *or* drippings	
⅓ cup parsley, minced	
⅓ cup pimiento, minced	
Medium cream sauce *or* gravy (1 to 1½ quarts), to moisten	
Salt and pepper, to taste	

For dipping:

6 cups crumbs	3. Combine the eggs and milk. Roll the croquettes in the crumbs, then dip these in the egg-milk mixture and again roll in crumbs. Chill them. Fry in deep fat at 360° F. until brown. Drain them on brown paper.
10 eggs, beaten	
1 cup milk	

Serve with:

4 quarts gravy, vegetable gravy,
 tomato sauce *or* cream sauce
 with peas.

MEAT LOAVES

General directions:

1. For the crumbs, use chopped *soft* bread (1 pound measures approximately 2½ quarts).

2. If onions are used, cook them with butter, fortified margarine, *or* drippings.

3. Beat the eggs slightly and add the milk or other liquid; pour this mixture over the chopped bread and combine with the meat and other ingredients and mix lightly. (Overmixing makes a compact and tough loaf.)

4. Divide the mixture into loaf pans of similar size; have the pans well greased and level off the tops, so that the loaves will be an even shape.

5. Bake the loaves in a moderate oven (350° F.) for from 1¼ to 1½ hours. If fresh pork is used in the mixture, the loaves should be cooked thoroughly. Use a meat thermometer and cook to an internal temperature of 175° to 185° F.

6. Allow the loaves to stand in a warm place for 20 to 30 minutes before slicing.

7. Drain off the liquid and use for gravy.

8. Cut the loaves into uniform servings (figure 3).

9. Serve with gravy, jelly, pickle, relish, catsup, parsley sauce, tomato sauce or other accompaniments.

Yield: 4 loaves of from 4 to 4½ pounds of raw mixture per loaf, 48 to 72 servings   Size of serving: 1 slice

BEEF LOAF I

11 pounds beef* raw, ground

1 pound fresh *or* fat salt pork, raw, ground

2 quarts bread, soft, chopped

6 eggs, slightly beaten

5 cups milk

½ cup onions, chopped

½ cup drippings, butter, *or* fortified margarine

¼ cup salt

½ teaspoon pepper

2 quarts tomato soup (may be poured over top of loaves before baking, if desired)

*8 pounds of beef and 4 pounds of pork and veal may be used.

BEEF LOAF II

10 pounds beef, raw, ground

2½ pounds (6 quarts) soft bread crumbs

1¼ quarts water *or* milk

9 eggs, slightly beaten

¼ cup salt

1 teaspoon pepper

2 tablespoons onion, minced

HAM AND PORK LOAF

8 pounds fresh pork, raw, ground

4 pounds smoked ham, raw, ground

1 quart bread, soft, chopped

8 eggs, slightly beaten

2 cups milk

1 tablespoon salt

½ teaspoon pepper

2 quarts (⅔ can, No. 10) tomatoes, poured over the tops of the loaves before baking

BEEF-OAT LOAF

7½ pounds beef, raw, ground
1½ pounds (2¼ quarts) oatmeal
8 eggs, slightly beaten
2¼ quarts milk
1 cup onions, minced
2½ cups catsup
¼ cup salt
1½ teaspoons pepper
4 teaspoons celery salt

HAM AND NOODLE LOAF

1 pound noodles (cook, drain, and chop
  the noodles)
3½ pounds ham,* ground
7 pounds fresh pork,* ground
7 eggs, slightly beaten
2 cups bread crumbs, soft
1¾ cups milk
2 teaspoons salt
½ teaspoon pepper

*Other kinds of raw, ground meat may
be used.

MEAT-VEGETABLE SQUARES

¾ pound noodles (cook, drain and
  chop the noodles)
6 pounds beef, raw, ground
3 cups onions, chopped fine
2 quarts celery, chopped fine, cooked
1 quart potatoes, chopped, cooked
1 quart green beans, chopped, cooked
1 quart carrots, chopped fine, cooked
1 cup green peppers, chopped
1 quart bread crumbs, soft
1 quart milk
1 dozen eggs, slightly beaten
⅓ cup salt
½ teaspoon pepper

SPANISH MEAT LOAF

12 pounds beef, raw, ground
4 cups (12 ounces) oatmeal, uncooked
5 cups (2 cans, No. 2½) tomatoes
2½ cups bread, soft, chopped
5 eggs, slightly beaten
5 cups cream sauce, heavy (¾ cup of
  fat, 1 cup of flour, 5 cups of milk)
5 tablespoons salt
¾ teaspoon pepper
2½ cups celery, diced
½ cup green peppers, diced

*This mixture may be baked in flat baking
pans and cut into squares. The mixture
should be about 2 inches thick in the pan.

VEAL LOAF

13 pounds veal,* raw, ground
2½ quarts bread, soft, chopped
9 eggs, slightly beaten
1½ quarts milk
3½ tablespoons salt
½ teaspoon pepper

*¾ pound of ground salt pork may be substi-
tuted for ¾ pound of the veal.

Variations

Meat patties: Use recipe for beef loaf II, page 60. Form the mixture into patties (3 per pound of mixture). Place in baking pans or in muffin pans; bake them in a moderate oven (350° F.) for about 25 minutes, until done throughout.

Meat squares: Spread the mixture about 1-inch thick in baking pans and bake in the same way as the patties. Cut into squares for serving.

MEAT, NOODLE, AND CHEESE CASSEROLE

Yield: 50 to 55 servings   Size of serving: ¾ cup

7 pounds, beef *or* pork, raw, ground, *or* sausage
1 pound (3 cups) onions, chopped

1. Brown the meat and onions in a hot oven (400° F.) or on top of a range.

2¼ pounds noodles

2. Cook the noodles in 2 gallons of boiling water and ¼ cup salt. Drain them in a colander and rinse them with water.

5 quarts (1½ cans, No. 10) condensed tomato soup
½ teaspoon salt
1 pound (1 quart) cheese, chopped or grated

3. Combine the meat, noodles, soup, salt, and one-half of the cheese and put into baking pans. Sprinkle the remaining cheese over the top of the mixture. Bake the mixture in a moderate oven (350° F.) for from 20 to 30 minutes until heated throughout. This mixture may be heated in a double boiler on the top of a range.

MEAT PATTIES

See variation of meat loaves, page 61.

MEAT PIE

See variation of meat and vegetable stew, page 57.

MEAT SHORTCAKE

Yield: 50 to 55 servings   Size of serving: ⅔ cup of the meat sauce and 1 biscuit

5 pounds (5 quarts) beef,* cooked,† diced
1 cup catsup
¼ cup horseradish
1 gallon brown gravy (1½ cups of fat, 2 cups of flour, 1 gallon of stock‡)

1. Heat the beef, catsup, horseradish, and gravy together. Season to taste.

Biscuits

3 quarts (3 pounds) flour, all-purpose
½ cup (3 ounces) baking powder
2 teaspoons salt

1. Sift the dry ingredients together.

1½ cups (11 ounces) vegetable fat
4½ to 5 cups milk

2. Rub in the fat and add the milk, handling lightly; knead the dough on a lightly floured board for a few seconds until smooth. Roll the dough ½ inch thick and cut into 2½-inch rounds. Bake them in a hot oven (425° F.)

¾ cup butter *or* fortified margarine

3. Split the biscuits and butter lightly if desired. Serve the meat mixture over the biscuits.

*Other cooked meats as lamb, liver, pork, or veal may be used.
†Raw ground meat may be used; brown 10 pounds with a little fat in a hot oven (400° F.) for about 1 hour.
‡Commercial meat concentrate may be used for making the meat stock.

Variation

This mixture may be served on boiled or baked potatoes, boiled rice or noodles, or toast. It may be divided into baking pans and covered with a batter crust for a ground beef pie.

MEAT SQUARES

See variation of meat loaves, page 61.

MEAT TURNOVERS

Yield: 50 to 55 servings

Size of serving: 1 turnover and ¼ cup gravy

8 pounds (6 quarts) beef, *or* other meat, cooked, chopped

2¼ quarts potatoes, raw, chopped (about 4 pounds before peeling)

1 quart meat stock

4 to 5 tablespoons salt

1 teaspoon pepper

1. Combine all the ingredients, mixing thoroughly. Add further seasoning if needed.

Pastry

3 quarts (3 pounds) flour, all-purpose

4½ tablespoons salt

1. Sift the flour and then weigh it; add the salt.

5¼ cups (2¼ pounds) shortening

2. Work in the shortening carefully, handling the mixture as little as possible.

1½ cups ice water

3. Add the ice water quickly, handling lightly. Chill the dough before rolling it. Roll out the dough ⅛ inch thick, cut it into circles 4½ inches in diameter. Place a No. 20 scoopful of the meat mixture on each circle; fold over and press the edges firmly together. Make 2 gashes in the top and brush top with milk. Bake in a hot oven (400° F.) until the crust is evenly browned.

Serve with:

4 quarts gravy *or* tomato sauce

MEAT UPSIDE-DOWN CAKE

See variation of hamburg deep-dish pie, page 52.

PEPPERS STUFFED WITH MEAT FILLING

Yield: 50 servings

Size of serving: ½ pepper with ½ cup of filling and ¼ cup of sauce

25 green peppers

1. Wash the peppers, cut them in halves, and remove the seeds.

1¾ pounds (3¾ cups) rice

2. Cook the rice in 2 gallons of boiling water and ¼ cup of salt; drain it in a colander and rinse it with water.

5 pounds (4 quarts) meat, cooked, ground

3. Mix the cooked rice, meat, and tomatoes, using enough tomatoes to moisten the mixture. Season

3 to 4 cups (1 can, No. 2½)
tomatoes
Salt and pepper to taste

to taste. Fill the peppers with the mixture. Place them in greased baking pans, put very little water in the bottom of the pans, and bake the peppers in a moderate oven (350° F) until they are tender.

Topping:

1 quart coarse bread crumbs
½ cup melted butter *or* fortified
margarine (may be omitted)

1. Butter the crumbs and spread them over the tops of the peppers. Return them to a hot oven and brown.

Serve with:

4 quarts tomato, cheese, *or*
mushroom sauce

Variation

Stuffed peppers with vegetable filling: Omit the meat. Use 3 cups diced cooked celery, 3 cups diced cooked carrots, 1 cup chopped cooked onions, 1½ quarts whole kernel corn, and tomatoes to moisten (about 2 cups).

PORK À LA KING

See variation of chicken à la king, page 74.

POTATO BEEFBURGERS

Yield: 50 cakes

Size of serving: 1 cake with ¼ cup gravy *or* sauce

6 pounds hamburg
3 quarts potato, raw, chopped
(about 6 pounds of potatoes
before peeling)
1½ cups onions, grated or
chopped very fine
3 tablespoons salt
1 teaspoon pepper

1. Combine all the ingredients, mixing thoroughly. Divide each pound of mixture into 4 portions and shape each into a flat cake. Place these in baking pans and bake in a moderate oven (350° F.) for from 20 to 30 minutes until potatoes and meat are cooked throughout.

Serve with:

4 quarts gravy *or* tomato sauce

SALISBURY STEAK

Yield: 55 to 60 servings (3 patties
per pound of raw mixture).

Size of serving: 1 patty

17 pounds beef, raw, coarsely
ground
6 tablespoons salt
1½ teaspoons pepper
2 quarts water

1. Mix the meat, seasonings, and water lightly; form flat patties.

For rolling:

2½ quarts bread crumbs

2. Coat the patties with the crumbs. Place them in well-greased baking pans. Bake them in a moderate oven (350° F.). Remove them from the pans. Add water to the fat in the pans, bring

the mixture to a boil, and pour it over the patties.

SAUSAGE AND APPLE CAKES

Yield: 50 servings   Size of serving: 1 cake

10½ pounds, sausage, bulk   1. Combine all the ingredients, mixing thorough-
5 eggs, slightly beaten   ly. Form into cakes using 1 pound of mixture
2 quarts (¾ pound) bread   for each 4 cakes. Bake in a moderate oven (350°
   crumbs, soft   F.) for from 25 to 30 minutes until done through-
1¼ quarts (2¼ pounds) apple,   out and browned.
   grated or chopped fine
2 tablespoons salt

SAUSAGE IN ACORN SQUASH

Yield: 50 servings   Size of serving: ½ acorn squash and 1 ball of sausage

25 acorn squash, medium size   1. Wash the squash, cut them in half, either
                                                     crosswise or lengthwise and place in baking pans
                                                     with cut surface down. Steam or bake them until
                                                     tender. If squash are baked add small quantity
                                                     of water to each pan.

Salt   2. Sprinkle each half with salt, pepper, and a
Pepper   little brown sugar.
Sugar, brown

6 pounds sausage, bulk   3. Combine the sausage, bread crumbs, water,
3 quarts (1¼ pounds) bread   and salt and mix thoroughly. Divide each pound
   crumbs, soft   in 6 portions and shape these portions into balls.
2 cups ice water   Place the balls in baking pans and bake in a
2 tablespoons salt   moderate oven (350° F.) for about 30 minutes.
                                                     Place a sausage ball in each squash half, and
                                                     return them to the oven to heat thoroughly and
                                                     brown the sausage.

Garnish with:
Parsley sprigs

SAUSAGE ROLLS

Yield: 50 servings   Size of serving: 2 rolls and ¼ cup of gravy

12½ pounds (100 links) sausage   1. Bake the sausage links in a hot oven (400° F.)
                                                     until partially done; drain them from the fat.

Biscuit dough
4 pounds (4 quarts) flour, all-   1. Mix and sift the dry ingredients.
   purpose
4 ounces (½ cup plus 2 tablespoons) baking powder
1 tablespoon salt
13 ounces (2 cups) vegetable fat   2. Rub the fat in the dry mixture; combine this
5 to 5½ cups milk   with the milk, handling lightly; knead the dough
                                                     on a lightly floured board for a few seconds until
                                                     smooth. Divide the dough into thirds; roll each

65

Serve with:
4 quarts sausage gravy
  4 quarts top milk
  2 cups sausage drippings
  2 cups flour
  Salt, pepper to taste

piece into a rectangular sheet about ⅛ inch thick or thinner. Measuring with a sausage link and allowing for lapping, cut the dough into pieces for wrapping the links lengthwise. Wrap each length with dough lapping over the ends. Place the rolls in baking pans with the lapped edges on the bottom. Bake them in a hot oven (425° F.) for from 20 to 25 minutes.

SAUSAGE STUFFED IN APPLES

Yield: 50 servings   Size of serving: 1 stuffed apple

50 apples, medium-sized

1. Wash and core the apples, making the hole quite large at the top.

6¼ pounds sausage, bulk

2. Divide each pound of sausage into eighths; stuff one portion into each apple. Put the apples in pans generously greased with bacon or sausage fat. Bake them in a moderate oven (350° F.) for 1 hour or until the apples are tender.

If desired, sugar may be sprinkled over the top.

SHEPHERD'S PIE

See variation of meat and vegetable stew, page 57.

BAKED ROUND STEAK

Yield: 50 to 55 servings   Size of serving: 4 ounces before cooking

14 pounds steak, round,
  (¾-inch thick)
Flour
Salt
Pepper

1. Cut the steak into 4-ounce servings. They may be pounded to aid in breaking up the connective tissue. Dredge them with seasoned flour.

1 cup beef drippings *or* other
  fat
½ cup salt
1 teaspoon pepper

2. Melt the fat in baking pans. Arrange the pieces of meat in the pans and sprinkle with salt and pepper. Brown them in a hot oven (400° F.) turning them as necessary. Add a small quantity of water and cover. Reduce the temperature to 300° F. and bake until tender, 1 to 1½ hours. Add more water as needed.

Variations

Mushroom or Spanish sauce may be served with the baked steak.

Swiss steak: Add 2 quarts of canned tomatoes in place of the water.

Spanish steak: Add 1 cup chopped green peppers, 1 cup chopped onions, ¼ cup chopped pimientos. Use canned tomatoes in place of the water.

CHICKEN FRIED STEAK

Yield: 50 servings

Size of serving: 4 to 5 ounces before cooking

13 to 17 pounds round steak,
⅜-inch thick
Flour
Salt
Pepper

1. Cut the steak into servings and pound until about ¼ inch thick. Dredge each piece with seasoned flour.

For dipping:

3 cups milk
8 eggs
2 quarts crumbs, fine

2. Dip the floured steak in the egg-milk mixture; then dip in crumbs. Pack the crumbs on and shake off any excess. Fry in deep fat at 360° F. Drain well and serve immediately.

SWISS STEAK

See variation of baked round steak, page 66.

VEAL À LA KING

See variation of chicken à la king, page 74.

BARBECUED VEAL* BALLS

Yield: 50 servings

Size of serving: 2 balls

6 pounds veal, raw, ground
3 pounds fresh pork, raw, ground
½ cup onions, chopped fine
3 tablespoons salt
½ teaspoon pepper
1¼ quarts milk
3 quarts (1¼ pounds) bread crumbs, soft
5 eggs, slightly beaten

1. Mix all the ingredients together thoroughly. Using a No. 20 scoop, divide the mixture into equal portions; shape these into balls and place them in baking pans.

Barbecue sauce

¾ cup dill pickles, chopped
2 cups dill pickle juice
2 cups chili sauce
¼ cup Worcestershire sauce
1 teaspoon Tabasco sauce
1 tablespoon salt

2. Mix all the ingredients of the sauce; pour this over the balls and bake in a moderate oven (350° F.) for from 25 to 30 minutes.

*Other raw, ground meat may be use.

JELLIED VEAL LOAF

See variation of jellied chicken loaf, page 76.

WIENERS AND MACARONI AU GRATIN

See variation of macaroni and cheese, page 87.

POULTRY COOKERY[1]

Poultry is available either feather dressed (New York dressed) or table dressed. Feather dressed poultry is that which has been bled and feathers removed; table dressed poultry is ready to cook, having had the entrails, head, and feet removed. These parts are approximately one-fourth of the feather dressed weight. Poultry may be purchased fresh killed or frozen.

Tender poultry is usually under a year old and has little tough connective tissue. Broilers, fryers, and roasters are cooked by dry-heat methods: broiling, oven-broiling, frying, and roasting. They may also be cooked by moist heat, adding various liquids for flavoring. Fowl (over one year) is less tender and should be cooked with added liquid as in fricasseeing and stewing (simmering). They may be fried if they are first stewed, then drained well, and wiped dry.

Turkey is more generally roasted whole. However, it may be purchased in parts such as breasts, thighs, drumsticks, and wings. The parts may be best cooked by braising. The less tender muscles such as the drumsticks and thighs will take longer to cook than the breast. Turkeys with a short body and a broad breast give a greater yield of meat with a larger proportion of breast. The heavier leg tendons should be removed before cooking.

The time necessary for defrosting frozen poultry depends on the size of the bird and the method of defrosting.

1. Birds may be immersed in cold running water for 2 to 5 hours.

2. They may be placed (in original wrapping) on a refrigerator shelf for 1 to 3 days.

3. They may be left (in original wrapping) at room temperature for 4 to 12 hours. However, they should not be left standing at room temperature once they are completely thawed.

Initial preparation of a drawn bird consists of removing any pin feathers, singeing it over an open flame and washing it thoroughly.

Improperly handled poultry products are often the cause of food poisoning outbreaks. Follow these precautions.

1. Do not allow workers with sores, colds, or other infectious diseases to handle poultry or dressing.

2. Keep frozen poultry in storage at 0° F. or below until time to thaw.

3. Store fresh and thawed poultry in a refrigerator under 50° F. and use within 24 hours. Do not allow a prolonged warming period at kitchen temperature. This is especially serious if the bird is stuffed with a warm dressing.

---

[1]Directions (with photographs) on how to prepare chicken and fowl ready for the different methods of cooking may be found in *How to Prepare and Cook Poultry.* By L. Shaben and L. M. Hurd, Cornell Extension Bulletin 785.

4. If birds are stuffed
   a) Roast immediately after stuffing *or*
   b) Refrigerate under 50° F. until time to cook — not longer than 12 hours.

   Dressing baked separately must be handled with the same precaution.

5. If carved and served within one hour after roasting, keep bird or the carved meat hot. Do not allow temperature to drop below 125° F. If *not* served shortly after roasting, refrigerate the bird. Slice the cold meat, stack it, and cover with a damp cheesecloth or with aluminum foil. Add a little hot stock, heat, and serve immediately. Do not allow meat to stand at room temperature.

6. The stock or gravy made from the stock should be handled with the same precautions. Either keep it hot (at least 125° F.) until served or refrigerate it and heat just before serving. Never hold it longer than 24 hours.

Roasting

The drawn bird is first salted inside, and may then be trussed for even cooking and browning, and to conserve space, particularly necessary when several birds are being roasted at one time. In quantity preparation, oftentimes birds are roasted without stuffing. A quartered onion may be placed in the body cavity.

Directions for trussing

1. Loosen the skin of the neck, after drawing it back, cut off the neck close to the body. Fasten the neck skin to the back with skewers.

2. Lift the wings up and out forcing the tips back until they rest flat against the neck skin.

3. Draw the thighs close to the body and hold them in place by the band of skin across the abdomen, or tie them to the tail piece with clean string.

Directions for stuffing the bird

1. Prepare stuffing according to recipe page 72. Allow approximately:
   a) 1 cup per pound of New York dressed weight.
   b) 1½ cup per pound of drawn (table dressed) weight.
2. Fill the neck cavity and skewer neck skin to the back.
3. Fill the body cavity loosely. Tightly packed dressing will be soggy and will likely cause the bird to burst during cooking.
4. Fasten with skewers and a string lacing.
5. Fasten the lacing around the tail.
6. Tie the legs together and fasten to the tail.

Directions for making giblet gravy

How to prepare the giblets

1. Simmer the neck, gizzard, and heart until tender, 2 to 3½ hours. Add liver and cook only 10 to 20 minutes.

2. Chop or grind the meat.

How to make the gravy

1. Use 2 to 3 cups of flour for each gallon of gravy. Proceed according to directions for making gravy, page 42.

2. Add the chopped giblets.

3. Keep hot for serving.

Directions for roasting turkey

(Directions for carving are given with figures 8 to 11 inclusive).

1. Preheat oven to correct temperature according to the weight of the birds (see chart, page 40).

2. Grease the skins thoroughly with melted or softened cooking fat.

3. Cover the top and sides with a fat-moistened cloth unless the bird is well streaked with fat.*

4. Place the birds in an uncovered roasting pan and cook them at the designated temperature for the entire period.

5. Baste the cloth with fat from the pan or with a fat and hot water mixture.

6. Test for doneness by one of the following methods:

a) Use a meat thermometer. (1) Insert it in the center of the inside thigh muscle and cook the bird to 190° F. or (2) Insert the thermometer in the center of the dressing and cook the bird to 180° F.

b) Press the fleshy part of the drumstick with the fingers protected with a paper towel. The meat will feel soft when done.

Directions for roasting chicken and fowl

(Directions for carving are given with figures 8 to 11 inclusive).

Method 1 (for chicken)

1. Preheat the oven to 300° F.†

2. Place the bird on a rack in an uncovered roasting pan and cook it at 300° F. for the entire period.

3. Baste with fat and hot water as necessary (1 cup of fat to 1 quart of hot water).*

Method 2 (for fowl)

1. Preheat the oven to 450° to 475° F.

2. Brown the bird for approximately 20 minutes or until it is well browned.

3. Reduce the heat to 275° F. for the remainder of the cooking.

4. Add a little water; cover the roasting pan tightly; add more water as needed.

---

*Another method of keeping turkey and chicken from becoming too brown during roasting is either to wrap the bird in aluminum foil, splitting the foil near the end of the cooking if the skin is not sufficiently browned, or to cover the top of the bird with foil. This method also helps to retain the moisture of the bird.

†If searing is preferred, preheat the oven to 475° F. and sear the bird for approximately 20 minutes; reduce the heat to 300° F. for the remainder of the cooking.

Fricasseeing

The fowl is cut into eight portions. First it is split from neck to tail; then each half cut into four portions: (1) wing, upper part of breast, and ribs; (2) remainder of breast; (3) thigh and back; (4) drumstick.

Directions for fricasseeing

1. Season by rubbing the pieces with salt and pepper.
2. Dip each piece into flour.
3. Brown each piece in cooking fat.
4. Place the pieces in a pan; cover them with boiling water. Cover the pan tightly.
5. Simmer the chicken at 180° F. on top of the range or in an oven at 275° F.
6. Remove the pieces and make a gravy, using a paste made of ½ cup of flour and ½ cup of cold water for each quart of stock.

Broiling

Broiling chickens are usually divided into servings by splitting them in two from neck to tail; the backbone and neck are removed and may be cooked together to give stock for gravy.

Cooked broilers may be held in a slow oven for serving; the pieces should be stacked loosely to keep them crisp.

Directions for broiling

1. Preheat the broiler.
2. Brush the chicken with unsalted fat (vegetable).
3. Place the pieces, skin side up, on the broiler pan.
4. Broil them under a low flame.*
5. Turn each piece after 12 or 15 minutes.
6. Brush them with melted butter and season.

*The heat may be increased at the end of cooking if a browner product is desired.

Frying

Frying chickens are cut into quarters or smaller pieces.

Method 1 (Shallow-fat)	Method 2 (Deep-fat)
1. Place cooking fat in a large heavy frying pan to a depth of 1 to 1½ inches and heat it.	1. Place cooking fat in a frying kettle and heat it to 375° F. (Use 6 pounds of fat for each one pound of chicken).
2. Dip the pieces of chicken in cold water and then roll them in seasoned flour.	2. Dip the pieces in cold water and then roll them in seasoned flour. If desired, pieces may be dipped in a batter* before frying.

*Batter dip for approximately 50 servings: 1 pound 12 ounces flour, 2½ tablespoons salt; 8 eggs slightly beaten, 7 cups milk, ⅓ cup melted shortening.

71

3. Place the dredged pieces in the hot fat and lower the heat so that the pieces will brown slowly. Fry for from 5 to 10 minutes until pieces are brown, turning them over to brown them on both sides.

3. Fry the pieces in hot fat at about 360° F. for about 3 minutes until just browned.

4. Place the pieces one layer deep in a baking pan and brush the tops with a mixture of melted butter and chicken broth. Cook in a 350° F. oven for from 30 to 40 minutes, turning the pieces once and brushing again with the butter-chicken-broth mixture.

Stewing

Stewed fowl may be served with thickened gravy; it may be drained and dried for frying; or it may be used for creaming, for salad and other dishes calling for cooked chicken. If the recipe calls for diced meat, the dicing may be done the day before and the chicken refrigerated; the stock should be cooled quickly and also refrigerated.

Directions

1. Cook the fowl whole or cut it into four or more pieces as for fricasseeing.
2. Add seasoning and just enough water to cover, simmer from 2 to 4 hours; the fowl is tender when the meat begins to fall away from the bone.

Recipes

BREAD DRESSING FOR STUFFING POULTRY

Yield: Stuffing for one 15-pound bird.
  (1 cup of stuffing for each pound of bird)

4 quarts (1½ pounds) bread, soft, chopped
1¼ cups butter or fortified margarine
¼ cup onions, chopped
2 tablespoons parsley, chopped
1 cup celery, chopped
1 tablespoon salt
½ teaspoon pepper
1 tablespoon poultry seasoning
Hot milk or stock to moisten

1. Cook the onion, parsley, and celery with the butter. Combine these with the bread and seasonings. Moisten with the hot milk or stock.

NOTE: For a dry dressing toast the bread; add only enough hot stock to just moisten the mixture. For a variation of this dry dressing use 1 quart of crumbled cornbread in place of 1 quart of bread and add 1 cup of chopped walnuts.

CHICKEN AND CELERY LOAF

Yield: 3 loaves, 36 to 48 servings

Size of serving: 1 slice or 1 square and ¼ cup of sauce or gravy

3 pounds cooked chicken* removed from bones
5½ quarts celery, chopped fine
2 quarts bread crumbs, soft
9 eggs, slightly beaten

1. Prepare the fowl; chop the meat fine.

2. Mix the chicken, celery, bread crumbs, and eggs together.

72

2¼ quarts milk
1 cup chicken fat, butter *or* fortified margarine
1 cup plus 2 tablespoons flour
1½ tablespoons salt
¾ teaspoon pepper

Serve with:

4 quarts mushroom sauce, cream sauce with peas, *or* chicken gravy

3. Heat the milk; melt the fat and stir in the flour; add this to the hot milk and cook until thickened, stirring constantly with a wire whip. Add the seasonings, and then add the the sauce to the above ingredients mixing thoroughly. Put the mixture into well-greased loaf pans, using 4 pounds for each pan; pack well. Set these in pans of hot water and bake in a moderate oven (350° F.) for about 1 hour. Test for doneness by inserting a knife blade into the center of the loaf; knife will come out clean when the loaf is done. Let the loaves stand in a warm place for from 20 to 30 minutes before slicing.

*Use approximately 12 pounds of New York dressed fowl or 9 pounds of table-dressed for the 3 pounds of clear meat.

Variation

Turkey and celery loaf: Use cooked turkey in place of the chicken.

CHICKEN AND NOODLES

Yield: 50 to 55 servings

Size of serving: ⅔ cup

10 pounds fowl, purchased weight*
5 cups tomatoes (2 cans, No. 2)
2 cloves garlic
3 tablespoons Worcestershire sauce
6 small red peppers
3 pounds noodles

1. Cook the fowl, tomatoes, garlic, sauce, and peppers together with enough water to yield 2 gallons of stock. Remove the garlic and peppers, but do not strain out the tomatoes. Cool the fowl, remove the meat from the bones and cut it into pieces. There should be 2½ pounds of clear meat.

2. Cook the noodles in 3 gallons of boiling water with ½ cup of salt; drain them in a colander and rinse with water.

2 gallons chicken stock

3. Heat the stock.

2 cups chicken fat, butter, *or* fortified margarine
1 quart flour
Salt and pepper to taste

4. Melt the fat and stir in the flour; add this to the hot stock and cook until thickened, stirring constantly with a wire whip. Season to taste. Combine with the chicken and noodles. Add further seasoning as needed. Heat throughout.

NOTE: A smaller amount of chicken may be used to decrease the cost of the recipe.

*New York dressed or 7½ pounds of table-dressed fowl.

Variation

Turkey and noodles: Use cooked turkey in place of the fowl.

CHICKEN À LA KING

Yield: 50 to 55 servings

Size of serving: ⅔ cup of mixture on a slice of toast, a patty shell, a baking powder biscuit, or a No. 16 scoop of rice.

3½ pounds cooked chicken,* removed from bones

1. Prepare the fowl; cut it into medium-sized pieces.

73

½ 4-ounce can pimientos, cut
in strips
1 cup green peppers, diced
1½ pounds mushrooms, sliced
(or 3 8-ounce cans)
1 cup chicken fat, fortified margarine *or* butter
3 quarts chicken stock
2 cups chicken fat
3½ cups flour
2 cups milk
2 cups cream, light *or* evaporated
milk
16 eggs, hard-cooked, diced
⅓ cup salt
½ teaspoon pepper
Serve on:
50 slices bread, toasted *or*
50 patty shells *or*
50 baking powder biscuits *or*
2½ pounds (5¼ cups) rice

2. Cook the vegetables with the fat until they
are tender.

3. Heat the stock; melt the fat and stir in the
flour; add this to the hot stock and cook until
thickened, stirring constantly with a wire whip.
Add the milk, cream, chicken, eggs, and vegetables. Add the seasonings and heat. Add further
seasoning as needed.

4. Serve the chicken mixture over toast, patty
shells, baking powder biscusits, or a No. 16 scoop
of rice. Cook the rice in 2½ gallons boiling water
with ⅓ cup salt; drain it in a colander and rinse
it with water; reheat it in the oven.

Variations

Ham à la king: Use cooked diced ham in place of the chicken. May be served on
cornbread squares.

Pork à la king: Use cooked diced pork in place of the chicken. May be served on
cornbread squares.

Turkey à la King: Use cooked diced turkey in place of the chicken.

Veal à la king: Use cooked diced veal in place of the chicken.

*Use approximately 14 pounds of New York dressed fowl or 10½ pounds of table-dressed for
the 3½ pounds of clear meat.

ESCALLOPED CHICKEN

Yield: 50 to 55 servings

Size of serving: ¾ cup and ¼ cup gravy

5 pounds cooked chicken* removed from bones

1. Cut the meat into cubes.

Gravy

1½ gallons chicken stock

1. Remove fat from the chicken stock; then heat
the stock.

3 cups chicken fat *or* other fat
3 cups flour
3 tablespoons salt

2. Melt the fat and stir in the flour; add this to
the hot stock and cook until thickened, stirring
constantly with a wire whip. Add the salt.

Dressing

⅓ cup onions, chopped
¼ cup butter *or* fortified margarine

1. Cook the onions with the fat.

6½ quarts bread, soft, broken

2. Combine all the ingredients of the dressing,

74

1½ cups chicken fat *or* other fat
1 tablespoon sage *or* poultry seasoning
2 tablespoons salt
¼ teaspoon pepper
Hot stock to moisten

Serve with:
4 quarts chicken gravy

*Use approximately 20 pounds of New York dressed chicken *or* 15 pounds of table-dressed for the 5 pounds of clear meat.

mixing thoroughly. Moisten with the hot stock. Arrange in greased baking pans in layers as follows: dressing, gravy, cubed chicken, gravy, dressing. Bake in a moderate oven (350° F.) for from 30 to 40 minutes.

NOTE: The chicken may be cooked and the gravy made the day before using, cooled, and stored in a refrigerator.

Variation

Escalloped turkey: Use cooked turkey in place of the fowl.

CHICKEN PIE

Yield: 50 to 55 servings

Size of serving: ⅔ cup of mixture

4 pounds cooked chicken* removed from bones
3 quarts potatoes, diced (about 7 pounds before peeling)
1½ cups carrots, diced
1½ quarts peas (2½ pounds frozen *or* 3 cans, No. 2) *or* green beans
1 cup onions, chopped
1½ gallons chicken stock
2 cups chicken fat, fortified margarine *or* butter
3½ cups flour
Salt, pepper, and celery salt to taste

1. Prepare the fowl; cut it into large cubes.

2. Cook the vegetables until just tender.

3. Cook the onions in the stock for 10 minutes; strain them from the stock.

4. Melt the fat; stir in the flour; add this to the hot stock and cook until thickened, stirring constantly with a wire whip. Combine all the ingredients, seasoning as needed. Place the mixture in individual casseroles or baking pans (figure 3).

Drop crust†
8 eggs (1½ cups)
1 quart milk
1½ teaspoons sugar
1 quart (1 pound) flour, all-purpose
3 tablespoons baking powder
1 tablespoon salt
½ cup butter *or* shortening, melted

1. Combine the eggs, milk, and sugar.

2. Sift the flour, baking powder, and salt together; combine them with the liquid mixture.

3. Add the melted shortening. Pour the batter over the top of the *hot* chicken mixture. Bake in a hot oven (425° F.) for from 25 to 30 minutes until crust is done.

*Use approximately 16 pounds of New York dressed fowl or 12 pounds of table-dressed for the 4 pounds of clear meat.
†A baking-powder biscuit crust may be used.

Variation

Chicken (or turkey), vegetable, and rice casserole: Omit the potatoes. Cook 1¾ pounds (3¾ cups) of rice in 1½ gallons of water and 3 tablespoons of salt. Drain it in a colander and rinse it with water. Place a No. 20 scoop of rice in the bottom of individual buttered casseroles. Put the chicken mixture over the rice (about ⅔ cup for each casserole) and top with buttered bread cubes (about 2 quarts will be required). Buttered baking pans may be used instead of casseroles. Bake at 350° F. until mixture is well heated and bread cubes browned.

NOTE: The quantity of fowl may be decreased and more vegetables added to lessen the cost of these recipes.

JELLIED CHICKEN OR VEAL LOAF

Yield: 4 loaves (48 slices) or 65 ring molds (3 ounces each)

Size of serving: 1 slice or 1 mold*

5 pounds (5 quarts) veal† *or* chicken,‡ cooked and diced

2½ to 3 ounces (7½ to 9 table-spoons) gelatin, granulated§

2½ cups cold water

1. Soak the gelatin in the cold water.

1 gallon veal *or* chicken stock from which the fat has been removed

1 tablespoon onion juice

6 tablespoons salt

1 teaspoon pepper

2 cups lemon juice *or* vinegar

2. Heat half of the stock; add the soaked gelatin to it and stir until the gelatin is dissolved, then add the seasonings. Add the cold stock and chill.

1 quart carrots, diced

1½ quarts peas (2½ pounds frozen *or* 3 cans, No. 2)

3 cups green peppers, diced

3. Cook the vegetables until tender; drain and cool them. When the gelatin mixture begins to set, add the vegetables. Mold in loaf pans or individual molds that have been rinsed with cold water.

*If ring molds are used, turn out the mixture and garnish the center; Waldorf or potato salad is suggested.
†Purchase 12 pounds of shoulder veal for the 5 pounds of clear cooked veal.
‡Use approximately 20 pounds New York dressed fowl or 15 pounds table-dressed for the 5 pounds of clear chicken.
§If gelatin must be set quickly or if gelatin is made during hot weather, use the large amount.

TURKEY AND CELERY LOAF

See variation of chicken and celery loaf, page 73.

TURKEY AND NOODLES

See variation of chicken and noodles, page 73.

TURKEY À LA KING

See variation of chicken à la king, page 74.

ESCALLOPED TURKEY

See variation of escalloped chicken, page 75.

FISH

Single fillets are most commonly used in quantity food service. They may or may not have the skin removed. Allow 1 pound of fillet for each 3 or 4 portions. Usually, the fillets are cut into portions before cooking.

Raw and cooked fish are very perishable and should be kept under refrigeration.

Frozen fish should be kept frozen until used and thawed immediately before cooking. Thawed fish should never be refrozen. Dressed frozen fish, fillets, and steaks may be cooked as if they were in the unfrozen form, allowing additional time. However if fish is to be breaded and fried or baked, it should first be thawed. The best method for defrosting is to place the wrapped fish in a refrigerator allowing it to thaw only long enough for ease in preparation. Completely defrosted fish and fish thawed at room temperature have considerable leakage. Thawing fish in water causes loss of flavor.

ACCOMPANIMENTS

Well-seasoned cream sauce, plain, or with parsley, hard-cooked chopped egg, chopped green peppers or pimientos; creole sauce; tomato sauce; tartar sauce; drawn butter sauce; lemon or mock hollandaise sauce.

Watercress, chopped parsley, paprika, lemon wedge, tomato slice.

Lemon butter: 1½ pounds of soft butter creamed with ¼ cup lemon juice and ½ cup chopped parsley yields 50 garnishes. The lemon butter may be chilled and cut into cubes.

COOKERY

Steaming

1. Cut the fish fillets or steaks into servings.
2. Place them one layer deep in flat pans.
3. Steam for from 10 to 20 minutes depending on the amount cooked at one time and thickness of the pieces.
4. Brush with melted butter and serve with a garnish or sauce.

Poaching

Use any of the following liquids for poaching:

Salted water, fish stock, milk, or milk and water; use 1 tablespoon salt for each quart of liquid.

Acidulated water: use 1 tablespoon salt and 3 tablespoons lemon juice or vinegar for each quart of water.

Court bouillon: Tie 1 teaspoon peppercorns and 12 cloves in a cheesecloth bag. Prepare 4 sliced carrots, 4 sliced onions, 8 pieces of celery cut into rings and a bunch of chopped parsley. Boil all with 1 gallon water, ¼ cup salt, 1 cup vinegar or lemon juice, 6 sprigs thyme and 6 bay leaves for 30 minutes. Remove the spices and herbs.

1. Cut the fish into servings.

2. Prepare the liquid.

3. Place the portions of fish in this and *simmer* for from 10 to 20 minutes according to the thickness of the fish.

4. Remove the fish from the liquid and drain.

5. Serve with a sauce or garnish.

Baking

1. Cut the fish into servings.

2. Roll the pieces in salted flour or sifted bread crumbs.

3. Place these in baking pans which have been generously oiled with cooking oil or fat.

4. Sprinkle the top of each piece with cooking oil or melted fat.

5. Bake them in a very hot oven (450° F.) for from 10 to 15 minutes depending on the thickness of the pieces.

6. Serve with a garnish or sauce.

Frying

1. Wipe the fish fillets or steaks as dry as possible; cut these into servings.

2. Roll them in seasoned flour, dip in an egg-milk mixture (6 beaten eggs and 2 cups milk), then roll them in fine bread crumbs or cracker crumbs.

3. Place them in a wire basket, one layer deep.

4. Fry them in deep fat at 365° to 370° F. for from 5 to 10 minutes depending on the kind of fish and on the thickness of the pieces.

5. Drain and serve with a sauce or garnish.

Broiling

1. Heat the broiler.

2. Wipe the fish fillets or steaks as dry as possible; cut them into servings.

3. Place the pieces in greased shallow pans or on a greased broiler rack.

4. Sprinkle them with salt and pepper; brush with melted fat if dry-meated fish is used.

5. Place these under the broiler about 2 inches from the flame.

6. After the fish is browned on one side, turn carefully; brown on the other side.

7. Serve with a sauce or garnish.

RECIPES

CODFISH CAKES

Yield: 55 to 60 cakes

Size of serving: 1 cake and ¼ cup sauce

4½ pounds codfish, dried

1. Cover the codfish with water and soak it overnight. Drain. Cover it with fresh water and steam or boil it until tender. Drain and cool it. Shred it into fine pieces (this may be done on a chopping machine).

10 pounds potatoes (about 13 pounds before peeling)
1 tablespoon salt

2. Cook the potatoes, add the salt and mash them. Do not add any milk.

9 eggs, beaten

3. Mix the codfish, potatoes, and eggs. Add further seasonings as needed. Chill the mixture. Using a No. 16 scoop, measure the mixture and shape each scoopful into a cake. Place the cakes in well-greased baking pans. Bake them in a moderately hot oven (400° F.) until browned *or* shape the mixture into balls, roll them in flour, then dip them in an egg-milk mixture and roll them in bread crumbs. Fry them in deep fat at 380° F.

Serve with:
4 quarts egg, parsley, *or* tomato sauce

CREAMED CODFISH

Yield: 50 to 55 servings

Size of serving: ⅔ cup

5 pounds codfish, dried
2 gallons cream sauce
  2 gallons milk
  2½ cups butter *or* fortified margarine
  5 cups flour
12 egg yolks, beaten
Salt and pepper to taste

1. Prepare the codfish as for codfish cakes.
2. Make the cream sauce.

3. Add a small amount of the hot cream sauce to the egg yolks, combine, and return this to the remaining cream sauce. Add the flaked codfish and add seasoning as needed. Keep the mixture hot over water that is maintained just below the boiling point.

Garnish with:
⅓ cup parsley, chopped
Serve on:
50 slices bread, toasted *or* 50 boiled or baked potatoes

79

ESCALLOPED FISH, NOODLES, AND MUSHROOMS

Yield: 50 to 55 servings   Size of serving: ¾ cup

3 pounds noodles

1. Cook the noodles in 3 gallons boiling water with 6 tablespoons salt; drain them into a colander and rinse with water.

2 quarts milk
1½ quarts chicken* or veal stock
1 cup onions, finely chopped

2. Heat the milk, stock, and onions together.

2 cups butter or fortified margarine
1¾ cups flour
4 tablespoons salt

3. Melt the fat and stir in the flour; add this to the hot stock and cook until thickened stirring constantly with a wire whip. Add the salt.

4 8-ounce cans mushrooms
4 15-ounce cans fish flakes

4. Add the mushrooms to the cream sauce. Put a layer of noodles in greased baking pans and then a layer of flaked fish. Cover with the mushroom sauce.

For topping:
1½ quarts bread cubes or other topping (see page 14)

5. Put the bread cubes over the top. Bake in a moderate oven (350° F.) for from 20 to 25 minutes until the mixture is heated throughout and the top is browned.

*Commercial chicken concentrate may be used to make the stock.

Variations

Escalloped tunafish, noodles, and mushrooms: Use 5 13-ounce cans of tunafish in place of the fish flakes.

Escalloped salmon, noodles, and mushrooms: Use 4 1-pound cans of salmon in place of the fish flakes.

ESCALLOPED OYSTERS

Yield: 55 to 60 servings   Size of serving: ¾ cup

1½ gallons oysters
1 cup butter or fortified margarine

1. Remove any shells from the oysters. Cook them with the butter until edges of oysters begin to curl. Drain the liquor from the oysters and save it.

3 quarts milk
3 tablespoons onion juice
3 tablespoons Worchestershire sauce
3 tablespoons salt
½ teaspoon pepper

2. Heat the milk and oyster liquor together. Add the onion juice, Worcestershire sauce, salt, and pepper.

3 pounds (8 quarts) crackers, broken or coarsely chopped
1 cup butter or fortified margarine, melted
Paprika

3. Arrange a layer of crackers in each baking pan, then a layer of oysters, and another layer of crackers. Pour hot milk mixture over this. Cover with a thin layer of crackers and pour melted butter over the crackers. Sprinkle the top with paprika. Bake in a moderate oven (350° F.) for from 20 to 25 minutes.

Garnish with:

⅓ cup chopped parsley

NOTE: If mixture seems dry, add 2 cups of hot milk after removing it from the oven.

FRIED OYSTERS

Yield: 50 servings   Size of serving: 4 to 6 oysters

1½ gallons oysters, large

1. Remove any shells from the oysters and drain them.

2 quarts sifted bread or cracker crumbs

2. Roll the oysters in bread or cracker crumbs.

1 cup milk
1 dozen eggs
2 tablespoons salt
1 teaspoon pepper

3. Make a mixture of the milk, eggs, and seasonings, and dip the oysters in this mixture. Roll again in bread or cracker crumbs. Fry the oysters in deep fat at 355° to 360° F. for from 2½ to 3 mintues until browned.

SALMON *OR* TUNAFISH AND RICE CROQUETTES

Yield: 50 servings   Size or serving: 2 croquettes and ¼ cup sauce

3 1-pound cans salmon *or* 4 13-ounce cans tunafish

1. Drain the fish, reserving the liquid for the cream sauce; remove the bones and skin. Flake the fish.

2½ pounds (5⅓ cups) rice

2. Cook the rice in 2½ gallons boiling water and ⅔ cup salt. Drain it into a colander and rinse it with water.

1¼ quarts milk and fish liquid

3. Heat the liquid.

¾ cup butter *or* fortified margarine
1¼ cups flour
1 tablespoon salt

4. Melt the fat and stir in the flour; add this to the hot liquid and cook until thickened, stirring constantly with a wire whip. Add the salt.

3 eggs, beaten

5. Add a small amount of the hot sauce to the beaten eggs and add this mixture to the remaining sauce. Cook for about 1 minute, stirring constantly. Cool the sauce.

1 4-ounce can pimientos, chopped
3 tablespoons onion, grated

6. Combine the fish, rice, cream sauce, onions, and pimientos mixing lightly. Chill the mixture. Using a No. 20 scoop, divide the mixture into uniform portions; roll these balls into croquettes.

For dipping:

3 eggs
1 cup milk

7. Beat the eggs and milk together.

2 quarts fine bread crumbs, dry

8. Dip the croquettes in the egg-milk mixture and then roll them in the crumbs. Fry the croquettes in deep fat at 380° F.

Serve with:

4 quarts cream sauce with peas *or* parsley *or* tomato sauce

81

SALMON *OR* TUNAFISH LOAF

Yield: 4 loaves (from 48 to 56 slices)

9 1-pound cans salmon flaked *or* 11 13-ounce cans tunafish

4½ quarts bread crumbs, soft
2 quarts milk and fish liquid
1 dozen eggs, beaten
1½ quarts celery, finely diced or minced
1 teaspoon paprika
3 tablespoons salt
⅓ cup butter *or* fortified margarine, melted

Serve with:

4 quarts tomato sauce *or* cream sauce with parsley, chopped hard-cooked eggs, or peas

Size of serving: 1 slice and ¼ cup sauce

1. Drain the fish saving the liquid. Remove skin and bones from salmon.

2. Combine all the ingredients. Put from 4 to 4½ pounds of the mixture into each of four greased loaf pans and bake them in a moderate oven (350° F.) until firm. Remove the loaves from the pans and allow them to remain in a warm place for from 15 to 20 minutes before slicing.

SALMON BISCUIT ROLL

See variation of meat biscuit roll, page 58.

SEAFOOD NEWBURG

Yield: 50 to 55 servings

2 pounds shrimp, cooked
13 ounces crabmeat, flaked
18 eggs, hard-cooked

5 quarts cream sauce
   3¾ quarts milk
   2 cups butter *or* fortified margarine
   2½ cups flour
1¼ quarts cream, light

½ cup catsup (may be omitted)
¼ cup sherry
1 tablespoon salt
1 teaspoon pepper

Serve on:

50 slices bread, toasted *or* other base (see page 14)

Size of serving: ⅔ cup on 1 slice of toast

1. Clean the shrimp; leave them whole. Remove any pieces of shell from crab meat.

2. To hard cook the eggs, cover them with cold water, bring to simmering temperature and cook over low heat for 10 to 15 minutes. Drain off the hot water and cover them with cold water. Remove the shells and quarter the eggs.

3. Make the cream sauce.

4. Add the cream to the sauce. Add the fish and eggs, folding them in carefully. Heat the mixture throughout.

5. Add the catsup, sherry, and seasonings just before serving.

CREAMED TUNAFISH *OR* SALMON WITH PEAS I

Yield: 50 to 55 servings

Size of serving: ⅔ cup on 1 slice of toast

6 1-pound cans salmon *or* 7 13-ounce cans tunafish

1. Drain the fish, reserving the liquid for the cream sauce. Remove the bones and skin; flake the fish.

3 quarts peas (5 pounds frozen *or* 1 can, No. 10)

2. If frozen peas are used, cook them until just tender.

6 quarts cream sauce
  6 quarts milk and fish liquid
  1½ cups butter *or* fortified margarine
  3 cups flour
  3 tablespoons salt
  ¼ teaspoon pepper

3. Make the cream sauce; combine it with the fish and peas, stirring carefully to prevent breaking the flakes. Add further seasoning as needed.

Serve on:
50 slices bread, toasted *or* other base (see page 14)

CREAMED TUNAFISH *OR* SALMON WITH PEAS II

Use 4 pounds of fish and 5 quarts of peas for a cheaper dish.

Variations

Creamed tunafish or salmon and asparagus or green beans: Use asparagus cuts or green beans in place of the peas. An attractive entree consists of placing asparagus spears on toast and adding a cream sauce containing the flaked salmon or tunafish.

Creamed tunafish or salmon, eggs, and peas: Replace part of the fish with sliced hard-cooked eggs.

ESCALLOPED TUNAFISH *OR* SALMON AND EGGS

Yield: 50 to 55 servings

Size of serving: ¾ cup

6 13-ounce cans tunafish *or* 5 1-pound cans salmon

1. Drain the fish, reserving the liquid for the cream sauce. Remove the bones and skin; flake the fish.

4½ dozen eggs, hard-cooked

2. To hard cook the eggs, cover them with cold water, bring to simmering temperature and cook over low heat for from 10 to 15 minutes. Drain off the hot water and cover them with cold water. Remove the shells.

4½ quarts cream sauce
  4½ quarts milk and fish liquid
  1½ cups butter *or* fortified margarine
  3 cups flour

3. Make the cream sauce. Add the fish, folding it in carefully.

4. Arrange quartered hard-cooked eggs on greased baking pans and cover with a layer of the creamed fish.

Topping:
1 quart bread crumbs, soft *or* other topping (see page 14)

5. Place bread crumbs over the top. Bake in a moderate over (350° F.) for from 20 to 25 min-

83

utes until the mixture is heated throughout and the top is browned.

Variations

Escalloped tunafish or salmon, peas, and celery: Use 7 13-ounce cans tunafish *or* 6 1-pound cans salmon, 3 quarts cooked peas (5 pounds frozen or 5 cans, No. 2), 4 quarts cooked, diced celery, 5 quarts cream sauce.

Escalloped tunafish or salmon, noodles, peas, and eggs: Use 4 13-ounce cans tunafish *or* 3 1-pound cans salmon, 3 pounds noodles, 2¼ quarts cooked peas (3½ pounds frozen or 4 cans, No. 2), 2½ dozen sliced hard-cooked eggs, 6 quarts cream sauce.

NOTE: Asparagus cuts may be used in place of the peas.

ESCALLOPED TUNAFISH *OR* SALMON WITH NOODLES AND MUSHROOMS

See variation of escalloped fish, noodles, and mushrooms, page 80.

TUNAFISH *OR* SALMON BISCUIT ROLL

See variation of meat biscuit roll, page 58.

TUNAFISH *OR* SALMON PIE I

Yield: 50 to 55 servings | Size of serving: ¾ cup and 1 biscuit

8 13-ounce cans tunafish *or* 6 1-pound cans salmon

1. Drain the fish, reserving the liquid for the cream sauce. Remove the bones and skin, and break the fish into large pieces.

1 quart celery rings
2 cups green peppers, chopped
2 quarts potatoes, cooked, diced (about 4 pounds of potatoes before peeling)
1 dozen eggs, hard-cooked
1 7-ounce can pimientos, cut into strips

2. Cook the celery until tender; cook the peppers slightly.

3. Prepare the potatoes, eggs, and pimientos. To hard cook the eggs, cover them with cold water, bring to simmering temperature and cook over low heat for 10 to 15 minutes. Drain off the hot water and cover them with cold water. Remove the shells and dice the eggs.

1½ gallons cream sauce
  1½ gallons milk and fish liquid
  1½ cups butter *or* fortified margarine
  3 cups flour

4. Make the cream sauce. Add the fish, vegetables, and eggs, folding them in carefully. Add further seasoning as needed. Place the mixture into greased baking pans and heat throughout.

Biscuit crust

3 pounds (3 quarts) flour, all-purpose
3 ounces (½ cup) baking powder
2 teaspoons salt

1. Sift the dry ingredients together.

11 ounces (1½ cups) vegetable fat
4½ to 5 cups milk

2. Rub in the fat and add the milk, handling lightly; knead the dough on a lightly floured board for a few seconds until smooth. Roll the dough ½ inch thick and cut it into 2½-inch

rounds. Place the biscuits on top of the *hot* mixture and bake them in a hot oven (425° F.) or the biscuits may be baked separately and placed on the hot mixture just before serving.

TUNAFISH *OR* SALMON PIE II

4 13-ounce cans tunafish *or* 3 1-pound cans salmon
5 cups potatoes, cubed, cooked
18 eggs, hard-cooked
2 quarts peas, cooked (3½ pounds frozen *or* 4 cans, No. 2)

2 quarts celery rings
1½ cups green peppers, chopped
1 15-ounce can pimientos
1¼ gallons cream sauce

Follow procedure given in recipe I.

TUNAFISH *OR* SALMON SOUFFLÉ

Yield: 50 to 55 servings

Size of serving: ¾ cup

2 quarts milk

1. Scald the milk in a double boiler.

2 cups butter *or* fortified margarine
4 cups flour
2½ tablespoons salt

2. Melt the fat and stir in the flour; add this to the hot milk and cook the mixture until thickened, stirring constantly with a wire whip. Add the salt.

4 dozen (4 cups) egg yolks, beaten

3. Add a little of the hot mixture to the egg yolks and combine. Return this to the hot mixture and cook for about 5 minutes. Cool.

6 13-ounce cans tuna fish *or* 5 1-pound cans salmon

4. Drain the fish, remove the bones and skin, and shred the fish. Add this to the cream sauce, folding fish in carefully.

4 dozen (6 cups) egg whites, stiffly beaten

5. Fold in the egg whites. Put the mixture into slightly greased baking pans and set them into pans of water. Bake in a moderate oven (325° F.) for approximately 1 hour. The soufflé is done when a knife blade inserted in the center comes out clean.

Serve with:

4 quarts cheese, parsley, tomato *or* mushroom sauce

CHEESE RECIPES

CHEESE AND CORN, ESCALLOPED

Yield: 50 to 55 servings

Size of serving: ¾ cup

1¼ cups drippings, butter, *or* fortified margarine
1¼ cups green peppers, chopped
20 (1⅔ cups) egg yolks, beaten
4¼ quarts milk, scalded
2½ pounds (2½ quarts) cheese, chopped

1. Cook the peppers with the fat.

2. Add the egg yolks to the milk; combine all the ingredients except the egg whites; fold them in last. Pour the mixture into greased baking pans; set these into pans of water. Bake them in

2½ quarts bread, soft, chopped
2½ tablespoons salt
2½ quarts (4 cans, No. 2) corn,
  cream style
½ teaspoon paprika
⅛ teaspoon cayenne pepper
¾ teaspoon black pepper
20 (2½ cups) egg whites, stiffly
  beaten

a very moderate oven (325° F.). Remove them
from the oven before the mixture becomes completely firm, and keep them in a warm place
for from 15 to 20 minutes before serving.

CHEESE FONDUE

Yield: 50 to 55 servings — Size of serving: ¾ cup

5 quarts milk, scalded
7½ quarts bread, soft, chopped
4¼ pounds (4¼ quarts) cheese,
  chopped
2½ dozen (2½ cups) egg yolks,
  beaten
½ cup butter, fortified margarine *or* bacon fat
2 teaspoons mustard
2 tablespoons salt
2 teaspoons paprika
2½ dozen (4 cups) egg whites,
  stiffly beaten

1. Combine all the ingredients except the egg
whites; fold them in last. Pour the mixture into
greased baking pans; set these into pans of water.
Bake in a very moderate oven (325° F.) until firm.

MARCARONI AND CHEESE

Yield: 50 to 55 servings — Size of serving: ¾ cup

3½ pounds (4 quarts) macaroni

1. Cook the macaroni in 3½ gallons of boiling
water with ½ cup of salt; drain it in a colander,
and rinse it with water.

1 gallon cheese sauce
  1 gallon milk
  1 cup butter *or* fortified mar-
    garine
  2 cups flour
  ¼ cup salt
  ½ teaspoon pepper
  1 teaspoon paprika
  2½ pounds (2½ quarts)
    cheese, chopped

2. Make the cream sauce. Add the seasonings
and chopped cheese.

1 cup (1 7-ounce can) pimiento
  strips, if desired

3. Mix the macaroni and cheese sauce; pour the
mixture into greased baking pans and garnish
it with pimiento strips. Bake in a moderate oven
(375° F.) for 30 minutes until the top is browned.

Variations

Macaroni with tomato and cheese sauce: Use 1 gallon of tomatoes in place of the
milk in the sauce; heat the tomatoes with 1 tablespoon of whole cloves, and remove
them before thickening the tomatoes.

86

Wieners and macaroni au gratin: Reduce the cheese to 1 pound (1 quart). Add 7½ pounds of wieners cut into ¼-inch circles. Mix 1½ quarts of soft bread crumbs and ½ pound (2 cups) of chopped or grated cheese. Spread this over the top of the macaroni mixture and bake in a moderate oven (350° F.) until the mixture is heated throughout and the top is browned.

QUICK TOMATO RAREBIT

Yield: 50 to 55 servings   Size of serving: ⅔ cup of mixture on 1 slice of toast

4 50-ounce cans condensed tomato soup

1. Heat the soup and cheese over hot water until the cheese melts.

4 pounds (4 quarts) American cheese, chopped or grated

1 14½-ounce can evaporated milk

2. Add the milk and seasonings. Reduce heat until water in bottom of double boiler is simmering.

2½ teaspoons salt

¼ cup Worcestershire sauce

16 (3 cups) eggs, beaten

3. Add the beaten eggs and cook until slightly thickened.

Serve on:

50 slices of bread, toasted *or* other base (page 14)

WELSH RABBIT

Yield: 50 to 55 servings   Size of serving: ⅔ cup on toast

5 quarts milk

1. Heat the milk.

2½ cups butter *or* fortified margarine

3¾ cups flour

2 tablespoons salt

¼ teaspoon pepper

2. Melt the fat and stir in the flour; add this to the hot milk and cook the mixture until thickened, stirring constantly with a wire whip. Add the seasonings.

3 pounds (3 quarts) cheese, chopped

½ teaspoon mustard

2 tablespoons Worcestershire sauce

3. Add the cheese, mustard, and Worcestershire sauce.

8 (⅔ cup) egg yolks, beaten

8 (1 cup) egg whites, stiffly beaten

4. Add a little of the hot mixture to the egg yolks, and combine. Return this to the hot mixture and cook for 3 or 4 minutes. Fold in the whites just before serving.

Serve on:

50 slices bread, toasted *or* other base (see page 14)

Variation

Scotch woodcock: To ¾ of the Welsh rabbit recipe add:

2 cups stuffed olives, sliced

1 quart celery, raw, chopped fine

1. Add to the mixture before folding in the egg whites.

87

EGG RECIPES

EGG CUTLETS

Yield: 50 servings

4 dozen eggs, hard-cooked

Size of serving: 2 cutlets and ¼ cup sauce

1. To hard cook the eggs, cover them with cold water, bring to simmering temperature and cook over low heat for 10 to 15 minutes. Drain off the hot water and cover them with cold water. Remove the shells and chop the eggs quite fine.

2 quarts cream sauce
   2 quarts milk
   1½ cups butter *or* fortified margarine
   3 cups flour
   1½ tablespoons salt
1 tablespoon Worcestershire sauce
1 tablespoon mustard, dry

2. Make the cream sauce.

3. Add the salt, Worcestershire sauce, and mustard. Add the chopped eggs to the cream sauce and mix thoroughly. Chill the mixture thoroughly. Using a No. 24 scoop divide the mixture into uniform portions and shape the balls into cutlets.

For dipping:
3 cups milk
4 eggs
1 quart bread crumbs, dry

4. Beat the eggs and milk together.

5. Roll the cutlets in the crumbs, dip them into the egg-milk mixture, and then in crumbs again. Chill the dipped cutlets. Fry them in deep fat at 380° F.

Serve with:
4 quarts tomato *or* cream sauce sauce

NOTE: This mixture may be placed in baking pans, sprinkled over the top with crumbs, and baked in a moderate oven (350° F.) until the mixture is heated throughout.

Eggs à la goldenrod
Eggs à la king
Creamed eggs and asparagus, green beans or peas
Creamed eggs and mushrooms

See variation of creamed eggs, page 89.

CREAMED EGGS ON TOAST

Yield: 50 to 55 servings

5 dozen eggs, hard-cooked

Size of serving: ⅔ cup on 1 slice of toast

1. To hard cook the eggs, cover them with cold water, bring to simmering temperature and cook over low heat for from 10 to 15 minutes. Drain off the hot water and cover them with cold water. Remove the shells and slice the eggs.

5 quarts cream sauce
   5 quarts milk
   1½ cups butter or fortified

2. Make the cream sauce and add the sliced eggs, folding them in carefully. Combine only as needed.

88

margarine
3 cups flour
2½ tablespoons salt

For garnishing:
1 teaspoon paprika
⅓ cup parsley, chopped

3. Sprinkle paprika and parsley over the top.

Serve on:
50 slices bread, toasted, *or* other
   base (see page 14)

Variations

Eggs à la goldenrod: Cut the hard-cooked eggs in halves and remove the yolks. Cut the whites into pieces and fold them into the cream sauce. Put the yolks through a strainer or ricer. Serve the creamed whites on toast and sprinkle a spoonful of finely divided yolk over the top or place the creamed whites in serving pans and sprinkle the yolks over top and serve all on toast.

Eggs à la king: Add 1 cup chopped pimientos, 1 cup chopped green peppers, and ¼ cup chopped parsley. Combine these with the eggs and cream sauce.

Creamed eggs and: Substitute from one-third to one-half of the vegetables for the
   asparagus   eggs.
   green beans
   peas

Creamed eggs and mushrooms: Add 1¼ pounds of fresh mushrooms which have been browned in a little fat *or* 2 cans drained canned mushrooms.

BAKED EGGS CREOLE

Yield: 50 to 55 servings

Size of serving: ¾ cup

50 eggs, hard-cooked

1. To hard cook the eggs, cover them with cold water, bring to simmering temperature and cook over low heat for 10 to 15 minutes. Drain off the hot water and cover them with cold water. Remove the shells and slice the eggs.

5½ quarts (1¾ cans, No. 10) tomatoes, heated
1¼ cups onions, chopped
2 cups green peppers, chopped
2 cups pimientos, chopped

2. Cook the onions and peppers with the fat; add them with the pimientos to the tomatoes.

2 cups bacon fat, butter, *or* fortified margarine
4 cups flour
⅓ cup salt
½ teaspoon pepper
¼ cup sugar

3. Melt the fat and stir in the flour; add this to the hot tomatoes and cook the mixture until thickened, stirring constantly with a wire whip. Add the seasonings. Add further seasoning as needed. Arrange alternate layers of the sliced eggs and sauce in greased baking pans or casseroles.

Topping:
1½ quarts bread cubes
1 cup butter, melted (may be omitted)

4. Top the mixture with buttered bread cubes. Bake the mixture in a moderate oven (350° F.) until the bread cubes are browned.

89

DEVILED EGGS ON TOAST

Yield: 50 to 55 servings

Size of serving: 1 egg (2 halves) on 1 slice of toast

50 eggs, hard-cooked
2 teaspoons salt
¼ teaspoon pepper
1 tablespoon mustard
¼ cup green peppers, chopped fine
¼ cup pimientos, chopped
1 quart mayonnaise
2 tablespoons vinegar
3½ quarts sauce, tomato, cheese, or cream

Serve on:
50 slices bread, toasted

1. To hard cook the eggs, cover them with cold water, bring to simmering temperature and cook over low heat for 10 to 15 minutes. Drain off the hot water and cover them with cold water. Remove the shells, cut the eggs lengthwise, and remove the yolks. Put the yolks through a sieve and add all the ingredients to them; mix thoroughly. Fill the whites with the yolk mixture (a pastry tube may be used).

2. Place the deviled eggs in shallow baking pans and pour the hot sauce over the eggs. Place them in a very slow oven and heat throughout.

ESCALLOPED EGGS AND GREEN BEANS

Yield: 50 to 55 servings

Size of serving: ¾ cup

7½ pounds green beans, frozen or 2 cans, No. 10
3 dozen eggs, hard-cooked

1. If frozen beans are used, cook them until just tender; drain.

2. To hard cook the eggs, cover them with cold water, bring to simmering temperature and cook over low heat for from 10 to 15 minutes. Drain off the hot water and cover them with cold water. Remove the shells.

1 gallon cream sauce
1 gallon milk
1¼ cups butter *or* fortified margarine
2½ cups flour
2 tablespoons salt

3. Make the cream sauce.

4. Arrange layers of sliced hard-cooked eggs and beans in greased baking pans. Cover these with the cream sauce.

Topping:
1½ quarts bread cubes *or* other topping (see page 14)

5. Put the bread cubes over the top. Bake in a moderate oven (350° F.) for from 20 to 25 minutes until the mixture is heated throughout and the top is browned.

NOTE: Grated or finely chopped onion, pimiento, parsley, or crisp bacon pieces may be added to the cream sauce.

Variations

Escalloped eggs and:
asparagus
mixed vegetables
peas

Use cooked asparagus, mixed vegetables, or peas in place of the green beans.

Escalloped eggs and spinach: Clean and drain one bushel of spinach. Chop this coarsely and use it raw in making up the dish.

SCRAMBLED EGGS

(with cream sauce*)

Yield: 50 servings   Size of serving: ½ cup

1 quart cream sauce
  ⅓ cup butter *or* fortified
    margarine
  ⅓ cup flour
  1 quart milk
  1 teaspoon salt

1. Make the cream sauce.

6 dozen eggs
1 quart milk
3 tablespoons salt

2. Beat the eggs, milk, and salt together using a wire whip.

¾ cup butter *or* fortified margarine

3. Melt the fat in the top of a double boiler.†
Pour in the egg mixture and cook over hot water stirring occasionally as the mixture thickens. When it is thickened fold in the hot cream sauce carefully. Keep the mixture hot for serving.

*Scrambled eggs made by this method will hold satisfactorily for serving.
†If 2 double boilers are used the mixture will cook more quickly.

BAKED OMELET *OR* SOUFFLÉ

Yield: 55 to 60 servings   Size of serving: ¾ cup

3 quarts milk

1. Heat the milk in the top of a double boiler *or* in a hot water bath.

2½ cups butter *or* fortified
  margarine
5 cups flour
3½ tablespoons salt
¼ teaspoon pepper

2. Melt the fat and stir in the flour; add this to the hot milk and cook the mixture until thickened, stirring constantly with a wire whip. Add the seasonings.

6 dozen egg yolks, beaten
6 dozen egg whites, stiffly beaten

3. Add a little of the hot mixture to the egg yolks and combine. Return this to the hot mixture and cook for from 3 to 4 minutes. Cool. Divide the beaten whites and the sauce into halves. Combine, folding the whites into the sauce. Pour the mixture into greased baking pans; set these into pans of hot water. Bake in a slow oven (300° to 325° F.) for from 40 to 50 minutes until set.

Serve with:

1 quart jelly *or*
4 quarts cheese, mushroom, *or*
  Spanish sauce *or* cream sauce
  with parsley *or* peas

91

DRIED BEAN RECIPES
BAKED BEANS

Yield 55 to 60 servings   Size of serving: ¾ cup

6 pounds (3½ quarts) beans, navy *or* kidney dried

1 cup onions, chopped

1. Wash the beans, cover them with water, and soak them overnight. Cook them with the onions until tender in the water in which the beans were soaked.

1 cup molasses

¾ cup (5 ounces) sugar, brown

1 teaspoon mustard

1½ teaspoons paprika

5 tablespoons salt

1½ pounds bacon or salt pork, cut into cubes

⅔ cup catsup

2 tablespoons vinegar

2. Combine the remaining ingredients and add them to the cooked beans. Bake them until well-browned in a moderate oven (350° F.) for 3 hours or longer. Add water if needed.

LIMA BEANS AND BACON IN TOMATO SAUCE

Yield: 50 to 55 servings   Size of serving: ¾ cup

6 pounds (4 quarts) lima beans, dried

¼ cup onions, chopped

1. Wash the beans, cover them with water, and soak them overnight. Cook them with the onions until tender in the water in which the beans were soaked. Drain.

1½ quarts meat stock

3¼ quarts (1 can, No. 10) tomatoes *or* diluted tomato purée

2. Heat the stock and tomatoes together.

2 cups bacon fat

3½ cups flour

¼ cup sugar

4 tablespoons salt

½ teaspoon pepper

1 cup chili sauce

3. Melt the fat and stir in the flour; add this to the hot tomato, and cook the mixture until thickened, stirring constantly with a wire whip. Add the seasonings. Add this to the cooked beans.

2 pounds bacon strips

4. Place the mixture into baking pans or casseroles; place the bacon strips on top.* Bake in a moderate oven (350° F.), for from 1½ to 2 hours.

*The bacon may be cooked separately until crisp and a strip added to each serving.

BAKED LIMA BEANS AND MUSHROOMS

Yield: 50 to 55 servings   Size of serving: ¾ cup

4½ pounds (3 quarts) lima beans, dried

1. Wash the beans, cover them with water, and soak them overnight. Cook them until tender in the water in which they were soaked. Drain.

1½ pounds mushrooms

1 cup onions, chopped

½ cup bacon fat, butter, *or*

2. Clean and slice the mushroom caps and stems. Cook them and the onions in the fat.

fortified margarine
1 gallon cream sauce
1 gallon milk
1 cup fat
2 cups flour
½ cup (½ 7-ounce can)
pimientos, chopped

3. Make the cream sauce.

4. Combine all the ingredients carefully. Put the mixture into greased baking pans. Bake it in a moderate oven (350° F.) for 30 minutes.

Variation

Baked lima beans with mushroom soup: Omit the mushroom, fat, and cream sauce. Use 1 gallon of canned mushroom soup (5 cans, No. 2½) combined with 3 cups of milk. Bake as above.

OTHER MAIN-DISH RECIPES

CORN PILAFF*

Yield: 50 to 55 servings

Size of serving: ¾ cup

1 pound (2⅛ cups) rice
½ cup bacon fat, butter *or* fortified margarine
7 cups juice from corn and water
1½ tablespoons salt
1 cup onions, small whole

1. Brown the rice with the fat in a moderately hot oven (375° F.). Add the water, salt, and onions, and cook the mixture in the oven until the rice is tender; remove the onions.

5½ quarts (1¾ cans, No. 10) corn, whole kernel
1 cup pimientos, chopped
½ cup bacon fat, butter *or* fortified margarine

2. Heat the corn; add it, the pimientos, and the fat to the rice. Heat the mixture.

2 pounds bacon, diced

3. Cook the bacon until crisp; drain, and add it to the corn mixture.

*To serve this as a vegetable, prepare ¾ of the recipe and use from ⅓ to ½ cup for a serving; omit the bacon.

CORN PUDDING†

Yield: 50 to 55 servings

Size of serving: ¾ cup

7½ quarts (2¼ cans, No. 10) corn, cream style
2 tablespoons salt
4½ tablespoons sugar
3 quarts milk

1. Heat the corn, salt, sugar, and milk together.

18 (3½ cups) eggs, beaten
5½ cups bread, soft, chopped

2. Add the eggs and chopped bread to the hot corn mixture. Pour it into greased baking pans and set these into pans of hot water. Bake in a slow oven (300° F.) until firm.

†To serve as a vegetable, prepare ¾ of the recipe and use ½ cup for a serving.

93

CREOLE MACARONI OR SPAGHETTI

Yield: 50 to 55 servings — Size of serving: ¾ cup

3½ pounds macaroni or spaghetti

1. Cook the macaroni in 3½ gallons of boiling water with ½ cup of salt; drain it in a colander, and rinse it with water.

4 quarts (1¼ cans, No. 10) tomatoes
2½ tablespoons sugar
2 bay leaves
1 tablespoon whole cloves and peppercorns

2. Heat the tomatoes with the seasonings tied loosely in a cheesecloth bag; boil them for 5 minutes. Remove the spice bag.

1 cup bacon fat
1¼ cups flour

3. Melt the fat and stir in the flour; add this to the hot tomatoes and cook until thickened, stirring constantly with a wire whip.

1½ pounds salt pork or bacon ends, diced
1 cup onions, chopped
1½ cups green peppers, chopped
½ cup pimientos, chopped

4. Cook the bacon or pork until golden brown and crisp; drain it. Cook the peppers and onions in the fat. Add them with the pimientos to the tomato sauce. Combine the sauce and macaroni. Season to taste.

Topping:

½ pound (2 cups) cheese, chopped
1½ quarts bread, soft, chopped

5. Mix the cheese and bread together; spread this over the top of the mixture. Bake in a moderate oven (350° F.) for 30 minutes until the crumbs are browned.

PEPPERS STUFFED WITH VEGETABLE FILLING

See variation of peppers stuffed with meat, page 64.

NEAPOLITAN SPAGHETTI

Yield: 50 to 55 servings — Size of serving: ¾ cup

1 pound bacon, diced
1 cup onions, chopped
¼ cup parsley, chopped
3 cloves garlic
1½ pounds mushrooms, sliced

1. Fry the bacon, onions, parsley, garlic, and mushrooms until lightly browned.

2 pounds beef, raw, ground

2. Add the meat and cook until brown.

4 quarts (1¼ cans, No. 10) tomatoes

3. Add the tomatoes, tomato purée and water and simmer for a few minutes. Add seasonings as needed.

3¼ quarts (1 can, No. 10) tomato purée
3 quarts water

4 pounds spaghetti

4. Cook the spaghetti in 4 gallons of water and ½ cup salt. Drain it in a colander and rinse it with water.

½ pound Parmesan cheese, grated

5. Arrange the spaghetti in layers in baking pans. Sprinkle it with the cheese and pour the hot sauce over the top. Heat in a moderate oven (350° F.) until mixture is heated throughout.

SPANISH RICE

Yield: 50 to 55 servings

Size of serving: ¾ cup

3 pounds (6½ cups) rice

1. Cook the rice in 3 gallons of boiling water and ⅓ cup of salt. Drain it into a colander and rinse it with water.

1 pound bacon *or* salt pork, diced
3 cups onions, chopped (5 to 6 medium onions)
3 cups green peppers, chopped

2. Partially cook the bacon; add the onions and peppers to the bacon and cook them.

5 quarts (1½ cans, No. 10) tomatoes
3 bay leaves

3. Heat the tomatoes and bay leaves together. Remove the bay leaves.

1 cup bacon *or* other fat
1½ cups flour
⅓ cup sugar
¼ cup salt
1 15-ounce can pimientos

4. Melt the fat and stir in the flour. Add this to the hot tomatoes. Cook until thickened, stirring constantly with a wire whip. Add the seasonings and diced pimientos. Combine the tomato mixture, vegetables, and rice mixing carefully. Heat the mixture throughout.

SPOONBREAD WITH BACON

Yield: 50 to 55 servings

Size of serving: ½ cup and 1 or 2 slices of bacon

2 pounds (6 cups) cornmeal
¼ cup salt
3¼ quarts water, boiling

1. Add the salt to the boiling water and stir in the cornmeal. Cook over hot water until thickened stirring occasionally.

1 cup butter, shortening, *or* other fat

2. Add the fat to the above mixture, remove from the heat, and cool slightly.

2½ quarts milk
23 (4½ cups) eggs, beaten

3. Combine the milk and eggs. Add these gradually to the cornmeal mixture, stirring until well mixed.

2½ tablespoons baking powder

4. Stir in the baking powder just before baking.* Pour the mixture into greased baking pans. Set these into pans of hot water. Bake in a moderate oven (375° F.) for from 40 to 45 minutes or until set.

Serve with:

3 cups butter, melted
50 to 100 strips bacon, crisp

5. Serve with melted butter and 1 or 2 slices of crisp bacon.

*Because the mixture is warm, it is a good procedure to divide the mixture and baking powder and combine in small batches.

SWEET POTATO, PINEAPPLE, AND BACON

Yield: 50 servings   Size of serving: 1 No. 12 scoop of mashed sweet potato
on a slice of pineapple, and one strip of bacon

12 to 15 pounds sweet potatoes
2 to 4 cups milk, scalded
2 tablespoons salt
1 cup butter *or* fortified margarine

1. Peel and cook the sweet potatoes; mash them and add enough milk to moisten; add the salt and butter.

1½ cups butter *or* fortified margarine, melted
1¼ cups (8 ounces) sugar, brown, packed
50 pineapple slices*

2. Put the butter in baking pans; sprinkle the brown sugar over it; arrange the slices of pineapple on this. Glaze the pineapple slightly in a moderately hot oven (375° F.).

50 slices (3 pounds) bacon strips, long

3. Partially cook the bacon in the oven.

25 (½ pound) marshmallows, cut in halves

4. Put a No. 12 scoop of mashed potato on each slice of pineapple; wrap a slice of bacon around the outside of the potato and pineapple. Fasten it there with round toothpicks. Bake the balls in a hot oven (425° F.) until the bacon is done. Top each serving with a marshmallow half and return it to the oven until the marshmallows are brown.

*Apple rings may be used in place of the pineapple rings.

VEGETABLE CHOP SUEY

Yield: From 55 to 60 servings   Size of serving: ¾ cup on a scoop of rice *or* spoonful of fried noodles

2½ pounds mushrooms
1½ cups green peppers, diced
1 cup drippings, butter, *or* fortified margarine

1. Clean and slice the mushroom caps and stems; cook them and the peppers with the fat.

2½ quarts celery rings
3½ quarts onion rings

2. Cook the celery and onions until just tender.

3½ cups (1 can, No. 2½) tomatoes
2 quarts chicken *or* veal stock*

3. Heat the tomatoes and stock together.

2½ cups cornstarch
1 cup flour
⅓ cup salt
1 cup soybean sauce
1 cup pimientos, chopped
1 can, No. 10, *or* 6 cans, No. 2, bean sprouts

4. Make a paste of the cornstarch and flour with cold water; add this to the hot stock, using enough to make a medium-thick gravy. Cook this until thickened, stirring constantly with a wire whip. Add the soybean sauce, pimientos, and bean sprouts. Add the cooked vegetables. Add seasonings as needed.

*Commercial chicken concentrate may be used to make the stock.

Serve on:

3 pounds (6½ cups) rice *or* 2 pounds fried (Chinese) noodles

5. Cook the rice in 3 gallons of hot water with 6 tablespoons of salt; drain it in a colander, and rinse it with water. Reheat it in the oven. Serve a No. 12 scoop of rice or a spoonful of noodles with the sauce over it.

VEGETABLE PIE

Yield: From 50 to 55 servings (10 quarts of mixture)

Size of serving: ¾ cup of mixture and 1 biscuit

2½ quarts carrots, diced
4 quarts potatoes
2½ quarts celery

1. Cook the carrots, potatoes, and celery until just tender.

2½ quarts peas (4 pounds frozen or 5 cans, No. 2)

2. Cook the frozen peas or heat the canned ones.

2 quarts (⅔ can, No. 10) tomatoes

3. Heat the tomatoes and stock together.

2½ quarts meat stock
1½ cups onions
½ cup bacon fat *or* drippings

4. Cook the onions with the fat and add them to the tomatoes.

1½ cups bacon fat *or* drippings
2½ cups flour
4 tablespoons salt
4 tablespoons sugar
2 tablespoons Worcestershire sauce

5. Melt the fat and stir in the flour; add this to the hot tomatoes and cook the mixture until thickened, stirring constantly with a wire whip. Add the sasonings. Combine the sauce with the vegetables carefully. Add further seasoning as needed. Place the mixture into baking pans.

*Biscuit**

3 pounds (3 quarts) flour, all-purpose

1. Sift the dry ingredients together.

3 ounces (½ cup) baking powder
2 teaspoons salt
11 ounces (1½ cups) vegetable fat
1 pound (1 quart) cheese, grated
4½ to 5 cups milk

2. Rub in the fat; mix in the grated cheese; combine this with the milk, handling lightly; knead the dough on a lightly floured board for a few seconds until smooth. Roll the dough ½ inch thick and cut into 2½-inch rounds. Place the biscuits on top of the *hot* mixture. Bake the mixture in a hot oven (425° to 450° F.).

*The biscuits may be baked separately and placed over the hot mixture just before serving.

VEGETABLES

Vegetables add much to the appearance and nutritive value of the meal; therefore, they should look attractive and taste good. Individual tastes and preferences vary, but, in general, the accepted standard for palatability of cooked vegetables includes the following characteristics: a bright, fresh color; the natural flavor and form of the raw product; a texture that is tender and at the same time a little crisp; as much of the nutritive value retained as is possible. To attain this standard, good quality is the first essential, and care in preparation and cooking is needed to retain all of the original goodness.

FRESH AND FROZEN VEGETABLES

Pare fresh vegetables carefully to prevent excess waste and to conserve as much nutritive value as possible.

Wash all fresh vegetables thoroughly in lukewarm water before cooking. Greens should be washed in several waters to remove all sand and dirt. It is best to use lukewarm water. Broccoli, cauliflower, and brussels sprouts should be soaked in salted water to aid in removing worms and insects. If broccoli is particularly wormy, the head may be held under hot running water.

Keep vegetables crisp and cool until time to cook them. Crisp them in water if necessary, but do not soak too long. Other ways to crisp vegetables are: 1) Place layers of crushed ice between layers of prepared vegetable, 2) Keep the prepared vegetable, covered with a heavy damp cloth, in a refrigerator or other cool place. Large glass jars with friction tops or similar equipment with tight fitting lids aid in keeping vegetables crisp when they stand before cooking.

FIGURE 14.   CUTTING LARGE
QUANTITIES OF CELERY

A specially designed holder attached to a cutting board holds the point of the French knife, leaving the left hand free to hold the stalks of celery. A pan placed on a lower table catches the celery rings as they are cut.

Select the method of cooking according to the vegetable and to the equipment available and keep the cooking time as short as possible. Most vegetables, except those of the cabbage family, may be steamed or baked, thus preserving the greatest amount of flavor and nutritive value. Cooking in the skins also helps to retain nutritive value. Overcooking impairs color, flavor, texture, and nutritive value. Succulent vegetables, which are easily overcooked and which tend to break in handling, should be cooked in quantities that can be handled easily; root vegetables, which hold their shape and color in cooking and serving, may be cooked in relatively large quantities.

Place the vegetables in actively boiling water and bring the water back to boiling as quickly as possible. Vegetables to be boiled on top of the range should be cooked in relatively small quantities in order to cook them quickly. Use as little water as practical and cover the container tightly. Cook only until crisp-tender. Fresh greens require very little water since they wilt down. Other fresh green vegetables such as broccoli require just enough water to cover.

Cook vegetables, particularly the green and succulent ones which require a short cooking period, as needed to insure attractiveness.

Hold cooked vegetables as short a time as possible before serving; vegetables have a fresher appearance if the butter or sauce is added just before serving. A measured amount of butter or sauce gives a standard product and establishes a basis for figuring the total food cost of the vegetable. Sugar added to the cooked vegetable in the proportions of 1 or 2 teaspoons per pound of vegetables improves the flavor of many vegetables, particularly if they are overmature. It is usually added after the vegetable has been drained.

Use shallow pans for holding and serving vegetables, especially for those that break up easily (figure 3). Vegetables may be steamed and served from the same pans to aid in keeping them intact.

Left-over vegetables are often more attractive when served with a cream sauce or made into an escalloped dish.

Cooking Directions

Directions for cooking specific vegetables in a steam-jacketed kettle, a steamer, and a utensil on a range are given on page 100. The use of an interval timer is recommended. Set timer for the minimum time given in the chart. Test the vegetable for doneness; cook it longer if necessary. Drain the vegetable when done and keep it warm for serving.

Most frozen vegetables should be cooked without defrosting. The containers of broccoli, asparagus, and spinach may be opened and defrosted long enough to pull the pieces of vegetable apart, or these vegetables may be cut into smaller blocks before cooking. The length of cooking time depends on degree of defrosting and quality of the vegetable.

Steaming

(An institution type steamer is shown in figure 15)

In steaming frozen vegetables place them only one package deep in a perforated steamer basket. Steam only 5 to 10 pounds of prepared

Directions for Cooking Individual Vegetables

Vegetable	Boiling — Steam-jacketed kettle				Boiling — Utensil on a range				Steaming — Steamer	
	Amount of vegetable (Pounds)	Amount of water (Gallons)	Amount of salt (Cups)	Minimum time (Minutes)	Amount of vegetable (Pounds)	Amount of water (Quarts)	Amount of salt (Tablespoons)	Minimum time of actual boiling (Minutes)	Amount of vegetable* (Pounds)	Minimum steaming time (Minutes)
Asparagus, tips and stems, fresh†	20	4 to 5	1 to 1¼	{9 stems, 7 tips}	5	4	3	{11 stems, 9 tips}	...	...
Asparagus, cuts, frozen	10	2 to 3	½ to ¾	7	5	2	1	9	5 to 6	8
Beans, green, cut, frozen	20	3 to 4	¾ to 1	6	5	2	1	5	5	13
Beans, green, lima, frozen	20	3 to 4	¾ to 1	7	5	2	1	7	6	7
Beet greens, young, fresh, cut up	15	2 to 3	½ to ¾	3	5	4	3	3	...	...
Beets, new whole	...	...	...	...	20	16	12	60	full basket	40
Beets, old	...	...	...	...	...	...	...	...	full basket	90
Broccoli, fresh	20	4 to 5	1 to 1¼	7	5	4	3	8	...	...
Broccoli, frozen§	20	3 to 4	¾ to 1	5	5	2	1	10	6	10
Brussels sprouts, fresh	10	2 to 3	½ to ¾	8	5	4	3	5	...	...
Brussels sprouts, frozen	20	2 to 3	½ to ¾	6	5	2	1	6	...	...
Cabbage, cut-up	20	4 to 5	1 to 1¼	6	5	4	3	7	10	9
Cabbage, shredded	20	3 to 4	¾ to 1	4	5	3	2	4	10	4
Cabbage, wedges	10‖	9 to 10		8	5	4	3	8	5	10
Carrots, new, cut-up	20	3 to 4	½ to ¾	20	20	8	8	15	full basket	25

Carrots, old, cut-up	20	3 to 4	½ to ¾	25	20	12	12	20	full basket	30
Cauliflower, broken-up										
Fresh	10	3 to 4	¾ to 1	5	5	4	4	4	10	10
Frozen	10	2 to 3	½ to ¾	6	5	3	3	2	5	4
Celery, cut-up	10	3 to 4	¾ to 1	6	5	3	3	10	10	10
Corn, fresh on cob	..	......	....	..	..	..	..	..	full basket	5
Corn, frozen kernels	20	3 to 4	¾ to 1	5	5	2	1	3	5	3
Kale, mid-ribs removed	5	1½	⅓	3	5	6	4	3	..	..
Onions, medium, whole	20	3 to 4	½ to ¾	28	20	12	12	35	full basket	30
Onions, rings	20	2 to 3	¼ to ⅓	15	5	4	3	22	full basket	15
Parsnips, halved or quartered	20	2½ to 3	⅓ to ½	19	20	10	8	12	full basket	25
Peas, fresh	20	3 to 4	¾ to 1	7	5	4	3	7	..	..
Peas, frozen	20	3 to 4	¾ to 1	6	5	2	1	3	5 to 6	4
Potatoes, sweet	20	3 to 4	....	30	20	12	..	25	full basket	30
Potatoes, white	20	3 to 4	½ to ¾	18	20	12	12	13	full basket	35
Rutabagas, cubed	20	3 to 4	½ to ¾	30	20	12	8	28	full basket	30
Spinach, fresh‡	15	2 to 3	½ to ¾	3	5	3	2	3	5	5
Spinach, frozen	10	2 to 3	½ to ¾	1	5	1½	2	3	5	7
Squash, winter	..	......	....	..	..	..	..	..	full basket	35
Squash, summer	..	......	....	..	..	..	..	..	full basket	20
Swiss chard, cut-up	12	2 to 3	½ to ¾	6	5	4	3	6	4	8
Turnips	20	2 to 3	⅓ to ½	15	20	8	8	20	full basket	20

*In one steamer basket.
†In boiling add stems to boiling water, cook 2 minutes; then add tips and continue boiling.
§Cooking time of frozen broccoli varies due to quality of vegetable and to blanching process used.
||Use round basket in a 25-gallon kettle.
‡Boil fresh spinach with steam-jacketed cover down for 1 minute; then raise cover for remainder of cooking.

Photograph from Cleveland Range Company　　　*Photograph from Aluminum Cooking Utensil Company*

FIGURE 15.　AN INSTITUTIONAL TYPE STEAMER

Used for steaming large quantities of food. It is especially useful in cooking root vegetables and some green vegetables. The steamer is connected to the steam line of a central plant. Another type of steamer produces steam for its operation.

FIGURE 16.　A STEAM-JACKETED KETTLE

Used for boiling large quantities of food: making soup, cooking vegetables, pot-roasting meat. This steam jacketed kettle is connected to the steam line of a central heating plant. Another type of steam jacketed kettle produces steam for its operation.

green, succulent vegetables in one perforated basket 22½ x 8 x 6½ inches. Steamer baskets may be filled with root vegetables.

Boiling

Steam-jacketed kettle (a steam-jacketed kettle is shown in figure 16)

1. Measure the water and salt into the kettle and heat to boiling.

2. Add the vegetable. Keep the steam on full until the water returns to boiling; then reduce the heat to keep the water just boiling to prevent breaking up the vegetable.

3. Turn off the heat; draw off the water.

NOTE: If the vegetable is tough, longer boiling will be required. Therefore, it will be necessary to use more water and a smaller proportion of salt (2 to 3 tablespoons per gallon of water).

Utensil on a range

1. Measure the water and salt into a utensil and heat to boiling.

2. Add the vegetable (about 5 to 6 pounds) and cover the utensil. Count cooking time when boiling begins. Vegetables cook some while coming to the boil. Therefore, the longer the time the vegetable requires to come to the boiling point, the shorter the actual boiling time.

Times given in the chart are for an open-burner gas range. If a pre-heated all hot-top range is used, the overall cooking time would be reduced somewhat.

3. Drain the vegetable. Save the vegetable liquid to use in soups, gravies, and sauces to the extent that this is practical.

HEATING CANNED VEGETABLES

Method 1	Method 2
(double-boiler or hot-water bath)	(steamer)
1. Pour off about half the liquid.	1. Drain the vegetable, and place it directly into serving pans.
2. Transfer the contents of the can, including the liquid, to the top of a double-boiler or other utensil.	2. Heat it in a steamer.
3. Season the vegetable, and heat it over hot water or over direct heat.	3. Add butter or sauce and seasonings, (see direction below).
4. Transfer it to serving pans, using a perforated ladle.	
5. Add butter or sauce (see directions below).	

NOTE: Prepare in moderate quantities as near serving time as possible.

SEASONING AND COMBINING VEGETABLES

Buttered Vegetables

Drain the cooked vegetable and add the fat just before serving. Use approximately ½ pound (1 cup) for each 10 pounds of cooked vegetable (1 No. 10 can yields about 5 pounds of drained vegetable). Butter is desirable but other fats as margarines, chicken fat, and bacon fat may be used. Bacon fat is particularly good with greens. Paprika or chopped parsley sprinkled over the vegetable adds color. Lemon butter gives a distinctive flavor to some vegetables such as green beans, broccoli, cabbage, and spinach.

Creamed Vegetables and Other Sauces for Vegetables

Drain the cooked vegetable thoroughly and add the sauce just before serving. For an attractive product, place the vegetable in the serving pan or dish and pour the sauce over it.

Sauces for vegetables

Cream sauce: Use 2 quarts medium-thin cream sauce for each 10 pounds of cooked drained vegetables. Proportions for 2 quarts of sauce: 2 quarts milk, ⅓ to ½ cup fat, ¾ cup flour, 1 tablespoon salt. Vegetable liquid may be substituted for part of the milk. In this case evaporated milk, light cream, or top milk will give a better sauce.

Variations

Cheese sauce: To 2 quarts of cream sauce add 3 cups grated cheese

Parsley sauce: To 2 quarts of cream sauce add 1 cup chopped parsley

Pimiento sauce: To 2 quarts of cream sauce add 1 cup chopped pimiento

Drawn butter sauce: The juices from several canned vegetables as asparagus, peas, and wax beans may be thickened and used as sauce for those vegetables. Proportions for 2 quarts of sauce: 2 quarts vegetable juice, 3/4 cup butter, 1/2 cup flour. For lemon flavor use 1/4 cup lemon juice in place of 1/4 cup vegetable juice adding it to the sauce just before pouring it over the vegetable.

Top milk or *light cream* seasoned with salt and pepper may be used with peas, green lima beans, and corn.

Escalloped Vegetables

Drain freshly cooked, canned, or reheated left-over vegetables thoroughly. Make a cream sauce as above. Arrange alternate layers of vegetable and cream sauce in greased baking pans or individual casseroles, ending with the cream sauce. Top with buttered or plain chopped bread or bread cubes, cracker crumbs, potato chips, cornflakes, or soybean flakes. Cheese may be chopped with soft bread for the topping. Bake in a moderate oven (350° F.) for from 20 to 25 minutes or until the mixture is heated thoroughly and the top is browned.

NOTE: Boiling certain vegetables such as carrots, soybeans sprouts, green or wax beans, celery, peas, mushrooms in chicken broth or veal stock adds to their flavor. This stock may be thickened for a sauce. Chicken concentrates may be used for this purpose. Follow the directions on the package for making the stock.

STANDARDIZING SERVINGS

It is difficult to estimate the yield from fresh vegetables because of differences in quality and therefore in the amount of waste; differences in the amount of waste due to methods and care in preparation; and difficulty in obtaining uniform servings. Frozen vegetables give a less variable yield than do fresh ones because they are purchased by the pound and are ready for cooking; yields from canned vegetables may vary somewhat, depending on the quality of the pack and the drained weight of the solids.

The total cost of vegetable servings includes the cost of the vegetable and of the butter or sauce and seasonings. The amount of butter or sauce used should be measured to obtain accurate figures.

The following methods may be used as aids to obtaining standard servings: (1) Put a known weight of the cooked vegetable into the serving pans, or fill the pans equally full; then add a standard amount of butter or sauce and seasonings, and gauge the servings to obtain a specified number per pan (figure 3); (2) Use standard serving utensils, such as ice-cream scoops for such items as mashed potatoes, rutabagas, squash, and buttered rice (figure 4); (3) Count servings from a given quantity by one of the methods mentioned on page 16.

RECIPES

APPLE RINGS, BAKED*

Yield: 50 servings   Size of serving: 3 rings

14 pounds (40 to 50) apples
1 cup bacon fat
2¼ cups (1 pound) sugar, brown, packed

1. Wash and core the apples; slice them about ¼ inch thick; arrange the slices in greased baking pans, overlapping them slightly (figure 3A). Brush with the melted bacon fat, sprinkle with the brown sugar, and add a little hot water. Bake them in a moderate oven (350° F.) until the apples are tender.

*Apple rings may be served with one or two strips of bacon or a sausage link as a main item in a luncheon menu.

Variation

Sliced cooked sweet potatoes or cooked carrot circles may be combined with the apples.

ESCALLOPED APPLES

Yield: 50 servings   Size of serving: ½ cup

12 pounds (35 to 40) apples, medium size

1. Peel and slice the apples.

2½ quarts bread, soft, chopped
1¼ cups (9 ounces) sugar, brown, packed
2¼ teaspoons nutmeg
1 teaspoon salt
1½ cups butter, or fortified margarine, melted

2. Combine the chopped bread, sugar, nutmeg, salt, and melted butter. Place alternate layers of apples and the crumb mixture in buttered baking pans, beginning and ending with the crumb mixture.

¾ cup lemon juice
2 quarts water or fruit juice, hot

3. Combine the lemon and fruit juices and pour them over the mixture. Bake the apples in a moderate oven (350° F.) for from 1¼ to 1½ hours.

Variation

Escalloped apples and onions: Use sliced raw onion rings in place of part of the apples.

105

SPANISH KIDNEY BEANS

Yield: 50 servings

Size of serving: ½ cup

4 pounds kidney beans, dried
or 2 cans, No. 10

1. Wash the beans, more than cover them with water, and soak them overnight. Simmer them until tender in the water in which they were soaked.

½ pound salt pork, diced
2 cups onions, sliced
1½ cups green peppers, chopped
4½ cups tomato puree
1 cup meat stock *or* water
2½ tablespoons salt
½ teaspoon pepper
½ teaspoon paprika

2. Add the remaining ingredients. Pour the mixture into baking pans. Bake them in a moderate oven (350° F.) for from 1½ to 2 hours.

SPICED BEETS

Yield: 50 servings

Size of serving: ½ cup

12 pounds beets, fresh *or* 2 cans, No. 10

1. Cook the cleaned beets in the skins until tender, remove the skins, and dice or slice the beets.

1½ quarts beet juice *or* water
3 cups vinegar
1½ teaspoons salt
½ teaspoon pepper
1¾ cups (12 ounces) sugar, brown, packed*
¾ cup sugar, granulated
1 small stick cinnamon
1 teaspoon cloves, whole

2. Combine the beet juice and vinegar; add the salt, pepper, brown and white sugar. Tie the cloves and cinnamon in a cheesecloth bag and add it to the beet juice and vinegar. Boil all together for 10 minutes. Remove the spice bag; pour the boiling liquid over the beets, and heat them.

¾ cup butter *or* fortified margarine

3. Add the butter to the beets.

*Reduce the amount of sugar if a more sour sauce is desired.

Variation

Pickled beets: Omit the butter and let whole or quartered beets stand in the spiced sauce. Serve cold.

Harvard beets: Thicken the juice with 6 tablespoons (2 ounces) cornstarch.

HOT CABBAGE SLAW*

Yield: 50 servings

Size of serving: ½ cup

10 pounds cabbage, shredded
½ pound bacon, diced

1. Brown the bacon lightly; drain it from the fat, and save the fat.

Sauce

2 cups vinegar, heated
2 cups water, heated
½ cup sugar
2 tablespoons salt

2. Add the sugar, salt, and bacon fat to the hot vinegar and water. Pour the sauce over the cabbage and add the crisp bacon just before serving.

*If stored cabbage is used, pour boiling water over it and let it stand about 10 minutes, or steam it for about the same length of time.

106

CELERY À LA KING

Yield: 50 servings (7 quarts)

Size or serving: ½ cup

8 quarts celery rings (1-inch pieces)

1. Cook the celery in salted water until just done; drain it well, saving the liquid.

3 quarts cream sauce
  2½ quarts milk
  2 cups liquid from celery
  ¾ cup butter *or* fortified margarine
  1¼ cups flour

2. Make the cream sauce.

½ pound fresh mushrooms, sliced (*or* 1½ 8-ounce cans)
2 tablespoons onions, minced
⅓ cup butter, fortified margarine, *or* bacon fat
1 4-ounce can pimientos, diced
1½ cups green peppers, diced
Salt and pepper to taste

3. Cook the mushrooms and onions in the butter. Add them, the pimientos, peppers, and celery to the cream sauce. Season the mixture to taste.

Variation

Carrots à la king: Carrots *or* a combination of carrots and celery may be used in place of the celery.

CELERY CABBAGE WITH TOMATOES

Yield: 50 servings

Size of serving: 3¼ ounces

12 pounds celery cabbage

1. Cut the cabbage into ¾-inch slices. Place it in flat pans; steam or boil it until just tender; drain it.

1½ quarts (½ can, No. 10) tomatoes
1 teaspoon salt
¼ teaspoon pepper
1½ tablespoons sugar
3 tablespoons butter *or* fortified margarine

2. Heat the tomatoes with the seasonings. Pour the tomato mixture over the cabbage just before serving.

CORN PILAFF

See recipe page 93.

CORN PUDDING

See recipe page 93.

ESCALLOPED EGGPLANT

Yield: 50 servings

Size of serving: ½ cup

14 pounds egg plant (10 pounds after preparation)
3 tablespoons salt

1. Peel the eggplant and cut it into 1-inch cubes. Boil it in salted water until tender. Drain it well.

1½ cups onions, chopped
½ cup parsley, chopped
¾ cup butter, fortified margarine, *or* bacon fat

2. Brown the onions and parsley with the fat. Add the chopped bread and brown it.

2 quarts bread, soft, chopped

2 quarts milk, heated

1 cup cheese, chopped

3. Arrange alternate layers of eggplant and bread mixture in well-greased baking pans. Sprinkle salt and pepper on each layer. Pour the milk over the top, then sprinkle the top with the cheese. Bake the mixture in a moderate oven (350° F.) for 1 hour.

ESCALLOPED EGGPLANT AND TOMATOES

Yield: 50 servings   Size of serving: 1/2 cup

15 pounds eggplant (15 medium)

1 1/2 tablespoons salt

2 1/2 quarts (3/4 can, No. 10) tomatoes

2 tablespoons sugar

1 1/2 teaspoons salt

1/2 teaspoon pepper

1. Peel and dice the eggplant; cook it in boiling salted water until just tender.

2. Heat the tomatoes and seasonings.

Topping:

6 cups onions, chopped

3/4 cup bacon fat, fortified margarine *or* butter

1 quart bread, soft, chopped

3. Cook the onions in the fat; mix them with the chopped bread, and brown it lightly. Place this with the eggplant and tomatoes in baking pans, topping with the onion-crumb, mixture. Bake the mixture in a moderate oven (350° F.) for about 30 minutes.

LETTUCE WITH BACON DRESSING

Yield: 50 servings   Size of serving: 1/2 cup

8 pounds (16 quarts) lettuce after preparation

1. Wash the lettuce; dry and crisp it, and put it in a cool place.

1 pound bacon, diced*

1/2 cup onions, chopped

2. Cook the onions with the bacon until they are lightly browned and the bacon crisp; drain off the fat.

Sauce

2 1/4 cups water

3 3/4 cups vinegar

1/2 cup bacon fat

1/2 cup flour

1 cup sugar

1 tablespoon salt

1/8 teaspoon pepper

3. Heat the water and vinegar to boiling. Stir the flour into the bacon fat; add this to the hot water-vinegar mixture and cook until thickened, stirring constantly with a wire whip. Add the sugar, salt, and pepper. Combine the lettuce with the cooked, diced bacon and the onions. Pour the hot sauce over the lettuce just before serving.

*Bacon may be omitted; cook the onions with bacon fat.

Variation

Other greens as spinach, chicory, escarole, very young beet greens, or dandelion greens may be used. Some greens may be blanched in rapidly boiling water for 3 to 5 minutes or in a steamer for 1 minute.

FRENCH FRIED ONION RINGS

Yield: 50 servings   Size of serving: 2½ to 3 ounces

12 pounds onions (use the large sweet onions)

1. Peel and slice the onions ¼-inch thick, then separate them into rings.

1 quart milk

2. Dip the onion rings in the milk and drain them well.

3 cups flour
2 tablespoons salt
½ teaspoon pepper

3. Combine the flour, salt and pepper. Dredge the onion rings with this mixture. Fry in deep fat at 350° F. until golden brown. Drain on brown paper.

NOTE: Onions may be dipped in a thin fritter batter and then fried.

BAKED POTATOES

Select potatoes of the desired size. Those weighing from 6 to 8 ounces are a good size for serving whole. Potatoes more than 10 ounces should be cut in half. Scrub them well and remove any defects. Potatoes may be baked in a hot oven (450° F.). The potatoes may be rubbed with beef drippings before putting them into the oven. As soon as the potatoes are done, remove them from the oven and crack or pierce the skins to allow the steam to escape and thus keep the potato mealy. Potatoes are attractive if they are cut with a crosswise slit, pressed open, garnished with butter, and sprinkled with paprika.

POTATOES BAKED IN CREAM

Yield: 50 servings   Size of serving: ⅔ cup

12 pounds (17 pounds before peeling) potatoes, raw, pared

1. Drain the potatoes well and chop them. Place them in flat baking pans.

3 cups evaporated milk*
3 cups water
2½ tablespoons salt

2. Mix the evaporated milk and water and add the salt. Pour this over the potatoes. Bake the potatoes in a moderately slow oven (325° F.) for 1½ hours until they are done.

*For a richer product, 3½ cups of heavy cream mixed with 2½ cups of milk may be used in place of the evaporated milk and water.

NOTE: This recipe should not be used for potatoes that blacken during cooking.

POTATOES BROWNED IN THEIR SKINS

Yield: 50 servings   Size of serving: 1 medium-sized potato

15 pounds new potatoes with thin skins
1½ cups butter, fortified margarine or beef drippings
Salt and pepper

1. Brush the potatoes and remove any spots; steam or boil the potatoes until almost tender. Cut them in halves or slices, arrange in well-greased baking pans, brush with melted butter, and sprinkle with salt and pepper. Brown them in a hot oven (400° F.) for about 30 minutes.

109

CREAMED POTATOES

Yield: 50 servings   Size of serving: ⅔ cup

15 to 20 pounds potatoes before   1. Prepare the potatoes. They may be cooked in
peeling (12 to 13 quarts cubed)   their jackets, then peeled, and cubed.
3 quarts cream sauce
   3 quarts milk   2. Make the cream sauce.
   ¾ cup butter *or* fortified mar-
    garine
   1¼ cups flour
3 tablespoons salt   3. Place the potatoes in serving pans or dishes;
   pour the cream sauce over them. Garnish them
   with melted butter and paprika or chopped
   pimientos or parsley.

Variations

Creamed potatoes with peas, green beans, or carrots: In place of part of the potatoes
use an equal quantity of cooked peas, green beans, or diced carrots.
Cream sauce variations for creamed potatoes: Add chopped parsley, chopped chives,
chopped green peppers, chopped pimiento, diced crisp bacon or salt pork, a small
quantity of minced onion.

ESCALLOPED POTATOES

Yield: 50 servings   Size of serving: ⅔ cup

15 to 20 pounds potatoes, be-   1. Peel and slice the potatoes. Arrange them in
fore peeling   baking pans.
3 quarts cream sauce   2. Make the cream sauce. Pour the cream sauce
   3 quarts milk*   over the potatoes. Bake them in a moderately
   ½ cup butter *or* fortified mar-   slow oven (325° F.) for about 2 hours.†
    garine
   ½ cup flour
   2 tablespoons salt
   ¼ teaspoon pepper

*Evaporated milk or dry milk solids may be substituted. See directions, page 22.
†To cook potatoes in a shorter time, steam or boil them for 10 minutes before adding the cream
sauce.

Variation

Pittsburg potatoes: Use cooked potatoes. Add to the cream sauce 1½ cups chopped
green peppers cooked with a little fat; 1 7-ounce can pimientos; 1½ tablespoons
minced onion. Arrange in baking pans in alternating layers of cooked potatoes and
cream sauce ending with cream sauce. Place soft chopped bread or bread cubes,
cornflakes, or soybean flakes over the top and bake in a moderate oven (350° F.) for
from 20 to 25 minutes or until heated throughout and the top is browned.

FRENCH FRIED POTATOES

Yield: 50 servings   Size of serving: ½ cup

12 pounds potatoes, peeled   1. Cut the peeled potatoes into long narrow
(Prepare about 16 pounds of   strips. Cover them with ice water until ready to
potatoes)   fry. Drain them and then dry between towels.

Frying methods

Use about 10 pounds of fat for frying 1-pound batches of potatoes.

One operation

1. Fry the potatoes at 380° F. for 7 to 8 minutes until brown and tender. Drain them on brown paper and sprinkle them with salt.

Partial cooking and browning

1. Fry the potatoes at 380° F. for about 5 minutes. Drain them.

or

Steam the potatoes for about 5 minutes.

2. Brown the potatoes at 380° F. for about 2 minutes until brown and tender. Drain them on brown paper and sprinkle them with salt.

NOTE: For best quality fry in amounts needed. If French fried potatoes are to be held, keep them warm in a 250° F. oven.

HASHED-BROWN POTATOES

Yield: 50 servings   Size of serving: ⅔ cup

12 pounds (9 quarts) potatoes, cooked, chopped

2 cups beef drippings, melted

2 tablespoons salt

¾ teaspoon pepper

1. Put part of the drippings into roasting pans, then put in the potatoes; pour the remaining drippings over them, and brown in a hot oven (450° to 500° F.) for from 20 to 25 minutes, turning them as they brown.

MASHED POTATOES*

Yield: 50 servings   Size of serving: ½ cup or 1 No. 10 scoop

15 to 20 pounds potatoes, before peeling

7 to 8 cups *hot* milk†

3 to 4 tablespoons salt

3 to 4 tablespoons butter *or* fortified margarine

1. Peel and cook the potatoes; drain them well. *Mash them immediately.*

2. Add the hot milk and seasonings; whip the mixture until fluffy.

*Mashed potatoes may be held for serving in a covered container in a very slow oven.
†Evaporated milk and water in equal quantities may be used in place of fresh milk.
NOTE: Dry milk solids may be added in proportions of one cup for the above recipe to increase the nutritive value.

PITTSBURG POTATOES

See variation of escalloped potatoes, page 110.

POTATO PUFF

Yield: 50 servings   Size of serving: ½ cup

7 quarts (from 15 to 20 pounds before peeling) potatoes, mashed

½ cup (6) egg yolks, slightly beaten

1. Reheat left-over mashed potatoes or use freshly mashed ones.

2. Add the egg yolks, butter, and milk to the potatoes; beat thoroughly, preferably in a mix-

¼ cup butter *or* fortified margarine

1½ cups milk, hot

Salt and pepper to taste

3 tablespoons butter *or* fortified margarine, melted

ing machine. Taste for seasoning.

3. Place the mixture into greased baking pans, brush the top with the melted butter, and bake them in a moderately hot oven (375° F.) until browned.

NOTE: Grated cheese may be sprinkled over the top before browning.

BAKED SWEET POTATOES AND APPLES

Yield: 50 servings

Size of serving: ⅔ cup

15 pounds sweet potatoes

1. Scrub the potatoes thoroughly and cook them in their skins until partially tender. Peel and slice them; arrange them in greased baking pans with the slices overlapping.

1 pound (2¼ cups) sugar, brown, packed

2 tablespoons salt

2. Sprinkle part of the sugar and the salt over the potato slices.

4 pounds, (12) apples, tart

3. Core and slice the apples and arrange a layer of them over the sweet potatoes. Sprinkle the remaining sugar over the top.

6 tablespoons butter *or* fortified margarine

4. Dot the top with the butter. Bake them in a moderate oven (350° F.) until the apples are tender when pricked with a fork. Occasionally baste the top with the mixture in the pan.

Variations

Baked sweet potatoes with marshmallows: Near the end of the baking, place quartered marshmallows over the top and return the potato to the oven long enough to brown the marshmallows.

Baked sweet potatoes with pineapple: Use pineapple slices or cubes in place of the apples. Then use only ½ pound (1 cup) sugar.

CANDIED SWEET POTATO

Yield: 50 servings

Size of serving: 2 to 3 slices

20 pounds sweet potatoes

1. Scrub the potatoes thoroughly and cook them; partially cool, skin, and slice them.

or

Pare raw potatoes and cook them; partially cool and then slice them.

2. Arrange in greased baking pans, overlapping the slices.

Glaze

1½ pounds (3½ cups) sugar, brown, packed

1 quart hot water

3. Boil the sugar and water together for a medium sirup: add the butter and salt. Pour this over the potato slices. Bake in a moderate oven

½ cup butter *or* fortified margarine

1 tablespoon salt

(350° F.) for from 30 to 45 minutes.

SWEET-POTATO PUFF

Yield: 50 servings

Size of serving: ½ cup

7 quarts (20 pounds before peeling) sweet potatoes, mashed

1 cup butter *or* fortified margarine

4 tablespoons salt

¼ teaspoon pepper

10 eggs

3 tablespoons sugar

3 tablespoons butter *or* fortified margarine, melted

1. Add the butter, salt, pepper, eggs, and sugar to the mashed sweet potato and mix all thoroughly, preferably with a mixing machine. Add further seasoning as needed.

2. Place the mixture into greased baking pans, brush the top with the melted butter, and bake in a moderately hot oven (375° F.) until browned.

Variation

Sweet potato croquettes: Use the above recipe and let the mixture cool thoroughly after mixing. Measure it with a No. 20 scoop and shape into balls or cylinders. Dip each in an egg-milk mixture (4 eggs and ½ cup milk) and roll in cornflakes. Fry in deep fat at 380° F. until brown, and drain each on absorbent paper. The balls may be baked. Drip melted butter or fortified margarine over the balls and bake in a moderate oven (350° F.) for about 30 minutes. Use 2 balls for a serving.

SPICED PRUNES

Yield: 50 servings

Size of serving: 4 prunes

4 pounds prunes

1. Wash the prunes, cover them with water and soak them overnight; drain them.

1 quart water

2 cups sugar

Pinch salt

1 5-inch piece stick cinnamon

1 tablespoon whole cloves

½ cup lemon juice

2. Combine the water, sugar, spice, and lemon juice, and bring to boiling. Pour over the prunes and let them simmer until tender.

BAKED RHUBARB SAUCE

Yield: 50 servings

Size of serving: ½ cup

12 to 14 pounds rhubarb

1. Cut and wash the rhubarb (do not peel it); place in baking pans.

1 teaspoon salt

2 quarts sugar

2½ cups water

2. Combine the salt and half the sugar with the water, and pour over the rhubarb. Bake in a moderate oven (350° F.) until tender but not mushy. Remove from the oven and add the remaining sugar.

113

BUTTERED RICE

Yield: 50 servings   Size of serving: 1 No. 12 scoop

3 pounds (6½ cups) rice   1. Wash the rice thoroughly. Cook it in 3 gallons of boiling water and 6 tablespoons of salt until tender; drain it in a colander; and rinse it with hot water; drain again thoroughly. Put the rice in a moderate oven (350° F.) to dry and to keep hot for serving.

1½ cups butter, *or* fortified margarine, melted   2. Add the butter just before serving.

NOTE: A method for steaming converted rice is given on page 13.

BAKED SQUASH

Yield: 50 servings   Size of serving: 5- or 6-ounce piece

20 to 22 pounds squash, winter   1. Cut the squash into pieces for one serving. Place these in shallow baking pans with cut surfaces down. Add a small quantity of water to pans and bake in a moderate oven (350° F.) for 40 minutes. (This cooking may be done in a steamer; do not add water to the pans.)

¾ cup butter *or* fortified margarine, melted
2 tablespoons salt
Pepper

2. Turn the cut surfaces up, brush them with melted butter, sprinkle them with seasonings. Bake them until done.

NOTE: One teaspoon of brown sugar may be placed on each piece before baking, if desired.

ESCALLOPED TOMATOES

Yield: 50 servings   Size of serving: ½ cup

6½ quarts (2 cans, No. 10) tomatoes
6 tablespoons sugar
1½ tablespoons salt
¼ teaspoon pepper
⅓ cup onions, minced
1 cup plus 2 tablespoons tapioca

1. Heat the tomatoes, sugar, salt, pepper, onion, and tapioca slowly.

¾ cup butter *or* fortified margarine
3 quarts bread, soft, chopped

2. Melt the fat and pour it over the chopped bread. Brown this lightly in a hot oven. Arrange the bread and tomato mixture in alternate layers in greased baking pans, beginning and ending with the bread. Bake the mixture in a moderate oven (375° F.) for from 30 to 45 minutes.

Variations

Cooked celery, corn, cauliflower, eggplant, onions, or summer squash may be used in combination with the tomatoes.

114

STEWED CANNED *OR* FRESH TOMATOES

Yield: 50 servings

Size of serving: ½ cup

2 cans, No. 10, tomatoes*
¾ cup (4 ounces) tapioca,†
  instant
½ cup sugar
½ teaspoon pepper
1½ tablespoons salt
3 tablespoons onions, minced

1. Heat the tomatoes with the tapioca and seasonings until tapioca is clear.

½ cup butter *or* fortified margarine

2. Add the butter before serving.

*For fresh tomatoes, use 16 pounds; peel and cook them, then add 1¼ cups (6½ ounces) tapioca and seasonings as above.
†Two quarts (6 ounces) of toasted bread cubes may be used in place of the tapioca. Add these just before serving.

Variations

Creole tomatoes: Brown 2½ cups of chopped onions and 2½ cups of chopped green peppers in fortified margarine, bacon fat *or* butter and add to the tomatoes and seasonings. Add the tapioca and cook until the tapioca is clear. Add 1½ cups of diced pimientos.

Spiced tomatoes: Tie 1 tablespoon each of stick cinnamon, peppercorns, and whole cloves and 2 small bay leaves in a cheesecloth, Add this bag of spices to the tomatoes and other seasonings. Add the tapioca and cook until the tapioca is clear. Remove the spice bag before serving.

STEWED TOMATOES AND CORN

Yield: 50 servings

Size of serving: ½ cup

1 can, No. 10, tomatoes
1 can, No. 10, corn, whole kernel
7 tablespoons (2½ ounces)
  tapioca, instant
⅓ cup sugar
1 tablespoon salt
½ teaspoon pepper
¼ cup onion, minced
⅔ cup butter *or* fortified margarine

1. Combine the tomatoes, drained corn, and seasonings. Heat the mixture throughout.

Variations

Tomatoes and celery: Use 4 quarts (4 pounds) of diced celery in place of the corn. Cook the celery until just tender and add it to the tomato mixture.

Tomatoes and hominy: Use 1 can, No. 10, drained hominy in place of the corn.

Tomatoes and okra: Use 1 can, No. 10, drained okra in place of the corn.

Tomatoes and onions: Use 7 pounds of onions in place of the corn. Peel the onions and cut them into halves or quarters and cook until tender. Drain them and add to the tomato mixture.

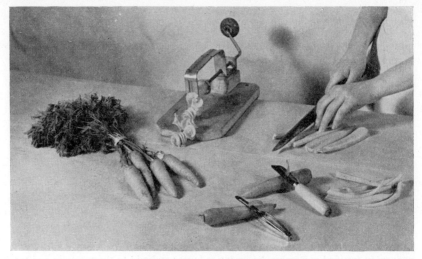

FIGURE 17. CARROT GARNISHES

Carrot curls (A) and sticks (B) are popular as relishes and garnishes. Here shown are special peelers (C) for thin paring of carrots

CREAMED MIXED VEGETABLES*

Yield: 50 servings   Size of serving: ½ cup

⅓ cup onions, chopped
¾ cup mushrooms
3 tablespoons butter, fortified
  margarine, *or* beef drippings
4½ cups peas, cooked

1. Clean and slice the mushroom caps and stems; cook them and the onions with the fat.

4½ cups corn, whole kernel
2 cups beans, green or lima
1½ quarts celery rings
1½ quarts carrots, diced

2. Combine the cooked, drained vegetables.

3 quarts cream sauce, medium
  2 quarts milk
  1 quart vegetable liquid
  1 cup fat
  1½ cups flour

3. Make the cream sauce. Add the vegetables to it. Add seasoning as needed.

*This mixture may be served on meat such as ham sausage curls or sliced canned ham loaf.

Variation

Mixed vegetables au gratin: Place the mixture in baking pans. Cover it with a mixture of chopped cheese and soft bread. Bake in a moderate oven (350° F.) for from 20 to 25 minutes until heated throughout and top is browned.

116

VEGETARIAN STEW

Yield: 50 servings   Size of serving: ½ cup

6 cups carrots, diced   1. Cook the carrots, potatoes, and celery in salted
6 cups potatoes, diced   water; drain them.
6 cups celery rings
5 cups beans, wax, canned,
   drained
5 cups peas, canned, drained
7 cups (2 cans, No. 2½) tomatoes   2. Heat the tomatoes with the tapioca and sea-
½ cup tapioca, instant   sonings.
3½ tablespoons sugar
1½ tablespoons salt
½ teaspoon pepper
¾ cup bacon fat, fortified mar-   3. Combine all the vegetables and add the fat.
   garine *or* butter

VEGETABLE COMBINATIONS

Carrots à la king
Carrots and celery, peas, or string beans, buttered or creamed
Cauliflower and celery, green beans, mushrooms, or peas, buttered or creamed
Celery and peas or mushrooms, buttered or creamed
Corn and peas, buttered
Green beans, celery, and onions, buttered or creamed
Onions and peas, buttered or creamed
Onions and tomatoes, buttered
Peas and new potatoes, creamed
Peas and white turnips, buttered
Shredded cabbage and celery, sauteed
Spinach and beets or carrots, buttered
Summer squash, onions, and tomatoes, buttered

Photograph from H. G. W. Young Company

FIGURE 18.   A VEGETABLE AND
FRUIT CUTTER

This cutter is especially useful for cutting carrots
to serve raw (carrot sticks) and cooked (lengthwise
pieces). Potatoes may be cut for French frying or
escalloping. Apples may be sliced for making pies or
sauce

117

VEGETABLE GARNISHES

Chopped bacon
Chopped chives
Cornflakes
Crisp buttered bread crumbs or
  cubes
Grated cheese mixed with
  crumbs
Mint leaves
Parsley lemon butter slices
Paprika
Shredded carrots

Chopped parsley
Pastry rounds
Pimiento, chopped or strips
Sauteed mushrooms
Shredded toasted almonds or pecans
Tomato slices or wedges
  (raw or slightly grilled)
Green pepper, chopped or strips
Watercress
Lemon wedges or slices
Onion ring, raw or French fried

RAW VEGETABLES USED AS RELISHES

Carrot strips (figures 17 and 18)
Celery sticks or curls
Green pepper strips or rings
Onion slices (Valencia or Bermuda onions)
Radishes
Lettuce leaves
Cucumber fingers
Flowerettes of raw cauliflower or broccoli
White turnip slices

SALADS AND SALAD DRESSINGS

SERVICE OF SALADS

Placed salads are those arranged on individual plates, with a definite pattern made with separate pieces of salad material and a garnish. Variety in garnishes may be obtained by using other greens for individual salads in place of iceberg or head lettuce. Some of these are: curly lettuce, endive, Boston or butter head lettuce, romaine, watercress, Chinese or celery cabbage, dandelion greens, hearts of escarole or chicory, parsley, spinach, cabbage, celery leaves, or nasturtium leaves.

Mixed, tossed, or combination salads may be served individually on a garnish, using a spoon or an ice-cream scoop to standardize the amount, or they may be served directly from a salad bowl. Tossed salads are an economical use of materials because all of a tossed salad is usually eaten.

STANDARDIZING SERVINGS

It is convenient to measure standard portions of some types of mixed salads with an ice-cream scoop. A number 16 scoop gives from 10 to 12 servings for each quart of mixture while a number 10 scoop gives from

118

Photograph from General Foods

FIGURE 19.   ATTRACTIVE MOLDED SALADS
The ring-mold salads shown ready to serve, have a scoop of cottage cheese in the center

6 to 8 servings. Placed salads are standardized by using an equal number of pieces of each ingredient for each serving. Gelatin salads may be "set" in oblong or square shallow pans of equal size and then cut into standard servings. Or the mixture may be put into individual molds (figure 19). Paper cups may be used as shown in figure 5. The amount of mayonnaise or dressing served should be measured.

To find the cost of individual servings total the cost of the salad ingredients, including lettuce and/or other garnish and mayonnaise or other dressings, and then divide this total cost by the number of servings.

STANDARDS FOR SALADS

Salads should be selected to balance the rest of the meal. They should be simple, palatable, colorful, and properly seasoned; the dressings and garnishes should be appropriate to the ingredients used.

Kind of salad	Dressings
Protein (meat, fish, egg)	Mayonnaise alone or combined with boiled dressing or a little vinegar. The ingredients may be marinated first with tart French dressing.
Vegetable	Mayonnaise; Thousand Island; boiled dressing; or French dressing. The vegetables may be marinated with French dressing before mayonnaise is added.
Fruit	Mayonnaise combined with whipped cream or a little fruit juice; boiled dressings made with fruit juice; French dressing; whipped cream.
Gelatin	Any of the above dressings according to the salad ingredients.

Salads should be served attractively to be tempting.

Greens that are clean, fresh, tender, and crisp should be prepared in advance to assure crispness and freedom of excess water at mealtime.

Cooked fruits or vegetables for salads should not be overcooked.

Gelatin salads should be selected only when it is possible to serve them attractively; if served in hot weather, some provision should be made to keep them chilled. Attractive gelatin salads have clear-cut edges; they are firm and have a delicate texture, but are not rubbery; they have a definite form but are not rigid. Molded salads give a diversity of shape (figures 5B, and 19).

In a combination fruit salad, the pieces should be of uniform size with clean-cut edges; melons and cantaloupe balls add interest to many combinations (figure 20).

Photograph from H. J. Heinz Company

FIGURE 20. BALLS FOR FRUIT CUP OR SALAD

These balls may be cut from cantaloupe, watermelon, or other fruits. Potato balls may also be cut with this French cutter. The cutting edge is pressed down firmly, and the handle twirled to make a complete circle

Care should be used in mixing a salad; lightly mixing with a perforated skimmer or a fork in reasonably small amounts helps to distribute the dressing thoroughly and to prevent a "mushy" appearance (figure 6). To improve the flavor of mixed salads, such as potato, meat, certain other cooked vegetables, or fish, the dressing may be added an hour before serving and the mixture allowed to chill.

The dressing for salads of succulent vegetables or of most fruits should be added just before serving, because it tends to draw out juices and to make the salad too wet. For community meals, if this type of salad is to be prepared at home, it is desirable to carry the salad ingredients and dressing separately and to combine them just before serving.

If a placed salad is used, the individual pieces of the ingredients should be consistently arranged in a definite pattern.

The garnish of lettuce or other greens should not extend over the edge of the plate.

Chilled plates tend to keep the garnish crisp; chilling salads until time of serving is desirable.

Photograph from H. J. Heinz Company

FIGURE 21.   AN EGG SLICER

This slicer has other uses than for slicing eggs. Cooked carrots, beets, and potatoes may be thus sliced to make attractive cuts

Photograph from H. J. Heinz Company

FIGURE 22.   PREPARING ORANGE AND GRAPEFRUIT SECTIONS

The white membrane of these fruits should be removed if they are to be used in salads and fruit cup. To peel, cut through the skin and the white membrane, removing strips around the fruit as in peeling an apple. Another method is to cut off a thick slice, top and bottom, then place the fruit on a board and cut the skin from tip to bottom, cutting deep enough to remove all the white membrane

To produce sections of fruit with clean cut edges, cut along the membrane of each section until the center is reached, using a sharp knife. Then turn the knife and force the blade along the membrane of the next section

To keep the sections intact, place the pieces in single layers on trays covered with wax paper

Another method of removing the skin with little membrane remaining, is to (1) steam the fruit in an institution type steamer for about 3 minutes (2) put a small quantity at a time in boiling water and let stand for about 3 minutes. For either method place the fruit immediately into cold water and peel.

121

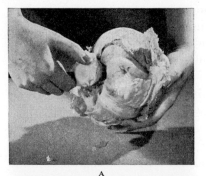

A

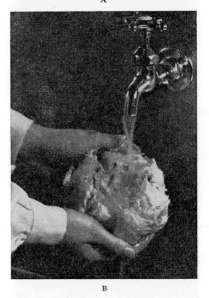

B

Photograph from H. J. Heinz Company

FIGURE 23.   PREPARING LETTUCE

1. Wash the head
2. Remove the outer leaves. Use the outer leaves for tossed greens salads, for sandwiches, or for lettuce with hot bacon dressing (recipe page 108)
3. Cut out the stem end and core (A), cutting to a depth of about 1 inch
4. Hold the head under the faucet and run cold water speedily into the cavity (B); the weight of the water helps to separate the leaves without tearing them. If running water is not available, submerge the head with the cavity-side-up in cold water and lift it in and out of the water several times
5. Finish separating the leaves, stack them like saucers with from 6 to 8 leaves in a pile
6. Invert each pile, put them into a covered container in a towel, and place them in a refrigerator for two or more hours to complete crisping. Use the attractive cup-shaped leaves for salad garnishes; and the small center leaves for holding garnishes of jelly, mayonnaise, relishes, and the like.

SUGGESTIONS FOR SALAD PREPARATION

Prepare the ingredients for salads in advance, keep them cold, and combine them just before serving (figures 20, 21, 22, and 23).

Clean, wash, and crisp greens in cold water for from 15 to 20 minutes; drain them thoroughly in a colander or in towels of linen or paper; pack them into a tightly covered container (with a rack in the bottom) or moistureproof bag, and put it into the refrigerator; or place the greens in a colander with layers of ice between and cover with a damp cloth for further crisping.

Shredding, can be done on a slicing machine or hand slicer (figure 24). This method is particularly successful for a vegetable such as cabbage.

FIGURE 24.   CONVENIENT TOOLS

A. A wax paper dispenser holds wax paper sheets, convenient for wrapping (B) sandwiches

C. A small grater has many uses; grating carrots, cheese, and cabbage are only a few. This one has a fine and a coarse grating attachment

D. Uniform squares of butter may be obtained by cutting quarter pounds with the inexpensive wire cutter

E. Cabbage slaw, grated carrots, or cheese may be made on the small slaw cutter which has fine and coarse grater knives

F. The edge of the butter will be clean-cut if the butter paper is placed over the blade of the knife

FIGURE 25.   MAKING INDIVIDUAL SALADS

Assemble all materials and equipment; distribute the plates on trays; arrange the green garnish, such as lettuce, on the plates; place salad pieces or mixture on the garnish (if an ice cream scoop is used, care must be taken not to pack the mixture too tightly); place an additional garnish and/or dressing. The salads on the trays are ready for serving

For community meals or other functions at which several workers are available, and it is desirable to put individual salads on the plates just before serving, the following procedure is efficient:

First worker: Lay out plates on trays or large work surface
Second worker: Follow the first worker and place the green garnish on each plate
Third worker: Follow the second worker and place salad pieces or mixture
Fourth worker: Place the additional garnish and/or dressing

123

Skin tomatoes for use in salads. To remove the skin, rotate the tomato, held on a fork, in a clear gas flame or over glowing coals until the skin begins to crack, then plunge the tomato into cold water and peel. Another way is to dip the tomatoes, held in a colander or wire basket, into boiling water until the skin begins to loosen, then plunge them into cold water. The skin peels easily. After the skin is removed, place the tomatoes in a covered container and put them into a refrigerator.

Kitchen shears may be used to cut marshmallows, figs, dates, and other sticky foods. Dip the blades into hot water occasionally to keep the pieces from sticking. Rolling sticky foods in powdered sugar beforehand also makes cutting easier.

Peel and dice apples, bananas, and peaches, and cover them with lemon or other acid-fruit juice, or combine them with salad dressing to prevent discoloration. The Cortland or Jonathan apples are particularly desirable for salads because the flesh does not darken on exposure to air.

The use of a large amount of lettuce to garnish salads usually is wasteful, for it may not be eaten; in general, one-half of a large leaf or one smaller leaf is enough. Shredded lettuce as a base is particularly useful in arranging placed salads.

Steps for making individual salads are given with figure 25.

RECIPES

(Use ⅔ of these recipes for a No. 16 scoop serving)

APPLE COMBINATIONS

Combine the ingredients lightly with 2 to 2½ cups of cream dressing (equal parts of boiled dressing *or* mayonnaise and whipped cream). Season the mixture to taste. Dates and nuts tend to cause other ingredients to darken and should be mixed in just before serving or added as a garnish.

Yield: 50 servings   Size of serving: ½ cup (scant) *or* 1 No. 10 scoop

Apple, carrot, and celery

 6 quarts apples, diced
 2 quarts carrots, raw shredded
 2 quarts celery rings

Apple and pineapple

 6 quarts apples, diced
 2 quarts celery rings
 2 quarts pineapple, diced

Apple and coconut

  6 quarts apples, diced
  2 pounds coconut, shredded
  1½ quarts celery rings

Apple and date

  9 quarts apples, diced
  4½ cups dates, quartered

Apple, carrot, and grape
  (Autumn salad)

  6 quarts apples, diced
  2 quarts Malaga grapes, seeded
  2 quarts raw carrots, shredded

Apple and orange

  6 quarts apples, diced
  2 quarts oranges, diced
  1½ quarts celery rings
  1½ cups nuts, coarsely chopped

Apple and peanut (Circus salad)

  5 quarts apples, diced
  4 quarts celery rings
  4 cups peanuts, coarsely chopped

Apple and raisin

  6 quarts apples, diced
  3 quarts celery rings
  4½ cups raisins

Apple and cranberry

  4½ pounds cranberries, raw ⎱ ground
  4 quarts apples, quartered ⎰ together
  4 quarts apples, diced
  4½ cups sugar

NOTE: May be used as a relish with meat.

Apple, celery, and date
  (Waldorf)

  6 quarts apples, diced
  3 quarts celery rings
  2 cups dates *or* raisins
  2 cups nuts, coarsely chopped

CABBAGE SLAW

Yield: 50 servings

8 quarts cabbage, shredded

Cream dressing

1½ cups cream, sweet or sour
½ cup vinegar
¾ cup sugar
2 tablespoons salt
½ teaspoon pepper

Slaw dressing

¾ cup sugar, brown, packed
2 cups vinegar
1 cup water
3 to 4 tablespoons celery seed
3 tablespoons salt
½ teaspoon pepper

Size of serving: ½ cup (scant) *or* 1 No. 10 scoop

1. Mix the ingredients of the dressing; add the mixture to the crisp cabbage just before serving.

NOTE: Allow this dressing to stand on the cabbage for about 30 minutes before serving.

CABBAGE COMBINATIONS

Toss the ingredients together lightly; add the dressing just before serving.

Yield: 50 servings   Size of serving: ½ cup (scant) *or* 1 No. 10 scoop

Cabbage, bacon, and egg
8 quarts cabbage, shredded
2 tablespoons salt
2 tablespoons sugar
½ teaspoon pepper
2 cups bacon, cooked, diced
12 eggs, hard-cooked, diced
1 cup green peppers, diced
2 tablespoons onions, minced
2 cups French dressing *or*
  1 cup cooked dressing
1½ cups mayonnaise

Cabbage, spinach, and apple
4 quarts cabbage, shredded
1½ quarts spinach, shredded
4 quarts apples,* diced
4 tablespoons salt
⅓ cup sugar
2 tablespoons vinegar
½ teaspoon pepper
2 cups mayonnaise

*Add the 2 cups of mayonnaise to the apples to prevent discoloration.

Cabbage, pimiento, pickle, and green pepper
8 quarts cabbage, shredded
1 cup green peppers, chopped
½ cup pimientos, chopped
1 cup sweet pickle relish
1½ tablespoons salt
1½ tablespoons sugar
¼ teaspoon pepper
1½ cups mayonnaise

Cabbage, carrot, green pepper, and Cottage Cheese
6 quarts cabbage, shredded
1 quart carrots, shredded
2 cups green peppers, chopped
4 pounds cottage cheese *or*
2 pounds diced American cheese
1½ tablespoons salt
1½ tablespoons sugar
1½ cups mayonnaise

Cabbage, pineapple, and banana
6 quarts cabbage, shredded
1½ quarts bananas, cubed
3 cups pineapple, crushed
¾ cup lemon juice
1 cup cream, heavy, sour
½ to ¾ cup sugar
1½ tablespoons salt

NOTE: Nuts may be used in place of pineapple.

Cabbage Waldorf
7 quarts cabbage, shredded
2 quarts apples,* diced
2 cups raisins
4 tablespoons salt
4 tablespoons sugar
½ teaspoon pepper

Dressing

1½ cups cream, sweet or sour
½ cup vinegar
¾ cup sugar
1 tablespoon salt

*Add the dressing to the apples to prevent discoloration.

Cabbage, carrot, and peanut
6 quarts cabbage, shredded
1½ quarts carrots, shredded
2 cups peanuts, chopped
1¼ cups cream dressing
1 tablespoon Worcestershire sauce
¼ teaspoon cayenne pepper
1½ tablespoons salt
1½ tablespoons sugar

NOTE: Raisins may be used to replace part or all of the peanuts.

CARROT COMBINATIONS

Combine the salad ingredients with the dressing and season the mixture with salt and sugar.

Yield: 50 servings Size of serving: ½ cup (scant) *or* 1 No. 10 scoop

Carrot and apple

7½ quarts carrots, raw, shredded
1½ quarts celery rings
1½ quarts apples, diced
Mayonnaise *or* cream* dressing

Carrot, celery, and peanut, *or* raisin

7½ quarts carrots, raw, shredded
1½ quarts celery rings
4½ cups peanuts, coarsely chopped,
   or raisins
Mayonnaise *or* cream* dressing

Carrot and coconut

9 quarts carrots, shredded
1½ pounds coconut
Mayonnaise *or* cream* dressing

Carrot, egg, and celery

5 quarts carrots, raw, shredded
2 quarts celery rings
14 eggs, hard-cooked, sliced
3 cups peas, cooked
3 cups cucumbers, diced
2 cups French dressing
2 cups mayonnaise

*Equal parts of boiled dressing *or* mayonnaise and whipped cream.

CIDER *OR* GINGERALE FRUIT GELATIN SALAD

Yield: 56 servings Size of serving: 2½-inch squares by ¾ to 1 inch thick

2½ to 3½ ounces (7½ to 10½ tablespoons) gelatin, granulated*
2 cups cold water
1 quart boiling water *or* fruit juice
1 cup sugar
1 teaspoon salt
2½ quarts cider *or* gingerale

1. Soak the gelatin in the cold water; add the boiling water, salt, and sugar, and stir until all are dissolved. Cool. Add the cider or gingerale; chill.

1 quart apples, diced
½ cup lemon juice
3 cups grapes, halved and seeded *or* Royal Ann cherries, pitted
2 cups celery rings
3 cups pineapple, diced

2. Cover the apples with lemon juice to flavor and to keep them from discoloring, drain before adding to the gelatin mixture. When the mixture begins to set, add the solid ingredients; chill.

*If gelatin must be set quickly or if gelatin is made during hot weather, use the larger amount.

COTTAGE CHEESE SALAD

Yield: 50 servings Size of serving: 1 No. 16 scoop

5 pounds cottage cheese
2 cups celery rings
1 cup green peppers, diced
1 cup nuts, coarsely chopped
2 cups carrots, raw, shredded

1. Combine all the ingredients.

2. Add mayonnaise and cream to moisten.

127

COMBINATION FRUIT SALAD

Yield: 8 quarts   Size of serving: 1 No. 10 scoop

I
6 cups oranges, sectioned*
6 cups grapefruit, sectioned*
3 quarts pineapple cubes
3 quarts grapes, seeded and cut
  in halves
1½ cups cream, heavy†
1 cup mayonnaise

*Instructions for sectioning oranges and grapefruit are given on page 121.
†Whip the cream and add it to the mayonnaise.

II
1½ quarts apple cubes
2 quarts pineapple cubes
1½ quarts oranges, diced
2 quarts bananas, diced
2 cups cream dressing *or* mayonnaise

NOTE: Cream cheese blended with lemon juice is an excellent topping.

OTHER FRUIT COMBINATIONS

Apple, grapefruit, melon
Avocado, celery, apple
Grapefruit, cantaloupe, avocado
Orange, pineapple, marshmallow cubes

Pineapple, strawberry, orange
Pineapple, orange, tomato
Strawberry, celery, almonds

CRANBERRY AND ORANGE GELATIN SALAD

Yield: 56 servings

2½ pounds cranberries, raw
3 oranges, whole
4 apples, cored

5 cups sugar
1½ teaspoons salt

3 ounces (9 tablespoons)
  gelatin, granulated
2 cups cold water
3½ quarts fruit juice

Size of serving: 2½-inch square by ¾ to 1 inch thick or individual molds ½ cup each

1. Grind the cranberries, oranges, and apples.

2. Add the sugar and salt and let stand for 2 hours.

3. Soften the gelatin in the cold water.

4. Heat part of the fruit juice and add it to the softened gelatin, stirring until gelatin is dissolved. Add the remaining cold fruit juice. Add the cranberry mixture. Chill.

CRANBERRY GELATIN SALAD

Yield: 56 servings   Size of serving: 2½-inch squares by ¾ to 1 inch thick

4 pounds (4 quarts) cranberries
2 quarts water

7 cups sugar

¾ cup (4 ounces) gelatin,
  granulated
3 cups cold water

1. Cook the cranberries in the water until tender. They may then be sieved or left whole.

2. Add the sugar to the cranberries and cook them for 5 minutes. Remove them from the heat.

3. Soak the gelatin in the cold water and add it to the hot cranberries, stirring until it is dissolved; chill.

1 quart celery rings
1½ cups nuts, coarsely chopped
4 oranges, diced

4. When the gelatin begins to set, stir in the solid ingredients; chill.

FROZEN FRUIT SALADS

Yield: 5 to 6 quarts

Size of serving: 1 slice

I

2½ quarts bananas, diced
3 cups oranges, diced
1¼ quarts peaches, diced
1 quart Royal Ann cherries, pitted
1 teaspoon salt
1 cup mayonnaise
1 pint cream, heavy
1 cup boiled dressing
½ cup sugar
¼ cup lemon juice

II

1½ quarts grapefruit, diced
3 quarts pineapple, diced
1½ quarts oranges, diced
3 quarts Royal Ann cherries, pitted
3 cups mayonnaise
3 cups cream, heavy
1 teaspoon salt

1. Drain the fruit well.
2. Whip the cream and combine it with the mayonnaise.
3. Combine the dressing and fruit lightly.
4. Put in quart paper cartons and freeze overnight.
5. Cut into slices for serving.

GELATIN SALAD VARIATIONS

General directions

The containers in which the salads are to be "set" should first be rinsed with cold water. Mold gelatin salad in square or oblong pans and cut it into squares for individual servings, or set it in individual molds (figures 5B and 19). Individual salads in ring molds are attractive; the center of these may be filled with a salad mixture or with shredded lettuce. Garnish gelatin salads with mayonnaise or some other dressing as given on page 120.

The amount of gelatin needed varies; the more acid used, the more gelatin is required; if the gelatin has to be set quickly, use a larger proportion; likewise, a larger proportion is needed in hot weather than is needed in cold weather, therefore a range in the amount of gelatin is given in the recipes.

Yield: One gallon of gelatin base and about 3 quarts of solid ingredients yield 56 servings 2½ inches square, and ¾ to 1 inch thick. One oblong pan, 16 by 10 inches, cuts 28 servings of this size.

For 1 gallon of base made with flavored gelatin

26 ounces (3¾ cups) prepared gelatin powder
1 gallon water and/or fruit juice

1. Heat part of the liquid; add this to the gelatin powder, and stir until it is dissolved. Add the remaining cold liquid. Chill the mixture. When it begins to set, add the solid ingredients; chill.

For 1 gallon of base made with granulated gelatin

2½ to 3½ ounces (7½ to 10½ tablespoons) gelatin, granulated

1. Soak the gelatin in the cold water; heat 2 quarts of the water or fruit juice to the boiling point; add it, the salt, and sugar to the soaked

129

2 cups cold water
3½ quarts fruit juice
and/or water
1 tablespoon salt
2½ cups sugar*
1 cup lemon juice *or* vinegar†

gelatin and stir until all are dissolved. Add the remaining cold liquid and acid liquid. Chill the mixture. When it begins to set, add the solid ingredients; chill.

*Vary the amount of sugar according to the kind of salad and sweetness of fruit juice used.
†Use vinegar or lemon juice according to the kind of salad; if the vinegar is very sour, dilute it with water.

Variations

Apple, cabbage, and stuffed olive
1½ quarts apples, diced
1½ quarts cabbage, shredded
1 cup stuffed olives, sliced

Nut and stuffed olive
2 cups stuffed olives, sliced
1 cup nuts, coarsely chopped
2 quarts celery rings
1 cup green peppers, chopped

Golden
1 quart pineapple, crushed, drained
1½ quarts carrots, raw, grated
2 cups celery rings

Pineapple and cucumber
1½ quarts pineapple tidbits
1½ quarts cucumbers, diced

Kentucky
1½ quarts pineapple, crushed, drained
1½ quarts celery, diced
1 cup maraschino cherries

Knickerbocker
6 grapefruit, sectioned
12 oranges, sectioned
3 cups pineapple cubes
12 small apples, cut into thin strips
½ cup pimiento strips
2 cups celery rings

Manhattan
1 quart celery, cut fine
1 quart Royal Ann cherries, pitted
1 quart pineapple tidbits
½ cup maraschino cherries, sliced thin

Pineapple relish
2½ quarts pineapple tidbits
1½ cups pickle relish

Sea green
Use a lime-gelatin base; substitute 1 cup of medium-sour vinegar for 1 cup of the liquid; add:

¼ cup onion juice
3 quarts grated cucumber (about 8 cucumbers)
2 tablespoons sweet pickle relish

JELLIED BEET AND HORSERADISH SALAD

Yield: 56 servings   Size of serving: 2½-inch square by ¾ to 1 inch thick

2½ to 3½ ounces (7½ to 10½ tablespoons) gelatin, granulated*
2½ cups cold water
6 cups hot water
2 tablespoons salt
¾ cup sugar
4 cups cold beet juice

1. Soak the gelatin in the cold water and add the hot water, salt, and sugar to it; stir until all are dissolved. Add the beet juice, onion juice, fruit juice, and vinegar; chill.

½ cup onion juice
1½ cups fruit juice
1½ cups vinegar
6 cups beets, cooked, and diced
   or sliced
1 cup horseradish
3 cups celery, diced

2. When the mixture begins to set, add the solid ingredients; chill.

*If gelatin must be set quickly or if gelatin is made during hot weather, use the larger amount.

HEALTH SALAD IN INDIVIDUAL MOLDS

Yield: 45 to 50 servings   Size of serving: ½ cup

2 quarts cabbage, chopped
2 quarts carrots, chopped
2 cups green peppers, chopped
Mayonnaise
Salt and pepper to taste

1. Mix each vegetable separately with mayonnaise and season to taste. Pack a small amount of the pepper mixture into the bottom of individual molds; fill one-half full with the carrot mixture; finish filling with the cabbage mixture. Pack the mixtures firmly into the molds and let them stand in a cool place. Turn them out on a lettuce leaf.

MACARONI *OR* SPAGHETTI SALAD

Yield: 6 quarts   Size of serving: ½ cup

1½ pounds macaroni or
   spaghetti

1. Cook the macaroni or spaghetti in 1½ gallons of water with 3 tablespoons of salt; drain it in a colander and rinse it with water. Chill the macaroni *or* spaghetti.

3 cups sweet pickles, diced
3½ cups cheese, cubed
¾ cup green peppers, chopped
½ cup pimiento strips
4 cups celery rings
8 eggs, hard-cooked, diced
3 tablespoons salt
1⅓ cups mayonnaise
1⅓ cups chili sauce

2. Mix all the ingredients with the cooked macaroni *or* spaghetti.

3. Add the salt, dressing, and chili sauce; mix it thoroughly and carefully.

MEAT SALAD

Yield: 7 to 7½ quarts   Size of serving: ½ cup

4 pounds (4 quarts) veal and
   pork, cooked, cubed
3 quarts celery rings
1 quart cucumbers, diced
2 tablespoons salt
2 cups cooked dressing
2 cups mayonnaise
⅓ cup vinegar
1 tablespoon Worcestershire
   sauce

1. Combine all the ingredients; add the dressing and mix it thoroughly and lightly.

131

MIXED GREENS COMBINATIONS

Toss the ingredients together lightly; add salt and the dressing just before serving.

Yield: 50 servings   Size of serving: ½ cup

I (Chef's)

7½ quarts lettuce, shredded
3 cups watercress, coarsely chopped
1 quart tomatoes, cut in large cubes
6 eggs, hard-cooked, cut in pieces
1 tablespoon onions, minced
2 cups cheese, cubed
¾ cup green peppers, diced
1 tablespoon salt
2 cups French or Spanish dressing

II

7½ quarts lettuce, shredded
3 quarts apples, diced
2 quarts carrots, raw, shredded
Cream dressing (equal parts of boiled
  dressing or mayonnaise and whipped
  cream)

III

9 quarts lettuce, shredded
3 cups cucumbers, sliced
1½ cups radish slices
¾ cup onions, diced
1½ cups green peppers, diced
1½ cups carrots, raw, shredded
4½ cups tomato wedges
French dressing

IV

6 quarts lettuce, shredded
3 quarts spinach, raw, cut-up
3 cups celery rings
3 cups carrots, raw, shredded
4½ cups cauliflower, raw, diced
1½ cups green peppers, diced
French dressing

V

8 quarts spinach, raw, cut-up
2 quarts carrots, raw, shredded
9 eggs, hard-cooked, sliced
French or Spanish dressing

VI

4½ quarts spinach, raw, cut-up
3 quarts carrots, raw, shredded
1½ quarts celery rings
2 quarts pineapple, diced

VII

4½ quarts spinach, shredded
5½ quarts lettuce, shredded
3 cups celery rings
1 tablespoon onions, minced or onion
  juice
1 tablespoon salt
15 strips bacon, diced and browned
2 cups French dressing
½ cup vinegar

Variations

1. Add 6 tablespoons grated orange rind.
2. Add diced fresh fruit such as apple,
   cantaloupe, pear, orange, or grapefruit.

VIII (Spring)

2 quarts cucumbers, diced
3 cups radishes, sliced
6 cups tomatoes, cut in wedges
1 cup green peppers, diced
1 quart celery, diced
8 quarts lettuce, shredded
1 cup French dressing
2 tablespoons salt

IX (Vitamin)

3 quarts spinach, raw, shredded
2 quarts cauliflower, raw, cut into tiny
  flowerettes
2½ quarts broccoli buds,* raw, diced
3 quarts celery rings
2 cups green peppers, chopped
4 tablespoons salt
2 cups Spanish dressing

*Frozen broccoli buds may be used.

PERFECTION SALAD

Yield: 56 servings   Size of serving: 2½-inch square by ¾ to 1 inch thick

4 to 5 ounces (¾ to 1 cup)   .   1. Soak the gelatin in the cold water; add the
  gelatin, granulated*   boiling water, salt, and sugar, and stir the mix-

2 cups cold water
3 quarts boiling water
2 tablespoons salt
4 cups sugar
1 cup lemon juice
2 cups vinegar

2 quarts cabbage, shredded
1½ quarts celery rings
1 cup pimientos, cut in strips
1 cup green peppers, chopped

ture until all are dissolved. Cool. Add the lemon juice and vinegar; chill.

2. When the gelatin mixture begins to set, add the vegetables; chill.

*If gelatin must be set quickly or if gelatin is made during hot weather, use the larger amount.

POTATO SALAD*

Yield: 5½ quarts   Size of serving: 1 No. 12 scoop

5 quarts potatoes, cooked and cubed (about 9 pounds before peeling)
1 tablespoon salt
1 tablespoon paprika
2 tablespoons onion juice
1 cup French dressing

1. Combine the salt, paprika, onion juice, and French dressing. Mix this with the potatoes and let them stand for 15 minutes.

6 eggs, hard-cooked, quartered
5 cups celery rings
½ cup pimientos, chopped
½ cup green peppers, chopped
½ cup parsley, chopped

2. Add the vegetables and the eggs: mix the ingredients together lightly.

1 cup mayonnaise
1 cup cooked dressing

3. Combine the mayonnaise and cooked dressing and add this to the salad; mix it lightly.

*2 cups of diced cucumbers may be added if desired.

HOT POTATO SALAD

Yield: 7 quarts   Size of serving: 1 No. 12 scoop

10 pounds (7½ quarts) potatoes, cooked, diced (about 13 pounds before peeling)

1. Prepare the potatoes.

¾ pound bacon, diced
10 eggs, hard-cooked, sliced
2 quarts celery, diced
½ cup green peppers, chopped
¼ cup onions, minced

2. Fry the bacon; drain the fat from it.

3. Combine the eggs, vegetables, potatoes, and bacon.

Sauce

2 cups vinegar
2 cups water
1¼ cups sugar
½ cup bacon fat
3 tablespoons salt

4. Combine all the ingredients of the sauce; add the sauce to the potato mixture and mix all lightly. Heat this in the top of a double boiler and keep it hot for serving.

133

SALMON OR TUNAFISH SALADS

Yield: 50 servings

Size of serving: ½ cup (scant) or 1 No. 10 scoop

I	II
7½ pounds salmon *or* tunafish, flaked	6 pounds salmon *or* tunafish, flaked
4½ cups pickles, chopped	2 quarts cucumbers, diced
3½ quarts celery rings	2½ quarts celery rings
2 cups mayonnaise	2 quarts (3 pounds, frozen) peas, cooked
¼ cup lemon juice	2 cups boiled dressing
Salt and pepper to taste	2 cups mayonnaise
	Salt and pepper to taste

SHRIMP OR CRABMEAT SALADS

Yield: 50 servings

Size of serving: ½ cup (scant) or 1 No. 10 scoop

Shrimp or crabmeat and orange	Shrimp or crabmeat and vegetable
4½ pounds shrimp or crabmeat, coarsely flaked	2¼ pounds shrimp or crabmeat, coarsely flaked
3 quarts oranges, diced	3 cups pickles, chopped
2 quarts celery rings	3 quarts cabbage, shredded
1½ quarts cucumbers, diced	3 quarts celery rings
2 cups mayonnaise	1½ quarts (2 pounds frozen) peas, cooked
Salt and pepper to taste	12 eggs, hard-cooked, diced
	¾ cup lemon juice
	1½ cups mayonnaise
	Salt and pepper to taste

TOMATO ASPIC SALAD

Yield: 56 servings:

Size of serving: 2½-inch square by ½ to ¾ inch thick

6 ounces (1⅛ cups) gelatin, granulated
2 cups tomato juice, cold

1. Soak the gelatin in the cold tomato juice.

5½ quarts tomato juice
1½ tablespoons salt
6 bay leaves
¾ cup sugar
1½ tablespoons cloves, whole
1½ pounds (6) carrots, cut up
¾ cup onion, cut up
3 cups celery tops, cut up
3 cups vinegar
¾ cup lemon juice
Solid ingredients (see variations)

2. Combine the tomato juice, salt, bay leaves, sugar, cloves, carrots, onion, and celery tops. Boil the mixture for 15 minutes; strain. Measure the strained juice and add enough more tomato juice to make 5½ quarts. Add this to the soaked gelatin and stir until it is dissolved. Cool the mixture. Add the vinegar and lemon juice; chill.

3. When the gelatin mixture begins to set, add the solid ingredients; chill.

Variations

Asparagus: Place stalks of cooked or canned asparagus in even rows on the bottom of flat pans. When the aspic begins to set, pour it over the asparagus.

Celery and olive: Add 1½ cups of celery rings and 1½ cups of sliced stuffed olives.

Cottage cheese and aspic sandwich: Pour one-half of the gelatin mixture into the bottom of the pans and allow this to harden. Over this spread from 2 to 3 quarts of cottage cheese. Pour the remaining gelatin mixture over the cheese. Cut it into squares.

Cream or cottage cheese balls: Place a ball of cream or cottage cheese on each square.

Deviled or sliced eggs: Place a half deviled egg or a slice of hard-cooked egg on each square.

Tunafish, shrimp or crabmeat: Add 3 cups of flaked fish.

VEGETABLE SALAD

Yield: 8½ quarts

Size of serving: ½ cup

4 quarts carrots, cooked, diced (about 8 pounds before peeling)
2 quarts potatoes, cooked, diced (about 4 pounds before peeling)
2 quarts peas, cooked (3 pounds frozen)
2 quarts green beans, cooked (3 pounds frozen)
2 cups pimientos, cut in strips
½ cup salt
½ teaspoon paprika
1 cup French dressing
2 cups Thousand Island dressing

1. Combine all the vegetables; add the salt, paprika, and French dressing, and let the mixture stand for 15 minutes before serving. Add the Thousand Island dressing and mix all well.

PLACED SALADS (INDIVIDUAL)

Banana fingers with fruit French dressing; whipped cream; peanut butter dressing; jelly dressing

Apricot halves stuffed with cream or cottage cheese, plain or rolled in nuts or chopped parsley; mayonnaise garnish

Figs, canned, stuffed with cream or cottage cheese; mayonnaise garnish

Grapefruit and apple and/or orange sections; French dressing

Orange slices with cottage cheese sandwich; fruit French dressing

Orange slices and prunes stuffed with nuts; mayonnaise garnish

Orange slices and stuffed figs; mayonnaise garnish

Orange and mild onion slices; French dressing

Orange slices and green pepper rings; French dressing

Peach or pear halves with: cream or cottage cheese, plain or rolled in nuts or shredded carrots; date or fig filling; mayonnaise garnish

Pineapple slices with: cottage or cream cheese, sandwich fashion; grated cheddar cheese; mayonnaise garnish

Prunes stuffed with peanut butter, nuts, or cottage cheese; mayonnaise garnish

Tomato stuffed with: chicken salad; cottage or cream cheese; ham and celery salad; mixed vegetable salad; cole slaw; potato salad; tunafish or shrimp salad

GARNISHES FOR SALADS

Beet slices

Carrot sticks or curls (figure 17)

Celery curl, celery heart, or celery stuffed with cheese

Cheese, American or Swiss, shredded or sliced

Cheese balls (American, cream, or cottage) rolled in chopped nuts, chives, paprika, or grated carrots

Coconut

Cucumber fingers or slices

Dates or prunes stuffed with peanut butter, cheese or nuts

Egg slices or deviled egg (figure 21)

Gherkins; burr, or pickle fans or slices

Green pepper strips or rings

Lemon wedges or slices

Melon balls, cubes, or slices

Nuts, whole, chopped, or slivered

Olives, whole, stuffed, or ripe

Onion rings or scallions

Orange sections

Peaches, pears, or watermelon rind, spiced

Pimiento strips

Radishes, plain or radish roses

Tomato wedge

Watercress, mint, or parsley sprig

Fresh berries

ACCOMPANIMENTS FOR SALADS

Biscuits, baking powder

Breads, hot: date, brown, prune, apricot, nut

Crackers spread with cheese

Muffins, hot or toasted

Muffins, English, toasted

Potato chips

Rolls, hard or soft, toasted or plain

Sandwiches with fillings, appropriate to the salad

Toast, plain, cinnamon, melba

Cheese pastry sticks

SALAD DRESSING RECIPES

BLUE CHEESE FRENCH DRESSING

See variation of French dressing, page 137.

COOKED DRESSING*

Yield: 2 quarts

1¼ cups sugar
2 tablespoons mustard
2 teaspoons salt
1½ cups flour
6 egg yolks, beaten
3 cups vinegar, heated
3 14½-ounce cans evaporated milk

1. Mix the dry ingredients and combine them with the egg yolks, then add the hot vinegar. Cook the mixture over hot water until thickened, stirring constantly with a wire whip. Add the milk, and cook until the mixture is creamy.

*This mixture will keep indefinitely if sealed in glass jars while hot.

FRENCH DRESSING

Yield: 3 quarts

2 tablespoons sugar, confectioners'
3 tablespoons salt
1 tablespoon mustard
1½ teaspoons paprika
1 tablespoon, pepper, white
4 tablespoons onion juice*
1 quart vinegar
2 quarts salad oil

1. Place the ingredients in a jar and shake
thoroughly or beat with a wire whip.

*May be omitted.

Variations

Roquefort or Blue Cheese French dressing: To 1 quart of French dressing add 4 to 5
ounces of crumbled Roquefort or Blue Cheese.

Tomato soup French dressing: To 1 quart of French dressing add ¾ cup of sugar,
1 teaspoon of onion juice, and 2 cups of condensed tomato soup. Shake the mixture
well.

COTTAGE CHEESE FRENCH DRESSING

Yield: 3 quarts

5 cups cottage cheese
1 cup sugar
3 tablespoons salt
2½ tablespoons dry mustard
4 teaspoons paprika
1½ cups vinegar
3 cups salad oil
1 cup catsup
¼ cup water
2½ tablespoons Worcestershire
sauce
4 teaspoons grated onion
4 cloves garlic (cut in small
pieces)
Dash of Tabasco sauce

1. Whip the cheese in a mixer until very creamy.

2. Mix together the sugar, salt, mustard, and
paprika and make a thin paste with a little
vinegar. Add this mixture to the cottage cheese.

3. Add the remaining ingredients and beat at
medium-fast speed until mixture is well blended.

FRUIT FRENCH DRESSING

Yield: 2 quarts.

1 cup lemon juice
1 cup orange juice
6 cups salad oil
2 tablespoons salt
¾ teaspoon white pepper
½ cup sugar, confectioners'
2 to 3 cups currant jelly, if
desired

1. Place the ingredients into a container and beat
the mixture with a wire whip, or make it in
smaller quantities and shake the ingredients together.

2. Beat the jelly into the dressing.

137

HONEY FRUIT DRESSING

Yield: 1½ quarts

2 cups strained honey
1 cup hot water
1½ cups lemon juice

1. Mix the honey with the water and lemon juice.

1 cup salad oil
½ teaspoon paprika
Salt to taste

2. Add the oil slowly, beating with an egg beater. Add seasoning as needed.

MAYONNAISE*

(electric mixer)

Yield: 1 gallon

10 egg yolks
1 cup vinegar†

1. Beat the yolks until thick and lemon colored. Add one-half of the vinegar.

3¼ quarts salad oil

2. Pour in gradually one-half of the oil, beating constantly. Once the oil and egg yolk are thoroughly combined to form a thickened product the oil may be added more rapidly without danger of breaking down the mayonnaise.

1½ tablespoons mustard
1½ tablespoons sugar, confectioners'
1½ tablespoons salt
1 teaspoon paprika

3. Combine the dry ingredients with the remaining vinegar, and add this to the mixture. Continue adding the oil and beat the mixture for about 5 minutes to thoroughly blend the ingredients.

*Mayonnaise may be thinned with water or milk.
†¼ cup of lemon juice may be used in place of ¼ cup of vinegar.

Variation

Thousand Island dressing: To 3 quarts of mayonnaise, add 1 cup of sweet relish, 1 cup of chili sauce, and 4 hard-cooked eggs, chopped.

MAYONNAISE WITH CORNSTARCH BASE

Yield: 2½ gallons

Cornstarch base
3 cups water

1. Heat the water to boiling.

1 cup cornstarch
1 cup vinegar

2. Combine the cornstarch and vinegar; add this to the boiling water and cook until thickened, stirring with a wire whip. Put the mixture in a large mixer bowl and whip until cool.

Mayonnaise
24 (2 cups) egg yolks

3. Add the egg yolks to cooled cornstarch base and whip until lemon colored.

2 gallons salad oil

4. Using the oil dropper attachment, allow ½ gallon of the oil to drip slowly into the egg mixture, beating at high speed.

2 cups vinegar
¼ cup mustard
¼ cup sugar, confectioners'
1 tablespoon paprika
¼ cup salt
1½ 14½-ounce cans evaporated
  milk

5. Combine the vinegar and seasonings; add this mixture to the oil mixture slowly, allowing the rest of the oil to drip in at the same time.

6. Continue to beat until all oil is added. The flow of oil may be increased as the emulsion is formed. After all the oil is blended, add the evaporated milk. Do not beat the mixture after the milk is blended.

PINEAPPLE DRESSING

Yield: 2½ quarts

1½ quarts milk

1. Heat the milk.

2 cups sugar
1¼ cups cornstarch
½ teaspoon mustard
½ teaspoon paprika
½ teaspoon salt

2. Mix the sugar, cornstarch, mustard, paprika, and salt; add 2 cups of the hot milk and blend all with a wire whip; return this to the other hot milk and cook the mixture until thickened, stirring constantly with a wire whip.

8 eggs yolks, beaten

3. Add a little of the hot mixture to the egg yolks and combine; return this to the remaining hot mixture and cook it for a few minutes, stirring constantly. Remove it from the heat.

¾ cup orange juice
¾ cup lemon juice
1 cup pineapple juice

4. Add the fruit juices; stir until the mixture is well blended.

ROQUEFORT CHEESE FRENCH DRESSING

See variation of French dressing, page 137.

SPANISH DRESSING

Yield: 2 quarts

4 cups salad oil
2 cups catsup
2 cups vinegar
2 cups sugar, confectioners'
1 tablespoon salt
2 teaspoons paprika
1 cup lemon juice
2 medium onions, grated

1. Place the ingredients into a container and beat the mixture with a wire whip, or make it in smaller quantities and shake the ingredients together.

THOUSAND ISLAND DRESSING

See variation of mayonnaise, page 138.

SANDWICHES

MATERIALS

Sandwiches vary in cost according to the amounts and kinds of ingredients used. If they are to be sold for a specific price, the ingredients can be adjusted; expensive fillings are prohibitive if the price is to be low, but smaller measures and thinner slices of meat or cheese decrease the cost. Too little filling, however, makes a sandwich unpalatable. Usually the slices of bread are cut from $\frac{1}{8}$ to $\frac{1}{2}$ inch thick, depending on the use. The amount of butter used should be kept constant by weighing or measuring out the specified amount to spread a given number of sandwiches, the amount depending on whether one slice or both

FIGURE 26.   FILLED SANDWICHES

Making sandwiches with a filling
Wrapping sandwiches individually

APPROXIMATE MEASURES FOR 50 SANDWICHES

Item	Amount for 1 sandwich	Amount for 50 sandwiches
Butter for spreading	1½ teaspoons for 1 slice	10 to 12 ounces (1¼ to 1½ cups) for spreading 1 slice of the sandwich; double this amount for spreading both slices. For spreading whole-grain bread, use 2 ounces (¼ cup) more for each 50 slices of bread
Bread	2 slices	3 pullman loaves (100 slices) (2-pound pullman loaf, 14 inches long, cuts 35 slices ⅜ inch thick)
Mayonnaise	2 teaspoons to 1 tablespoon	2 to 3 cups
Mixed fillings	3 tablespoons or No. 24 scoop 2 tablespoons or No. 30 scoop (for sweet fillings)	2½ to 3 quarts 1¾ to 2 quarts
Sliced meat and cheese	1½ ounces clear meat 1 to 1½ ounces cheese	5 pounds (10 slices per pound) 3 to 4 pounds (12 to 16 slices per pound)
Peanut butter	2 tablespoons or No. 30 scoop	4 pounds or 7 cups (1 pound equals 1¾ cups)
Lettuce	1 small or ½ large leaf	2½ to 3 heads

are to be spread. A leaf of lettuce used with other fillings is a good investment from a nutritional standpoint and it adds crispness to the sandwich; with its use the amount of filling may be decreased slightly to balance the cost. A thin layer of cole slaw is good with sliced meat fillings.

Bread

Day-old bread of a close, firm texture is desirable for sandwiches. Pullman or sandwich loaves of whole-grain or enriched white bread may be purchased from the bakery already sliced to the desired thickness. Sandwiches made with nut, orange, banana, date, raisin, fig, chocolate, steamed or baked brown bread and plain or flavored butter or seasoned cream cheese are attractive, varied, and good to eat. For sandwiches with other fillings, white, whole-wheat, rye and cracked-wheat breads are appropriate. Two-tone sandwiches, made with one slice each of whole-grain and white bread, appeal to children who might not otherwise choose whole-grain bread.

Meat and Cheese

Loaves or bricks of meat or cheese may be purchased ready sliced or in bulk for slicing to the desired thickness by a machine. Slicing to a specific number of slices per pound produces standardized sandwiches on which an accurate food cost may be figured.

Paper for Wrapping

Waxed paper for wrapping individual sandwiches may be purchased in sheets cut to the correct size. A dispenser for such sheets saves time if a large number of sandwiches is to be wrapped (figure 24A).

"Fortified" Sandwich Fillings

The nutritive value of sandwiches may be increased by adding yeast or wheat germ to the fillings. Fresh yeast and dried brewer's yeast may be combined with fillings as cheese spreads and peanut butter; wheat germ may be added to any mixed filling.

PROCEDURE FOR MAKING SANDWICHES

1. Use a wood-top table or large cutting board in order to have plenty of work space. Shelves above the work space are efficient for holding bread and other ingredients.

2. Assemble all materials in advance: knives, spoons, scoops, waxed paper, damp towels, and storage pans.

3. Prepare the fillings, refrigerating any perishable fillings until time to make the sandwiches. If lettuce is used, it should be washed, drained, and crisped beforehand.

4. Soften the butter, either by leaving it for some time at room temperature, or cream it with a wooden spoon or in an electric mixer, using the flat paddle. One-half cup of milk may be added to 1 pound of butter to make the butter pliable. Melted butter is undesirable in sandwiches.

FIGURE 27.   BREAD AND BUTTER
SANDWICHES

Quantities of sandwiches may be kept fresh by stacking them in large pans between waxed paper and covering them with a damp towel

5. Slice the bread, or if ready sliced, unwrap the loaves as needed.

6. Arrange the bread as described below and shown in figures 26 and 27.

7. Spread the butter to all edges on one or both slices of bread, using a wide spreader and allowing the slices to lie flat on the working surface (figures 26 and 27). When fillings such as cream cheese, peanut butter, or those containing may-

onnaise are used, the butter may be omitted on one slice. Butter both slices when using jelly or mixtures that contain considerable moisture or lettuce or tomatoes. Readily adherent mixtures such as peanut butter may be mixed with the butter and the sandwiches filled in one operation (figure 27).

8. To make bread and butter sandwiches and sandwiches with butter-filling mixtures (figure 27):
    a. Arrange about 2 or 3 stacks of bread of 8 to 10 slices each on the table from front to back.
    b. With the left hand place one slice of bread near the front edge of the table.
    c. Spread it with butter or butter-filling mixture.
    d. Again with the left hand remove 2 slices of bread from the next stack and place them on the buttered slice.
    e. Spread the top slice with butter or butter-filling mixture and repeat until 4 or 5 sandwiches are completed.
    f. Cut the sandwiches and prepare them for holding.

9. To make filled sandwiches (figure 26):
    a. Arrange the bread on the table as shown in figure 26.
    b. Spread alternate rows of slices with butter.
    c. Place filling on remaining slices.
    d. Arrange lettuce leaves on the filling, if they are being used.
    e. Using 2 hands, place the buttered slices on the filled slices.
    f. Cut the sandwiches and prepare them for holding.

HOLDING SANDWICHES FOR SERVING

Sandwiches for cafeteria service and the lunch box remain attractive and palatable if individually wrapped. An efficient method for keeping stacked sandwiches fresh is the following:

1. Place a damp towel on the bottom of a flat pan or tray; place waxed paper over the damp towel.

2. Stack the sandwiches on this tray and cover them with waxed paper (figure 27).

3. Place a damp towel over the waxed paper, being sure that the sandwiches are completely covered.

4. Refrigerate the sandwiches until used.

5. Some types of sandwiches may be frozen successfully for short-time holding.

143

RECIPES

Base for 50 sandwiches

100 slices bread*

10 to 12 ounces (1¼ to 1½ cups) butter for spreading 1 slice of the sandwich

1¼ to 1½ pounds (2½ to 3 cups) butter for spreading both slices of the sandwich

*Whole-grain bread, because of its coarser texture, requires more butter. Use 4 ounces (½ cup) more for each 50 slices of bread to be spread.

Fillings for 50 sandwiches

APRICOT OR PRUNE AND NUT

Amount of filling per sandwich:
1 No. 30 scoop (2 tablespoons)

3½ pounds apricots or prunes, dried
5 cups nuts, coarsely chopped
⅛ teaspoon salt
⅓ cup sugar
½ cup lemon juice

To moisten:

½ to 1 cup mayonnaise

1. Wash the fruit, cover it with water and let it soak overnight; drain it well, and put it through a hand food grinder. Mix this with the nuts, sugar and salt; add enough lemon juice just to moisten the mixture.

2. Spread one slice of bread with butter and then with mayonnaise; spread the other slice with fruit mixture.

NOTE: Apricots and prunes in equal proportions may be used.

BEAN AND VEGETABLE

Amount of filling per sandwich:
1 No. 24 scoop (3 tablespoons)

7½ cups dried beans, cooked, drained and mashed (1½ pounds before soaking)
1½ cups celery, chopped fine
1 cup green peppers, chopped fine
½ cup onion, chopped fine
3 tablespoons salt
¼ teaspoon pepper
¼ cup prepared mustard
¼ cup catsup
To moisten:
About ¼ cup mayonnaise

SNAPPY CHEESE

Amount of filling per sandwich:
1 No. 30 scoop (2 tablespoons)

3 pounds (3 quarts) sharp American cheese, chopped
1¼ cups mayonnaise
1 cup top milk or evaporated milk
2 teaspoons prepared mustard
1 tablespoon paprika
2 teaspoons Worcestershire sauce
1 teaspoon salt

Variation

Snappy cheese and peanut butter: In place of 1½ pounds cheese, use 2½ cups peanut butter.

144

COTTAGE CHEESE

Amount of filling per sandwich:
  1 No. 24 scoop (3 tablespoons)
3 pounds cottage cheese
1 cup celery, chopped
½ cup green peppers, chopped
½ cup nut meats, chopped
1 cup carrots, raw, grated
Salt to taste
To moisten:
Mayonnaise and cream

NOTE: Chopped olives may be added.

CORNED BEEF AND CABBAGE

Amount of filling per sandwich:
  1 No. 24 scoop (3 tablespoons)
2¼ pounds corned beef, cooked,
  chopped
3 quarts (1½ pounds) raw cabbage,
  chopped
⅓ cup prepared mustard
Salt and pepper to taste
To moisten:
2½ to 3 cups mayonnaise

CREOLE DRIED BEEF AND CHEESE*

Amount of filling per sandwich:

  1 No. 24 scoop (3 tablespoons).

6 cups tomato pulp, broken up

6 tablespoons cornstarch
½ cup cold water

1½ pounds (1½ quarts) snappy
  cheese, chopped
¾ pound dried beef, coarscly
  chopped
¼ teaspoon pepper
1 tablespoon mustard
1 teaspoon Worcestershire sauce

1. Heat the tomato.

2. Mix the cornstarch with the cold water; add this to the hot tomatoes and cook the mixture until thickened, stirring constantly with a wire whip.

3. Add the cheese, and cook the mixture over low heat until the cheese is melted; remove it from the heat. Add the dried beef and seasonings; cool.

*This filling may be served hot on toasted buns.

DEVILED MEAT

Amount of filling per sandwich:
  1 No. 24 scoop (3 tablespoons)
2½ pounds (7½ cups) meat, cooked,
  ground
3 cups raw carrots *or* celery, ground
¾ cup catsup
2 tablespoons Worcestershire sauce
2 teaspoons paprika
¼ cup onion, minced
3 tablespoons prepared mustard
1½ to 2 cups mayonnaise (or enough
  to moisten)
Salt and pepper to taste

EGG AND BACON

Amount of filling per sandwich:
  1 No. 24 scoop (3 tablespoons)
3 dozen eggs, hard-cooked, chopped
1 pound bacon (cook and dice it)
¼ cup lemon juice
2 to 3 cups mayonnaise
Salt and pepper to taste
2 medium heads lettuce

LIVER AND BACON

Amount of filling per sandwich:
1 No. 24 scoop (3 tablespoons)
6 cups liver, cooked, ground
3 cups bacon, cooked, diced*
3 tablespoons celery salt
1½ teaspoons onion juice or finely
minced onion
1 tablespoon prepared mustard
1 cup chili sauce
1 cup mayonnaise

*2 pounds before cooking.

TUNAFISH, CRABMEAT, OR SALMON SALAD

Amount of filling per sandwich:
1 No. 24 scoop (3 tablespoons)

2 pounds canned fish, flaked
8 eggs, hard-cooked, chopped
5 cups celery, chopped fine
1½ cups pickle relish or dill pickle,
chopped
2 teaspoons salt
¾ to 1 cup mayonnaise (or enough
to moisten)
2 tablespoons lemon juice

NOTE: A lettuce leaf in each sandwich
is a good addition.

MEAT SALAD

Amount of filling per sandwich:
1 No. 24 scoop (3 tablespoons)
6 cups cooked meat, coarsely ground
3 cups celery, finely cut
3 cups (or enough to moisten) cooked
dressing or mayonnaise
Lettuce leaf for each sandwich

Variations
Add:
Chopped sweet pickle
Chopped green peppers and pimiento
Chopped cheese
Chopped stuffed green or ripe olives
Minced onion

TUTTI FRUTTI

Amount of filling per sandwich:
1 No. 30 scoop (2 tablespoons)

2 pounds dates
12 ounces figs
2½ cups raisins, seeded
2½ cups walnuts
3½ to 4 cups orange juice

Grind the fruits and nuts together;
moisten with the orange juice

COMBINATIONS FOR SANDWICH FILLINGS

American cheese, prunes, mayonnaise
Apple, carrot, celery, raisins, mayonnaise
Apple, celery, nut, pimiento, mayonnaise
Bacon, dill pickle, mayonnaise
Cabbage, carrots, boiled dressing
Carrots (raw), peanuts, celery, lemon juice, mayonnaise
Carrots (raw), raisins, mayonnaise
Celery, nuts, dates, fruit juice, mayonnaise
Celery, nuts, olives, mayonnaise
Celery, pickle, mayonnaise
Cottage or cream cheese, celery, green pepper, mayonnaise
Cottage or cream cheese, green pepper, pimiento, onion juice, mayonnaise
Cottage or cream cheese, nuts, mayonnaise
Cottage or cream cheese, olives
Cottage or cream cheese, pineapple, mayonnaise

146

Cottage or cream cheese, raisins, prunes
Date and fig or nut, orange juice
Dried beef, chili sauce, mayonnaise
Egg, celery, green pepper, lemon juice, mayonnaise
Egg and pickle or olive, mayonnaise
Eggs, Thousand Island dressing
Ham (sliced), pickle relish, mayonnaise
Liver (cooked, minced), onions, sour pickles, mayonnaise
Meat (cooked, minced) egg, sweet pickle, tomato catsup
Meat (cooked, minced) pickles, horseradish, mayonnaise
Olive, nut, mayonnaise
Peanut butter, apple or peach butter
Peanut butter, bacon
Peanut butter, sliced banana (or jam)
Peanut butter, grated raw carrot, mayonnaise
Peanut butter, celery, mayonnaise
Peanut butter, cheese
Peanut butter, raisins or prunes; fruit juice *or* honey
Peanut butter, chili sauce or mixed pickles
Sardines, olives, catsup, lemon juice

HOT BREADS

BAKING POWDER BISCUITS

Baking powder biscuits should be symmetrical in shape and should double their volume in the baking. They should have a light golden crust free from yellow or brown spots, with a somewhat rough surface, and the interior should be creamy white in color. The biscuits should be tender and light, with small cells evenly distributed; fluffy, rather than compact; and composed of flaky layers that pull off in thin sheets. The correct amount of stirring and kneading is important to obtain a product of high quality.

Recipe

Yield: 6 to 7 dozen

Size of serving: 1½ biscuits

4 pounds (4 quarts) flour, all-purpose
4 ounces (½ cup plus 2 tablespoons) baking powder
3 tablespoons salt
13 ounces (2 cups) vegetable fat
6 to 7 cups milk

1. Mix and sift the dry ingredients.

2. Rub in the fat and add the milk, handling lightly; knead the dough on a lightly floured board for a few seconds until smooth. Roll the dough ½ inch thick and cut it into 2-inch rounds, or cut into 2-inch squares using a floured knife. Place biscuits apart on baking sheets if crusty sides are desired. Bake at 425° F.

NOTE: For a richer biscuit, increase the fat to 1 pound 5 ounces (3 cups) and reduce the milk to 4¼ to 5 cups.

Variations

Butterscotch biscuits: Divide the dough and roll it out ⅛ inch thick. Brush it with 1 cup of melted butter *or* fortified margarine and sprinkle it with 3 cups of brown sugar. Roll the dough up as for a jelly roll and cut off ¾-inch slices. Bake these in well-greased muffin tins.

Cheese biscuits: Add 1½ pounds (1½ quarts) of grated cheese to the dry ingredients. Grated dehydrated cheese may be used; then increase the amount of milk slightly.

Cinnamon biscuits: Roll out the dough as for butterscotch biscuits; brush it with 1 cup of melted butter *or* fortified margarine and sprinkle it with a mixture of 3 tablespoons of cinnamon and 2 cups of granulated sugar; spread 1½ cups of raisins over this. Roll this up as for butterscotch rolls.

Orange biscuits: Add the grated rind of 4 or 5 oranges to the dough. Before baking place a small lump of sugar soaked in orange juice on the top of each biscuit.

or

In place of all milk, use 2½ cups of orange juice and from 2½ to 3 cups milk. Before baking, put 1 teaspoon of orange marmalade on the top of each biscuit.

Orange marmalade: Prepare the dough as for butterscotch biscuits. Brush it with 1 cup of melted butter *or* fortified margarine and spread the top with 2 cups of orange marmalade. Roll the dough as for a jelly roll and cut off ¾-inch slices. Bake these in well-greased muffin tins.

MUFFINS

Muffins, to be attractive and palatable, should have a golden brown crust with a somewhat pebbled surface. They should have a well-rounded top, should not overrun the tins, and should not be peaked.

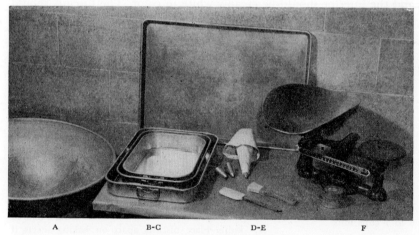

A	B-C	D-E	F

FIGURE 28.   BAKING EQUIPMENT

A. Large mixing bowl on a portable bowl rack	B. Baking pans of different sizes C. Bun or sheet cake pan (against wall)	D. Pastry tube, brush E. Rubber scraper

F. Balance scales for weighing dry ingredients and shortening

They should be light in texture and, when broken open, should show rather large, round, even cells throughout the interior. They should have a moist, tender crumb. For mixing in large quantities, a round-bottom mixing bowl is convenient (figure 28B); mixing the batter with the hands combines the ingredients thoroughly with little danger of overmixing, which is the major cause of a tunnelled interior. The mixture may be measured into the tins with an ice-cream scoop (a No. 16 scoop for a 2-inch muffin) (figure 5A). When baked, the muffins should be removed at once or tilted in the tins to allow for circulation of air, thus preventing sogginess.

A small sample may be baked. If the sample is not satisfactory, adjustments to the batter can be made.

PLAIN MUFFINS*

Yield: 6 dozen   Size of serving: 1½ muffins

1 pound (2½ cups) vegetable fat
13 ounces (1¾ cups) sugar
1½ cups (8) eggs

1. Cream the fat and sugar together until well blended; add the eggs and beat thoroughly.

4 pounds (4 quarts) flour, all-purpose
3¼ ounces (½ cup) baking powder
4 teaspoons salt
7 cups milk

2. Sift the dry ingredients together; add them and the milk to the mixture all at once; mix with the hands until just combined; avoid overmixing. Bake at 425° F. for about 20 minutes.

*For smaller quantities, the methods and proportions of ingredients ordinarily used may be more satisfactory.

Variations

Bacon: Add 1½ cups of cooked, chopped bacon to the batter.

Cranberry: Add 1 quart of washed cranberries (chopped), which have been dusted with some of the sugar; use ¼ cup additional sugar in the recipe.

Date or raisin: Add 2½ cups of chopped dates or raisins which have been mixed with some of the flour.

Honey Graham: In place of all sugar, use 2½ cups of honey and 1 cup of sugar; cream them with the fat. Substitute 5½ cups (1½ pounds) of graham flour for an equal amount of the white flour.

Marmalade: Place 1 teaspoon of orange marmalade or some other preserve on the top of each muffin before baking.

Nut: Add from 1½ to 2 cups of coarsely chopped nuts that have been mixed with some of the flour.

Orange: In place of all milk, use 1 quart of orange juice and 3 cups of milk; add the grated rind of 4 oranges.

Tomato juice: In place of all milk use 2½ cups of tomato juice and 4½ cups of milk. Sprinkle the top of each muffin with grated cheese before baking; this takes about ⅓ pound (1⅓ cups) of cheese.

DARK BRAN MUFFINS

Yield: 6 dozen   Size of serving: 1½ muffins

1½ pounds (1½ quarts) flour, all-purpose
1 pound (1 quart) cake crumbs
1 pound (3½ quarts) all-bran
¼ cup soda
3 tablespoons salt

1. Mix the dry ingredients.

4 eggs, beaten
2½ quarts sour milk
3 cups molasses

2. Mix the eggs, milk, and molasses; add them to the dry ingredients all at once; combine all with the hands, mixing only enough just to dampen the flour.

1½ cups vegetable fat, melted

3. Add the melted fat and mix the batter carefully. Bake at 400° to 425° F.

SUGARY APPLE MUFFINS

Yield: 6 dozen   Size of serving: 1½ muffins

1 pound, 8 ounces (3⅓ cups) sugar
1 tablespoon cinnamon

1. Mix the sugar and cinnamon. Reserve ¾ cup of this mixture for the topping.

12 ounces (1½ cups) vegetable fat
6 eggs, slightly beaten

2. Cream the fat with the remaining sugar-cinnamon mixture until well blended; add the eggs and beat the mixture thoroughly.

1½ quarts milk
3 pounds, 6 ounces (13½ cups) flour, all-purpose
3¼ ounces (½ cup) baking powder
1 tablespoon salt

3. Add the milk and the dry ingredients all at once, and mix the ingredients with the hands until all are just combined.

1 quart apples, chopped

4. Fold in the apples carefully. Put the mixture into muffin tins and sprinkle the tops with the reserved sugar-cinnamon mixture. Bake at 425° F. for from 20 to 25 minutes.

ROLLS

Homemade yeast rolls, plain or sweet, made with whole-grain or enriched flours, in a variety of shapes, are always popular (figures 29 and 30).

Rolls should be evenly browned and evenly shaped. They should be

150

FIGURE 29. ROLL SHAPES

light, with a tender, elastic crumb, and free from dryness or doughiness; they should have fine cells evenly distributed, with thin cell walls; they should be free from dark streaks.

151

Photograph from Wheat Flour Institute

FIGURE 30.   SHAPING BUTTERHORN OR POCKETBOOK ROLLS

One pound of dough is rolled into a thin round. It is then cut into wedge pieces. Wedges are rolled, beginning with the long end

PLAIN ROLLS

Yield: 6 dozen

Size of serving: 1½ rolls

1½ cakes yeast, compressed
¼ cup lukewarm water
1 tablespoon sugar
1½ cups milk
¾ cup butter *or* fortified margarine
1 cup sugar
1 tablespoon salt
1¼ cups water
4 eggs, beaten
3 quarts flour, all-purpose

1. Dissolve the yeast in the lukewarm water; add the sugar.

2. Scald the milk, add the butter, salt, sugar, and water; cool to lukewarm.

3. Add the eggs and mix; stir in part of the flour and beat. Add the dissolved yeast and the remaining flour to make a stiff dough. Knead and put the dough in a greased bowl; grease the top with melted fat. Let the dough rise until light. Weigh out 2 or 3 pounds of dough (1 pound should yield approximately 1 dozen rolls). Shape as desired (figures 29 and 30). Let rise in a warm place until light. Bake at 400° F.

152

Variations

Apple rolls: Prepare 6 cups of thinly sliced apples. When the dough is light, roll it out in rectangles about ½ inch thick; brush them with melted butter. Spread a thin layer of apples over the dough, and sprinkle these with about 6 cups of brown sugar. (Three tablespoons of cinnamon may be mixed with the sugar if desired.) Roll the dough as for a jelly roll and cut off ¾-inch slices. Place the slices onto greased flat pans or muffin tins. Sprinkle the tops with a little brown sugar. Let them rise until light. Bake them at 375° F.

Butterscotch: When the dough is light, roll it out in rectangles about ½ inch thick. Spread them lightly with ¾ to 1 cup of melted butter; sprinkle them with 3½ to 5 cups of brown sugar. Roll the dough as for a jelly roll and cut off ¾-inch slices. Generously grease flat baking pans or muffin tins with the melted butter, then sprinkle them with the brown sugar. Place the cut rolls on the sugar and let them rise until light. Bake them at 357° F.

Cinnamon-raisin rolls: When the dough is light, roll it out in rectangles about ½ inch thick. Spread them with melted butter. Sprinkle them with a mixture of 3 tablespoons of cinnamon and 2 cups of granulated sugar; spread 1½ cups of seedless raisins over this. Roll, cut, and bake them as for butterscotch rolls.

Pecan or walnut rolls: Use the same method as for butterscotch rolls, sprinkle coarsely chopped nuts over the brown sugar in the baking pans. Nuts may be sprinkled over the sugar before the dough is rolled.

Pineapple rolls*: Use the same method as for butterscotch rolls, spreading 1½ quarts of drained crushed pineapple over from 2½ to 3½ cups of brown sugar on the bottom of the baking pans.

Jelly or peanut butter buns: When the dough is light, roll it about ½ inch thick and cut it into 3-inch squares. Place 1 teaspoon of jelly (currant, apple, quince, grape) or peanut butter on each square. Fold the corners to the center and pinch them together firmly. Place the rolls in greased flat pans or muffin tins. Let them rise until light. Bake them at 375° F.

Whole wheat rolls: In place of all white flour, use 7 cups white flour and 5 cups whole wheat flour.

*The butterscotch, nut, and pineapple rolls are especially good when baked in heavy iron skillets.

OTHER HOT-BREAD RECIPES

BROWN NUT BREAD, BAKED

Yield: 3 loaves   Size of serving: 1 slice

2¼ cups cold water
11 ounces (1½ cups) sugar, brown, packed
1½ cups molasses
2¼ cups milk

1. Stir the sugar with the cold water. Add the molasses and the milk.

18 ounces (4½ cups) flour, all-purpose

2. Sift the all-purpose flour, baking powder, soda, and salt together; then mix these with the whole

153

1 ounce (7½ teaspoons) baking
powder
2¼ teaspoons soda
2 tablespoons salt
1 pound, 6 ounces (4½ cups)
whole wheat flour
8 ounces (2 cups) nuts, coarsely
chopped
¼ cup vegetable fat, melted

wheat flour. Combine the wet and dry ingredients, mixing them with the hands.

3. Stir in the nuts and fat. Bake the bread at
300° F. for from 1 to 1½ hours, until done.

BROWN BREAD, STEAMED

Yield: 6 tubes (from 60 to 70 slices)   Size of serving: 1 to 1½ slices

2 pounds (2 quarts) stale bread
or cake crumbs
3½ quarts cold water

1. Soak the crumbs in the cold water until soft.

2 cups molasses
2 pounds (1½ quarts) corn meal
3¼ pounds (3 quarts) flour,
graham
1½ ounces (3 tablespoons) soda
2 cups raisins, chopped
2 tablespoons salt

2. Mix the dry ingredients; add them with the
molasses to the soaked crumbs, and combine.
Fill well-greased tubes one-half full. Steam them
for from 2 to 2½ hours. Remove the loaves from
the tubes and slice them while hot. To do this,
loop a string around the loaf and cut slices by
pulling the ends of the string.

CORNBREAD

Yield: 6 dozen pieces   Size of serving: 1½ pieces (2½ x 3 inches)

2 pounds (2 quarts) flour, all-
purpose
2 pounds, 11 ounces (2 quarts)
cornmeal
11 ounces (1½ cups) sugar
5 teaspoons salt
5 ounces (¾ cup plus 1 tablespoon) baking powder

1. Mix the dry ingredients.

8 (1½ cups) eggs
2½ quarts milk
¾ cup butter or other shortening, melted

2. Beat the eggs and milk together; add them
to the dry ingredients, and then mix with the
hands or a machine. Add the melted butter when
the batter is about half mixed; continue to mix
until the ingredients are just combined. Pour
the mixture into well-greased baking pans to
the depth of 1 inch. Let the mixture stand for
30 minutes. Bake at 450° F. for from 20 to 30
minutes.

Variation

Bacon cornbread: Sprinkle 1 pound of crisp diced bacon over the batter before baking
the bread.

DATE LOAF

Yield: 4 loaves (from 60 to 70 slices)   Size of serving: 1 to 1½ slices

1½ pounds (4 cups) dates, diced
4 teaspoons soda
3 cups hot water

1. Mix the dates, soda, and hot water; allow them to cool.

4 eggs, slightly beaten
1 pound, 7 ounces (3 cups) sugar
2 teaspoons salt

2. Mix the eggs, sugar, and salt, and add them to the date mixture.

1 pound, 12 ounces (7 cups) flour, all-purpose
2 tablespoons baking powder
4 teaspoons vanilla

3. Sift the flour and baking powder and add them to the liquid mixture; mix until just combined.

½ cup butter *or* fortified margarine, melted
1 cup nuts, coarsely chopped

4. Add carefully the vanilla, butter, and nuts. Bake the mixture in loaf pans at 325° F. for about 1 hour.

GRIDDLE CAKES

Yield: 25 servings   Size of serving: 2 cakes (from 4½ to 5 inches in diameter)

2 pounds, 4 ounces (9 cups) flour, all-purpose
2 ounces (5 tablespoons) baking powder
3 teaspoons salt
¾ cup sugar

1. Mix the dry ingredients.

6 eggs, beaten
1½ quarts milk
5 ounces (¾ cup) fat, melted

2. Combine the eggs, milk, and fat. Add this to the dry ingredients and mix until just combined. Dip with a No. 16 scoop to a greased griddle. Bake on one side until brown; then turn and brown the other side.

WAFFLES

Yield: 25 servings   Size of serving: 1 waffle (7 inches in diameter)

2 pounds (2 quarts) flour, all-purpose
5 ounces (1 cup) cornstarch
¾ cup sugar
2 ounces (5 tablespoons) baking powder
4 teaspoons salt

1. Mix the dry ingredients.

1⅓ cups (about 16) egg yolks, beaten
2 quarts milk
1 pound (2 cups) butter *or* fortified margarine, melted
2 cups (about 16) egg whites, stiffly beaten

2. Combine the egg yolks, milk, and butter. Add the dry ingredients and stir until just combined. Fold in the egg whites. Preheat the waffle irons, then bake the waffles.

DESSERTS
CAKES

Cakes containing fat should be symmetrical, with an even top free from cracks and peaks. The crust of plain cakes should be tender and uniformly browned to a light golden color. The cakes should be light, and of a fine, even texture. The crumb should be tender and moist with a velvety feeling to the tongue.

Angel and sponge cakes should have a uniformly smooth level surface with a tender crust; they should be tender and feathery with a resilient crumb; and should have a fine, even texture. Proper manipulation and baking are important in producing good angel and sponge cakes.

Aids to producing good cakes are: a properly balanced recipe, ingredients at room temperature (75 to 80° F.), proper mixing, correct oven temperature, and correct baking time.

Ingredients

Weighing the ingredients is more accurate than measuring them.

A high-ratio shortening is used in the recipes in this bulletin for machine-mixed cakes. High-ratio shortenings are those containing an emulsifier in proportions which allow the use of larger quantities of sugar and liquid thus producing cakes of finer texture and better keeping qualities. They are available mainly in 50-pound containers.

Procedure for Baking Cakes

Baking a sample

A sample may be baked. If the sample is not satisfactory, adjustments to the batter can be made. Fill a greased and floured sample cup one-third full and bake at the temperature specified in the recipe.

Preparing the pans

Grease and flour the pans well to facilitate the removal of the cakes. A mixture of shortening and flour may be used for this purpose and may be prepared in quantity and kept on hand.

Weight of cake batter for specific sized pans and number of servings

Pans	Description	Weight or volume of batter	Number of servings
Cake tin (layer)	Round with knife blade, 10 x 1½ inches	20 to 22 ounces medium layer	2-layer cake cuts 14 to 16 wedges
Baking pan	Large oblong, 18 x 12 x 2 inches	80 to 96 ounces	Cuts from 28 to 32 pieces, depending on size of piece and volume of cake
Baking pan	Medium oblong, 15 x 10½ x 2¼ inches	48 to 56 ounces	Cuts 24 2½-inch squares or 20 3-x-2½-inch pieces
Baking pan	Small oblong, 13 x 8 x 1⅞ inches	32 to 36 ounces	Cuts 15 2½-x-2¾-inch pieces, or 12 3¼-x-2¾-inch pieces
Bun pan	24 ⅝ x 16⅝ x 1 inch	48 to 96 ounces depending on thickness desired	(Used for bars and jelly rolls)
Loaf pan (pullman pan)	12 x 2½ x 4 inches	27 to 36 ounces(equivalent to 1½ to 2 layers)	12 to 15 slices
Tube tin	Round 10-inch diameter x 4 inches high	25 to 32 ounces	10 to 14 wedges

Blend together 1 pound of hydrogenated vegetable shortening and 8 ounces of all-purpose flour. Hold this mixture at room temperature, but do not allow it to melt. Spread a heavy layer of the mixture on the bottom of each pan with a pastry brush. Weigh the amount of batter specified into the pans and level the top.

Baking the cake

Place pans in ovens heated to the proper temperature. Do not open the oven door until minimum baking time is reached, then test for doneness. Cakes are done if they spring back when touched lightly in the center. Do not bake longer as they shrink and dry out.

Remove the cake from the oven and leave in pans 15 to 20 minutes (but not longer) to cool.

Filling and frosting layer cakes

1. Tap side of pan on table to loosen the cake.

2. Remove to an inverted layer cake pan placing one-half of the layers with tops up and the other half with tops down.

3. Brush off loose crumbs to a tray (save the crumbs for use in puddings, muffins, or brown bread).

4. When cakes are cooled completely, spread filling or icing on the inverted layer to within ¼ inch of the edge.

5. Place the second layer on top (topside up); balance the layers to make the total cake symmetrical.

6. Spread frosting evenly on the top, and if desired, on the sides.

Recipes
LAYER CAKE, PLAIN
(conventional method)

6 layers (10-inch)	8 layers (10-inch)
1 pound (2½ cups) vegetable fat	1 pound, 5 ounces (3⅓ cups) vegetable fat
2 pounds, 2 ounces (4½ cups) sugar	2 pounds, 13 ounces (5¾ cups) sugar
1 pound (2 cups) eggs* (about 10 eggs)	1 pound, 5 ounces (2½ cups) eggs* (about 13 eggs)
3 teaspoons vanilla	
2 pounds, 2 ounces (8½ cups) flour, cake	1½ tablespoons vanilla
1½ ounces (3¾ tablespoons) baking powder	2 pounds, 13 ounces (11 cups) flour, cake
1½ teaspoons salt	2 ounces (5 tablespoons) baking powder
3½ cups milk	2 teaspoons salt
	5 cups milk

*In place of the whole eggs, fresh or frozen yolks and whites may be used as follows: *For 6 layers,* 6 ounces of egg yolks and 10 ounces of egg whites.
For 8 layers, 8 ounces of egg yolks and 13 ounces of egg whites.

Hand method	Machine method
1. Cream the fat until plastic but not melted.	1. Use low speed to cream the fat until plastic.
2. Add the sugar gradually and cream sugar and butter together until well blended.	2. Use low speed and allow about 3 minutes to incorporate the sugar; scrape down the sides of the bowl and continue the beating for 5 minutes; scrape down the sides of the bowl again.
3. Add the eggs and beat the mixture thoroughly. The whites may be beaten separately and folded in last.	3. Beat on second speed for 8 to 10 minutes to incorporate the eggs.
4. Add the flavoring.	4. Add the flavoring.
5. Sift the flour, salt, and baking powder and add this to the mixture alternately with the milk, beginning and ending with the flour. Beat until the batter is smooth.	5. Using low speed add the dry ingredients in three parts alternately with the milk, beginning and ending with the flour; scrape down the sides of the bowl and under the paddle several times.

6. Weigh out or divide the batter (20 ounces per layer). The filled pans may be dropped on the table two or three times to break the air bubbles.

7. Bake the batter at 325° to 375° F. according to the thickness of the batter in the pan; thick cakes may be started at the lower temperature, which is raised to the higher temperature toward the end of the baking period. Thin layers require about 15 minutes for baking; thick layers, from 20 to 25 minutes; sheet cake, 30 minutes; loaf cake, 60 minutes.

8. If nuts, raisins, or other fruits are added, save out a small quantity of the flour to mix with them and stir them into the batter last.

Variations

Boston cream pie: Split layers of plain cake and fill each cake with 1½ cups of cream filling (recipe, page 170). Sprinkle the tops with confectioners' sugar or spread with jam.

Lemon cake: For 6 layers, use 1½ teaspoons of vanilla, ¾ teaspoon of lemon extract, and 1½ teaspoons of grated lemon rind.

For 8 layers use 2 teaspoons of vanilla, 1 teaspoon of lemon extract and 2 teaspoons of grated lemon rind.

Nut cake: Use 1 ounce of chopped nuts per layers. Sift the nuts to get out the finer pieces. Add the nuts to the sifted dry ingredients *or* sprinkle over the batter in each layer. Weigh out 1 pound 5 ounces of batter in each layer pan.

LAYER CAKE, GOLD

(Dough-batter method) machine mixed

6 layers (10-inch)	8 layers (10-inch)
1 pound, 8 ounces (6 cups) flour, cake	2 pounds (8 cups) flour, cake
1 pound (2½ cups) shortening, high-ratio*	1 pound, 6 ounces (3½ cups) shortening, high-ratio*
1 pound, 14 ounces (4 cups) sugar	2 pounds, 8 ounces (5⅓ cups) sugar
1½ tablespoons salt	2½ tablespoons salt
1½ ounces (3¾ tablespoons) baking powder	2 ounces (5 tablespoons) baking powder
1¼ cups milk	1½ cups milk
1 pound, 6 ounces (2¾ cups) eggs,† unbeaten, (about 14 eggs)	1 pound, 13 ounces (3½ cups) eggs,† unbeaten, (about 18 eggs)
1 cup milk	1½ cups milk
4½ teaspoons vanilla	2 tablespoons vanilla

*A *high-ratio* shortening must be used for this method of making cake.
†In place of the whole eggs, fresh or frozen yolks and whites may be used as follows: *For 6 layers* 9 ounces of egg yolks and 13 ounces of egg whites.
For 8 layers 12 ounces of egg yolks and 17 ounces of egg whites.

1. Use low speed throughout the mixing.

2. Mix the flour and shortening for 3 to 5 minutes. (The mixture will have the appearance of a stiff dough.) Scrape down the bowl and the paddle once or twice during this time.

3. Add the sugar, salt, baking powder and first portion of the milk. Mix for 3 to 5 minutes. Scrape down the bowl and the paddle during this mixing time.

4. Mix together the eggs, second portion of the milk and the vanilla. Add half of this mixture and mix for 2 minutes. Scrape down and mix for 2 minutes longer.

5. Add the balance of the liquid mixture and mix the batter for 2 minutes. Scrape down and mix for from 1 to 3 minutes longer, until batter is smooth.

6. Weigh 1 pound, 3 ounces of batter into each layer pan.

7. Bake at 350° F. for from 15 to 20 minutes.

NOTE: Layer cakes made by this method give a better volume than those made by the conventional method; therefore a smaller weight (1 pound, 3 ounces) of batter is used for each layer.

Variations

Lord Baltimore Cake: Make boiled icing, recipe page 167. Divide this into 2 parts. To one part add the following:

For 3 cakes (6 layers)	*For 4 cakes (8 layers)*
Candied cherries, chopped, 1½ ounces	2 ounces
Macaroon crumbs, large, 2¼ ounces	3 ounces
Almonds, chopped, 2¼ ounces	3 ounces
Orange juice, ¾ tablespoon	1 tablespoon
Lemon juice, 1½ tablespoons	2 tablespoons

1. Fold the above ingredients into the icing using as few strokes as possible.

2. Spread this on the bottom layers.

3. Spread the top layer with the other part of the plain icing.

4. Dot the tops with chopped candied cherries and chopped almonds.

Orange Cake: In place of the vanilla use the following flavorings:

For 6 layers	*For 8 layers*
Vanilla, 3 teaspoons	4 teaspoons
Orange extract, ¾ teaspoon	1 teaspoon
Orange rind, grated, 1½ tablespoons	2 tablespoons

LAYER CAKE, WHITE
(Dough-batter method) machine mixed

6 layers (10-inch)	*8 layers (10-inch)*
1 pound, 14 ounces (7½ cups) flour, cake	2 pounds, 7 ounces (9¾ cups) flour, cake
2 pounds, 5 ounces (5 cups) sugar	3 pounds, 1 ounce (6½ cups) sugar
1½ ounces (3¾ tablespoons) baking powder	2½ ounces (6¼ tablespoons) baking powder
4 teaspoons salt	1½ tablespoons salt
15 ounces (2⅓ cups) shortening, high-ratio*	1 pound, 3½ ounces (3⅛ cups) shortening, high-ratio*
3 cups milk	4 cups milk
1 pound (2 cups) egg whites, unbeaten, (about 16 egg whites)	1 pound, 6 ounces (2¾ cups) egg whites, unbeaten, (about 22 egg whites)
2½ teaspoons vanilla	1 tablespoon vanilla

*A high-ratio shortening must be used.

1. Use low speed throughout the mixing.
2. Blend dry ingredients in mixing bowl for 2 minutes.
3. Add shortening and mix for 2 minutes. Scrape shortening from paddle.
4. Add ¾ of the milk and start and stop the mixer several times to blend sufficiently and to avoid splashing when the machine is in regular motion.
5. Mix for 3 minutes; stop and scrape the bowl.
6. Mix for 2 minutes; stop and scrape the bowl.
7. Mix for 2 minutes; stop and scrape the bowl.
8. Add remaining milk, egg whites, and vanilla and mix for 2 minutes; scrape the bowl using the hand to do a thorough job.
9. Mix for 3 minutes longer.
10. Weigh 1 pound, 4 ounces of batter into each greased and floured layer cake tin.
11. Bake at 350° F. for 20 minutes.

Variations

Almond cake: Replace half of the vanilla with almond extract.

Coconut cake: Half vanilla and half almond extract may be used for the flavoring. Frost the cakes with boiled icing (recipe page 167) and garnish each with 1 ounce of fresh, canned, or dried shredded coconut.

Lady Baltimore cake: Make a boiled icing (recipe page 167). Divide this into 2 parts. To half of the icing, add the following:

For 3 cakes (6 layers)	*For 4 cakes (8 layers)*
Raisins, chopped, 4 ounces	5 ounces
Dates, chopped, 1½ ounces	2 ounces
Pecans, chopped, 2¼ ounces	3 ounces

1. Fold the above ingredients into the icing, using as few strokes as possible.
2. Spread this on the bottom layers.
3. Spread the top layers with the plain icing.
4. Dot the tops with chopped, drained maraschino cherries, or candied cherries, or chopped pecans.

SHEET CAKE, PLAIN
(conventional method)

Yield: 2 large baking pans, 18 x 12 x 2 inches;   Size of serving: 1 piece (3 x 2¼ inches)
(56 to 64 squares)

2 pounds, 10 ounces (5½ cups) sugar

14 ounces (2⅓ cups) shortening

1 pound (2 cups) eggs* (about 10 eggs)

1⅓ tablespoons vanilla

3 pounds (3 quarts) flour, cake

2¾ ounces (7 tablespoons) baking powder

2 teaspoons salt

5¾ cups milk

1. Use plain layer cake method, page 158. Put 5 pounds of batter in each pan. Bake at 325° F. for from 35 to 40 minutes.

*In place of the whole eggs, fresh or frozen yolks and whites may be used as follows: 6 ounces of egg yolks and 10 ounces of egg whites.

ALMOND CAKE

See variation of white layer cake, page 161.

ANGEL CAKE

Yield: 4 cakes, 9½-inch diameter   Size of serving: $^1/_{12}$ or $^1/_{14}$ of a cake
(from 48 to 56 wedges)

2 pounds, 8 ounces (5 cups) egg whites (about 40 whites)
½ ounce (4 teaspoons) cream of tartar
½ teaspoon salt
1½ tablespoons vanilla
12 ounces (1½ cups) sugar
1 pound (1 quart) flour, cake
2 pounds (4¼ cups) sugar

Machine method

1. Using the whip on the machine, beat the egg whites for 1 minute on high speed.
2. Add the cream of tartar and salt; beat the mixture on high speed until the whites have passed the frothy stage but are not stiff enough to hold their shape (about 2 minutes).
3. Add the vanilla; beat the mixture until the egg whites are stiff enough to hold their shape but are still glossy (about 2 minutes).
4. Add the 1½ cups of sugar gradually in about 30 seconds. Beat the mixture 30 seconds.
5. Replace the whip with the paddle. Sift the flour and second quantity of sugar together. Start the machine at low speed and stop it 6 to 8 times to add the sugar-flour mixture, sprinkling it over the top of the egg whites (total mixing time about 1 minute). Remove the bowl from the mixer and with a few strokes of the hand, continue mixing until the ingredients are thoroughly blended.
6. Weigh 1 pound, 9 ounces of batter into each ungreased tube tin.
7. Bake at 300° F. for from 50 to 60 minutes.
8. Invert the cakes on racks to cool. Leave them in pans until completely cool.
9. To remove the cake, loosen it from the side of the pan and from the tube with a thin-bladed knife. Then apply a gas flame briefly to the bottom of the pan. Invert the pan and tap it on the table until the cake drops from pan.

APPLESAUCE CAKE

Yield: 2 large pans, 18 x 12 x 2 inches;   Size of serving: 1 piece (3 x 2¼ inches)
(from 56 to 64 pieces)

1¼ pounds (3 cups) vegetable fat

2 pounds, 8 ounces (5⅓ cups) sugar

1 cup (about 5) eggs

2½ pounds (2½ quarts) flour, cake

2 ounces (5 tablespoons) baking powder

5 teaspoons cinnamon

2½ teaspoons cloves

1. Cream the fat until plastic; add the sugar gradually, and continue creaming until well blended. Add the eggs and beat the mixture thoroughly.

2. Sift the dry ingredients together; dredge the raisins and nuts with a small quantity of the flour. Add the dry ingredients and applesauce alternately; beat until the batter is smooth. Stir in the floured raisins and nuts last. Bake the batter at 350° F. for from 35 to 40 minutes.

2½ teaspoons nutmeg
1¼ teaspoons salt
3¾ teaspoons soda
3 pounds, 12 ounces (7½ cups)
applesauce, unsweetened
1 pound (2½ cups) raisins,
chopped
10 ounces (2½ cups) nuts,
chopped

BOSTON CREAM PIE

See variation of plain layer cake, page 159.

COCONUT CAKE

See variation of white layer cake, page 161.

DEVIL'S FOOD CAKE

Yield: 2 large pans, 18 x 12 x 2 inches; Size of serving: 1 piece (3 x 2¼ inches)
(56 to 65 pieces *or* 8 layers) *or* $^1/_{14}$ or $^1/_{16}$ of a layer cake

6 ounces (1½ cups) cocoa
1 quart coffee brew

1. Cook the cocoa and the coffee together and cool.

1 pound (2½ cups) vegetable fat
3 pounds (6½ cups) sugar
2 cups (about 10) eggs

2. Cream the fat; add the sugar gradually and continue to cream until well blended; add the eggs and beat the mixture thoroughly.

2 pounds, 4 ounces (2¼ quarts) flour, cake
1 ounce (2½ teaspoons) baking powder
1 tablespoon salt
1¼ cups strong coffee brew
2 tablespoons soda
2 tablespoons vanilla

3. Sift the dry ingredients together and add them alternately to the first mixture with the cocoa-coffee mixture; beat until the batter is smooth.

4. Combine the coffee, soda, and vanilla, and stir them carefully into the batter. For the large pans weigh out 5 pounds of batter each. Bake these at 325° F. for from 40 to 50 minutes. For the layer tins, weigh out 1 pound, 4 ounces of batter in each. Bake at 350° F. for from 20 to 25 minutes.

Frosting*
½ cup coffee brew
½ cup cocoa
3 tablespoons butter *or* fortified margarine
¼ teaspoon salt
4½ cups (approximately) confectioners' sugar

1. Cook the coffee, cocoa, and butter together; cool and add the salt. Add enough confectioners' sugar to make the mixture stiff enough to spread.

*May be frosted with devil's food icing, recipe, page 167.

Variation

Domecon cake: Bake the cake in layers. Use a chocolate-cornstarch filling, recipe page 171, and top with boiled frosting, recipe page 167.

163

DOMECON CAKE

See variation of devil's food cake, page 163.

JELLY ROLL

Yield: 2 jelly rolls about 24 inches long (48 slices) Size of serving: 1-inch slice

14 ounces (1¾ cups) egg yolks (about 21 yolks)

2 pounds, 11 ounces (5¾ cups) sugar

1. Beat the egg yolks. Add the sugar gradually and continue beating the mixture until thick and lemon colored.

1 pound, 3 ounces (4¾ cups) flour, cake

4 ounces (¾ cup) cornstarch

2 tablespoons baking powder

1⅓ teaspoons salt

2. Sift together the flour, cornstarch, baking powder, and salt and fold this into the above mixture.

1 cup hot water

3. Add the hot water.

1 pound, 5 ounces (2⅔ cups) egg whites (about 21 whites)

4. Beat the whites until stiff and fold them into the batter. Pour the cake mixture into greased and floured bun pans to from ⅓- to ½-inch thickness. Bake the cakes at 375° F. for from 12 to 15 minutes. Remove them from the oven and invert them on a cloth which has been sprinkled with powdered sugar, removing the cakes from the pans.

Filling:

5 cups jelly *or* jam

5. Cover the cake with the filling and roll it up. Wrap in a cloth until ready to cut.

LAYER CAKE, PLAIN

See recipe page 158.

LAYER CAKE, GOLD

See recipe page 159.

LAYER CAKE, WHITE

See recipe page 160.

LEMON CAKE

See variation of plain layer cake, page 159.

LADY BALTIMORE CAKE

See variation of white layer cake, page 161.

LORD BALTIMORE CAKE

See variation of gold layer cake, page 160.

ORANGE CHIFFON CAKE
(machine mixed)

Yield: 4 10-inch tubes, from 48 to 56 pieces   Size of serving: $^1/_{12}$ or $^1/_{14}$ of a cake

1 pound, 13 ounces (7 cups) flour, cake

2 pounds, 7 ounces (5 cups) sugar

1 tablespoon salt

1¼ ounces (3 tablespoons) baking powder

1. Put the flour, sugar, salt, and baking powder into mixing bowl and blend thoroughly with the whip attachment.

12 ounces (1½ cups) salad oil

10 ounces (1¼ cups) egg yolks (about 15 yolks)

1¼ cups water

1¼ cups orange juice

2 ounces (6 tablespoons) grated orange rind

2. Add the salad oil, egg yolks, water, orange juice and orange rind and mix until satin smooth. Do not overmix this batter.

1 pound, 10 ounces (3¼ cups) egg whites (about 26 whites)

2 teaspoons cream of tartar

3. Beat the whites and cream of tartar in a large mixing bowl at high speed until very stiff. Do not *underbeat*. (The whites should be stiffer than for meringue or angel food cakes.) Replace the whip with a beater. Pour the egg yolk mixture over beaten egg whites while mixing on low speed. Mix only enough to blend the mixture. Remove the bowl from the machine and run the hand through the batter to make sure that the mixture is thoroughly blended. Put 2 pounds of batter into each ungreased tube tin. *Bake immediately* at 325° F. for from 50 to 55 minutes. Remove the cakes from the oven and invert the tins to cool. When cold, loosen the cake from the side of the pan and tube with a spatula. Invert the pan and tap the edge sharply on a table to loosen the cake.

ORANGE-DATE-NUT CAKE*

Yield: 2 pans 17 x 10½ inches; (48 pieces)   Size of serving: 1 piece (3 x 2½ inches)

1 pound, 7 ounces (3 cups) sugar

1 pound (2¼ cups) vegetable fat

1¼ cups eggs (about 6 eggs)

1. Cream the fat until plastic; add the sugar gradually and continue creaming until well blended. Add the eggs and beat the mixture thoroughly.

1 pound, 12 ounces (7 cups) flour, cake

1 tablespoon baking powder

1 tablespoon soda

1½ teaspoons salt

4 tablespoons grated rind of 6 oranges

2. Sift the dry ingredients together; dredge the dates and nuts with a small quantity of flour. Add the dry ingredients and sour milk alternately; beat until the batter is smooth. Stir in the orange rind and the floured dates and nuts last. Bake the batter at 350° F.

165

3 cups dates, cut up
1½ cups nuts, coarsely chopped
3 cups sour milk
2 cups sugar
1 cup orange juice

3. Mix the sugar and orange juice; carefully spread this over the cakes as soon as they are removed from the oven. Serve plain or with whipped cream.

*This may be served warm with whipped cream.

NUT CAKE

See variation of plain layer cake, page 159.

PRUNE-WHIP CAKE

Yield: 2 large pans, 18 x 12 x 2 inches; Size of serving: 1 piece (3 x 2¼ inches)
(from 56 to 64 pieces)

1½ pounds (3½ cups) vegetable fat
2½ pounds (5⅓ cups) sugar
1½ cups (about 8) eggs
3 pounds (3 quarts) flour, cake
2 tablespoons cinnamon
1 tablespoon cloves
2 tablespoons soda
¾ teaspoon baking powder
½ teaspoon salt
2⅔ cups prune juice
3½ pounds (7 cups) prunes, drained well and chopped

1. Cream the fat; add the sugar gradually and continue creaming until well blended; add the eggs and beat the mixture thoroughly.

2. Sift the dry ingredients together and add them to the first mixture alternately with the prune juice; beat until the batter is smooth. Fold in the prunes last. Weigh 6 pounds of batter into each pan and bake at 350° F. for about 30 minutes. Ice the cakes with prune whip boiled icing (recipe page 172).

SHEET CAKE

See recipe page 161.

SPONGE CAKE (hot water)

Yield: 4 10-inch tubes, from 48 to 56 wedges Size of serving: ¹/₁₂ or ¹/₁₄ of a cake

1 pound, 7 ounces (3 cups) egg yolks (about 36 yolks)
2 pounds, 14 ounces (6⅛ cups) sugar
3 cups boiling water
4 teaspoons grated lemon rind
1 teaspoon lemon extract
2 pounds 4 ounces (2¼ quarts) flour, cake
1¾ ounces (4½ tablespoons) baking powder
1⅔ tablespoons salt

166

Hand Method	Machine Method
1. Beat the egg yolks and sugar until light and lemon colored.	1. Beat the egg yolks and sugar with the whip at high speed until light and lemon colored.
2. Add the hot water gradually continuing to beat.	2. Add the hot water gradually continuing to beat.
3. Add the lemon juice and rind.	3. Add the lemon juice and rind.
4. Sift together the flour, baking powder, and salt. Add these to the above, mixing only enough to just blend the mixture.	4. Sift together the flour, baking powder, and salt. Change from the whip to the paddle. Using low speed, mix in the sifted dry ingredients, mixing only enough to blend them. Remove the bowl from the mixer and then remove the paddle. Using the hand, mix until ingredients are thoroughly blended.

5. Put 2 pounds of batter into each ungreased tube and bake at 325° F. for about 40 minutes. Invert the pans to cool. When cool, loosen the cake from the side of the pan and the tube with a spatula. Invert the pan and tap the edge sharply on a table to loosen the cake.

Frosting and Filling Recipes

BOILED FROSTING* (figure 31)

6 layers	8 layers	
3¾ cups sugar	5 cups sugar	1. Cook the sugar, salt, and water together to 238° F. (soft-ball stage) or until the sirup spins a thread. †
1 cup water	1⅓ cups water	
¼ teaspoon salt	½ teaspoon salt	
1¼ cups egg whites (about 10 whites)	1½ cups egg whites (about 12 whites)	2. Beat the egg whites until stiff but not dry. Pour the hot sirup slowly onto the egg whites beating continually until cool. Add the vanilla.
1½ teaspoons vanilla	2 teaspoons vanilla	

*This icing may be used immediately or held in the refrigerator, covered with waxed paper, for several days.
†The utensil should be covered for a few minutes after boiling begins, to wash down the crystals that collect on the sides of it. This helps to prevent a crystalline product.

Variation

Devil's food: Spread plain frosting on the cake. For 2 large cakes, recipe page 163, cover the top of the icing with a thin layer of: 5 ounces of butter, 5 ounces of sweet chocolate, 5 ounces of bitter chocolate, melted over hot water.

BROWN-SUGAR FUDGE FROSTING

6 layers	8 layers	
1 pound, 8 ounces (about 4 cups)	2 pounds (about 5 cups) sugar, brown	1. Combine the sugar, milk, salt, and cream of tartar. Cook over a low

sugar, brown
1 pound (2⅛ cups)
sugar, white
2½ cups milk
¼ teaspoon (scant)
salt
½ teaspoon cream
of tartar
¼ cup butter *or*
fortified margarine
1½ tablespoons
vanilla

1 pound, 8 ounces
(3⅓ cups) sugar, white
3½ cups milk
¼ teaspoon salt
¾ teaspoon cream of tartar

⅓ cup butter *or* fortified
margarine
2 tablespoons vanilla

flame to 234° F. (very soft-ball stage), stirring occasionally.

2. Remove from the fire, add the butter and vanilla and cool. When cool beat until stiff. Thin with cream or evaporated milk to a spreading consistency.

BUTTER-CREAM FROSTING
(Confectioners' sugar)

6 layers*

½ cup butter, vegetable fat, or fortified margarine
2¼ pounds (about 7 cups) sugar, confectioners'
½ cup egg whites (about 4 whites)

or

2 whole eggs
¾ teaspoon salt
1½ tablespoons vanilla
½ to ¾ cup top milk or evaporated milk

8 layers*

¾ cup butter, vegetable fat, *or* fortified margarine
3 pounds (about 9 cups) sugar, confectioners'
¾ cup egg whites (about 6 whites)

or

3 whole eggs
1 teaspoon salt
2 tablespoons vanilla
½ to 1 cup top milk or evaporated milk

1. Cream the fat until very soft; add the sugar slowly and cream it until well blended. Add the eggs, salt, and vanilla, and continue creaming. Add the milk, a little at a time, until the right consistency is reached.

*This quantity is sufficient to frost in between layers and the top of the cake. If sides are to be iced, increase the recipe by one-fourth.

Variations

Chocolate: Add melted bitter chocolate just before adding the milk; 2 ounces of chocolate for each pound of sugar.

Maple nut: In place of all vanilla use half maple flavoring and half vanilla; add from ⅓ to ½ cup of coarsely chopped nuts for each layer.

168

Mocha:

6 layers	8 layers	
½ cup butter, vegetable fat, or fortified margarine	⅔ cup butter, vegetable fat, *or* fortified margarine	1. Mix the sugar and cocoa together and proceed as above.
1¾ pounds (5 cups) sugar, confectioners'	2 pounds, 5 ounces (7 cups) sugar, confectioners'	
2 cups cocoa	2⅔ cups cocoa	
2 whole eggs	3 whole eggs	
¾ teaspoon salt	1 teaspoon salt	
1½ tablespoons vanilla	2 tablespoons vanilla	
⅓ to ¾ cup strong hot coffee	⅓ to 1 cup strong hot coffee	

Orange-lemon

Omit the vanilla
For *8 layers*, add 4 teaspoons of grated orange rind.
For *6 layers*, add 1 tablespoon of grated orange rind.
In place of the cream, use ¼ lemon juice and ¾ orange juice.
For a deeper color, use egg yolks in place of egg whites.

Peanut butter

6 layers	8 layers	
1½ cups peanut butter	2 cups peanut butter	1. Work part of the sugar into the peanut butter; heat the milk and add it, a little at a time, until the mixture is moistened. Add the remaining sugar, then enough of the hot milk to make the mixture the right consistency for spreading.
3 pounds (9 cups) sugar, confectioners'	4 pounds (3 quarts) sugar, confectioners'	
Top milk or evaporated milk	Top milk or evaporated milk	

DEVIL'S FOOD FROSTING

See variation of boiled frosting, page 167.

CHOCOLATE CREAM FILLING

See variation of cream filling, page 171.

CHOCOLATE BUTTER-CREAM FROSTING

See variation of butter-cream frosting, page 168.

CHOCOLATE FUDGE FROSTING

6 layers	8 layers	
6 ounces (6 squares) chocolate	8 ounces (8 squares) chocolate	1. Cut the chocolate into small pieces. Mix this with the sugar, milk, salt, and cream of tartar and cook over a low flame to 238° F. (soft-ball stage) stirring frequently to prevent burning.
1 pound (about 2½ cups) sugar, brown	1 pound, 4 ounces (about 3 cups) sugar, brown	
1¼ pounds (2½ cups) sugar, white	1 pound, 11 ounces (3¾ cups) sugar, white	
2 cups milk	2½ cups milk	
¼ teaspoon salt	¼ teaspoon salt	
½ teaspoon cream of tartar	¾ teaspoon cream of tartar	
1 teaspoon vanilla	1¼ teaspoons vanilla	2. Remove from the fire, and add the vanilla and butter. Cool the mixture. When cool beat it until stiff enough to hold its shape. Thin it with cream or evaporated milk until it is of spreading consistency.
3 tablespoons butter or fortified margarine	¼ cup butter or fortified margarine	

CHOCOLATE TUTTI-FRUTTI FUDGE FROSTING

2 large cakes (18 x 12 inches)

5 pounds, 4 ounces (11 cups) sugar	1. Cook the sugar, corn sirup, cocoa and milk together to 230° F. (soft-ball stage). Add the butter and the vanilla, cool the mixture and then beat it.
2 pounds (2⅔ cups) corn sirup	
4 ounces (1 cup) cocoa	
4½ cups milk	
1 cup butter or fortified margarine	
3 tablespoons vanilla	
2 cups raisins, chopped	2. Fold in the raisins and nuts.
2 cups nuts, coarsely chopped	
	3. Thin with cream or evaporated milk to a spreading consistency.

CREAM FILLING

3 cakes*	4 cakes*	
3½ cups milk	4½ cups milk	1. Heat the milk over hot water.
½ cup flour	2½ ounces (⅔ cup) flour	2. Mix the flour, cornstarch, and sugar. Add about 2 cups of the hot milk to this and stir until smooth. Add this to the remaining hot milk and cook until thickened stirring constantly. Cover the mixture and cook it over hot water for from 10 to 15 minutes.
2¼ tablespoons cornstarch	1 ounce (3 table-spoons) cornstarch	
⅓ cup sugar	½ cup sugar	
¼ cup egg yolks (about 3 yolks)	2½ ounces (⅓ cup) egg yolks (about 4 yolks)	3. Beat the egg yolks and combine with the sugar. Add this to the hot mixture and cook for about 2 minutes,

170

⅓ cup sugar	½ cup sugar	stirring constantly. Remove the mixture from the hot water.
3 tablespoons butter *or* fortified margarine ¼ teaspoon salt 1½ teaspoons vanilla	¼ cup butter *or* fortified margarine ½ teaspoon salt 2 teaspoons vanilla	4. Add the butter, salt, and vanilla. Pour the mixture into shallow pans. Cover this with waxed paper to prevent a scum on the top. Cool the mixture before spreading on the cakes.

*1½ cups filling per cake.

Variations

Chocolate filling: Add bitter chocolate to the hot milk, stirring until the chocolate is melted: 2 ounces for 3 cakes and 2½ ounces for 4 cakes.

Pineapple filling: For each cake add ¼ cup well-drained, crushed pineapple to the cream filling.

DATE FILLING

See variation of fig filling, below.

FIG FILLING

3 cakes	*4 cakes*	
6 cups (2½ pounds) figs, chopped 1¾ cups water 1½ cups sugar	8 cups (3¼ pounds) figs, chopped 2¼ cups water 2 cups sugar	1. Cook the figs, sugar, and water together until the figs become soft.
⅓ cup lemon juice	½ cup lemon juice	2. Add the lemon juice, and spread the mixture while hot. Thin with water if necessary.

Variation

Date filling: Use dates in place of figs.

LADY BALTIMORE FROSTING

See variation of white layer cake, page 161.

LORD BALTIMORE FROSTING

See variation of gold layer cake, page 160.

LEMON FILLING

*3 cakes**	*4 cakes**	
3 cups water 15 ounces (2 cups) sugar	4 cups water 1 pound, 4 ounces (2½ cups) sugar	1. Heat the water and sugar together.
2½ ounces (7½ table-	3¼ ounces (10 table-	2. Blend the cornstarch and cold water

spoons) cornstarch	spoons) cornstarch	together. Add this to the hot water
¾ cup cold water	1 cup cold water	and sugar and cook until thickened
		and clear, stirring constantly.
3 ounces egg yolks	4 ounces (½ cup) egg	3. Add a little of the hot mixture
(about 4 yolks)	yolks (about 6 yolks)	to the egg yolks. Return this to the
		hot mixture and cook for 2 minutes.
		Remove from the heat.
¾ teaspoon salt	1 teaspoon salt	4. Add the salt, lemon rind, juice,
1½ teaspoons lemon	2 teaspoons lemon	and butter. Pour the mixture
rind, grated	rind, grated	into shallow pans. Cover with
⅓ cup lemon juice	½ cup lemon juice	waxed paper to prevent a scum on
1½ tablespoons butter	2 tablespoons butter	the top. Cool.
or fortified margarine	or fortified margarine	

*1½ cups filling per cake.

MAPLE NUT FROSTING

See variation of butter-cream frosting page 168.

MOCHA FROSTING

See variation of butter-cream frosting page 169.

ORANGE-LEMON FROSTING

See variation of butter-cream frosting page 169.

PEANUT BUTTER FROSTING

See variation of butter-cream frosting page 169.

PINEAPPLE CREAM FILLING

See variation of cream filling, page 171.

PRUNE-WHIP FROSTING

2 large cakes, 18 x 12 inches, or 8 layers

3¾ cups sugar	1. Cook the sugar, salt, and prune juice together
¼ teaspoon salt	to 238° F. (soft-ball stage) or until the sirup spins
1 cup prune juice, thin	a thread.*
1¼ cups (10) egg whites	2. Beat the egg whites until stiff but not dry.
1½ teaspoons vanilla	Pour the hot sirup slowly onto the egg whites,
	beating continually until cool. Add the vanilla.
10 ounces (1¼ cups) prunes,	3. Add the well-drained prunes in small quanti-
cooked, chopped, and drained	ties, beating carefully while adding.

*Cover the utensil as directed under plain boiled frosting (page 167).

COOKIES

Although cookies may be soft, crisp, crunchy, or chewy, they should always be uniform in shape and color. Drop cookies should be soft, tender, and light, with a moist crumb. Thin cookies should be crisp yet tender.

Directions

If rolled cookie dough is chilled before handling it is easier to manipulate and less flour is needed for rolling, thus producing a tender product. Since re-rolling of the dough is likely to produce a less tender cookie, it is advisable to hold the scraps after each rolling until last and then work them together.

Drop cookies, in general, spread in baking, hence should be placed about 2 inches apart on the baking pan.

Molasses, fruit, and chocolate cookies require baking at a slightly lower temperature than do most others. In general, cookie pans do not need greasing, except for making molasses and fruit cookies, which are inclined to stick and burn. Pans for chewy bars should first be greased, then lined with heavy waxed paper.

SUGAR COOKIES
(rolled)

Yield: 6 dozen (2-inch)

4 ounces (½ cup) butter or fortified margarine

7½ ounces (1 cup) sugar

1 egg

½ teaspoon vanilla

12 ounces (3 cups) flour, all-purpose

¼ teaspoon salt

1 tablespoon baking powder

¼ cup milk

1. Cream the fat and sugar together.

2. Add the egg and flavoring, blending thoroughly.

3. Sift together the dry ingredients.

4. Add the dry ingredients and milk alternately to the fat-sugar-egg mixture, mixing only until all ingredients are blended. Chill overnight in refrigerator. Roll out ⅛-inch thick. Cut the dough into 2-inch rounds. Sprinkle with coarse granulated or colored sugar and place on lightly greased and floured baking sheets. Bake at 375° F. for about 6 minutes. Loosen the cookies from the pan immediately after removing them from the oven.

Variations

Cocoanut: After the cookies are partially rolled out, sprinkle chopped coconut over the top of the dough; finish rolling, and bake them as for plain sugar cookies.

Filled: Place a teaspoon of filling on one round; place a round on top and pinch the edges together, or use a fork to press them together. Mincemeat, thick jams, or other preserves may be used; a recipe for date filling is given on page 171.

Nut: Sprinkle the tops with coarsely chopped nuts; press the nuts into the dough slightly.

Tarts: Place a teaspoonful of jelly or jam on the top of a round; cover this with a round from which a round center has been cut.

BROWNIES

Yield: One pan (17 x 11 inches); 96 bars (1 inch x 2 inches)

8 1-ounce squares chocolate
10½ ounces (1⅓ cups) butter *or* fortified margarine

1. Melt the chocolate and butter together.

1 pound, 14 ounces (4 cups) sugar

2. Add the sugar.

13 ounces (1½ cups) eggs (about 8 eggs)

3. Beat in the eggs.

8 ounces (2 cups) flour, all-purpose
1 tablespoon salt
1 tablespoon vanilla
1 pound (4 cups) nuts, coarsely chopped

4. Add the flour, salt, vanilla, and nuts. Spread the mixture evenly on greased and floured pans, to about ¾-inch thickness. Bake the mixture at 325° F. for from 25 to 40 minutes. Remove pans from the oven when the mixture is still sticky but not doughy. Cool slightly, then cut into bars 1 inch x 2 inches.

CHOCOLATE DROP COOKIES

Yield: 5 dozen (medium size)

4 1-ounce squares chocolate, melted
½ pound (1 cup) butter, fortified margarine, *or* vegetable fat
1 pound (2¼ cups) sugar, brown
2 eggs, unbeaten

1. Combine the melted chocolate, fat, sugar, unbeaten eggs, and blend well.

1 pound (4 cups) flour, cake
½ teaspoon salt
1 teaspoon soda
1 cup milk

2. Sift together the flour, soda, and salt. Add these dry ingredients alternately with milk to creamed mixture and stir until thoroughly blended.

¼ pound (1 cup) nuts, coarsely chopped
1 teaspoon vanilla

3. Stir in the nuts and vanilla. Drop the batter by spoonfuls onto a greased and floured baking sheet. A No. 30 ice-cream dipper or a pastry bag may be used to advantage in quantity production. Bake cookies at 350° F. approximately 12 minutes.

COCONUT COOKIES

See variation of sugar cookies, page 173.

DATE WHIRLS

See variation of refrigerator cookies, page 176.

FILLED SUGAR COOKIES

See variation of sugar cookies, page 173.

FRUIT HERMITS

Yield: 5 dozen (medium size)

½ pound (1 cup) butter *or* fortified margarine

½ pound (1⅛ cups) sugar, brown, packed

3 eggs

12 ounces (3 cups) flour, all-purpose

1 teaspoon cloves

1 teaspoon cinnamon

1 teaspoon soda

4 ounces (1 cup) nuts, coarsely chopped

6 ounces (1 cup) raisins, chopped

6 ounces (1 cup) dates, chopped

Grated rind of 1 orange

1 tablespoon molasses

1. Cream the butter; add the sugar gradually, creaming until well blended.

2. Add one egg at a time, beating well.

3. Sift the dry ingredients together; add part of them and part of the fruit and nuts and mix the batter thoroughly; then add the remaining dry ingredients and fruit and nuts.

4. Stir in the orange rind and molasses. Drop by teaspoonfuls onto greased and floured baking sheets. Bake at 375° F. until done to the touch (about 12 minutes). Loosen the cookies from the pan immediately after removing them from the oven.

GRAHAM FINGERS

Yield: 5 dozen

60 graham crackers

¾ cup butter *or* fortified margarine

1 pound (2¼ cups) sugar, brown

Nut meats

1. Rub the butter and sugar together; spread this on the graham crackers. Place 2 or 4 nut meats on each cracker. Bake them at 350° F. until the sugar and the butter are blended. For tea cookies, cut each cracker in half while hot.

GUMDROP BARS

Yield: 64 bars (1 inch x 2 inches)

4 eggs

14 ounces (2 cups) sugar, brown

⅓ pound gum drops,* cut into small pieces

2 teaspoons vanilla

½ cup pecans, chopped

8 ounces (2 cups) flour, all-purpose

2 teaspoons baking powder

½ teaspoon salt

1. Beat the eggs until light.

2. Add the brown sugar, vanilla, sifted dry ingredients, gum drops, and nuts. Mix until well blended. Spread 1 inch thick in greased pans. Bake at 375° F. for from 12 to 15 minutes. Cut into bars 1 inch x 2 inches while warm. Roll the bars in powdered sugar.

*Do not use licorice or anise flavored gum drops.

175

HONEY-DATE BARS

Yield: From 40 to 50 bars (1 x 1½ inches)

4 ounces (1 cup) flour, all-purpose 2 teaspoons baking powder ¼ teaspoon salt 1 cup all-bran	1. Sift the flour, baking powder, and salt together. Mix the bran into this.
4 eggs, beaten 1½ cups honey	2. Combine the eggs and honey and add this mixture to the dry ingredients; stir the mixture until thoroughly blended.
12 ounces (2 cups) dates, chopped 4 ounces (1 cup) nuts, coarsely chopped	3. Stir in the dates and nuts. Spread this about ⅓-inch thick in a well-greased pan. Bake it at 350° F. for from 25 to 30 minutes. When done, cut into bars, remove them from the pan, cool, and roll them in confectioners' sugar.

REFRIGERATOR COOKIES

Yield: 100 (1½ inches)

8 ounces (1⅛ cups) sugar, brown 5 ounces (¾ cup) shortening	1. Cream the sugar and shortening together.
2 eggs ½ teaspoon vanilla	2. Add the eggs and vanilla and mix thoroughly.
10 ounces (2½ cups) flour, all-purpose ⅔ teaspoon soda ⅔ teaspoon baking powder ¼ teaspoon salt 2½ ounces (½ cup) nuts, chopped	3. Sift the flour, soda, baking powder, and salt together, add the nuts and combine with the above mixture. Form the mixture into rolls approximately 1¼ inches in diameter and 12 inches long. Wrap these in waxed paper and chill in a refrigerator overnight. Cut slices ⅛-inch thick and place them on very lightly greased cookie sheets. Bake at 375° F. for about 12 minutes. Loosen the cookies from the pans immediately after removing them from oven.

Variations

Orange: Add 1 tablespoon of grated orange rind to the mixture.

Pinwheel cookies: Omit the nuts. Divide the dough into 2 equal portions. Add ¾ ounce of melted chocolate to one portion. Roll or pat each portion on waxed paper into a rectangular sheet ⅛-inch thick or less. Place one on top of the other and roll as for a jelly roll. Chill the rolls and slice them.

Date whirls: Divide the dough into 2 or 3 portions. Place each portion on waxed paper and roll it into a rectangular shape about ¼-inch thick. Spread each with date paste. (Use ¼ the recipe for date paste, page 178.) Roll these as for a jelly roll. Chill the rolls and slice them.

MEXICAN WEDDING CAKE
(Pecan puffs)

Yield: 50 to 60 cookies

8 ounces (1 cup) butter *or* fortified margarine	1. Cream the fat and sugar until well blended.
¼ cup sugar, confectioners'	
8 ounces (2 cups) flour, cake	2. Add the flour, pecans, and vanilla. Roll the dough into 1-inch balls. Place them on lightly greased baking sheets and flatten slightly. Bake at 300° F. for about 45 minutes. Remove the cookies from the oven and roll them in confectioners' sugar while warm. When cool roll cookies again in confectioners' sugar.
8 ounces (2 cups) pecans, chopped	
2 teaspoons vanilla	

MOLASSES COOKIES (crisp)

Yield: From 5½ to 6 dozen (medium size)

5 ounces (⅔ cup) fat	1. Cream the fat; add the sugar gradually, creaming these together until well blended.
4 ounces (½ cup) sugar	
1 egg, slightly beaten	2. Add the egg, and beat the mixture thoroughly.
1 cup molasses	3. Mix the molasses, vinegar, and water; add them and beat well.
1 tablespoon vinegar	
2 tablespoons water	
1 pound, 2 ounces (4½ cups) flour, all-purpose	4. Sift the flour, soda, and ginger together; add this to the creamed mixture and stir until well blended. Chill the mixture in the refrigerator until stiff; roll it out about ⅛-inch thick and cut. Bake the dough on greased and floured cookie sheets at 375° F. for from 6 to 7 minutes. Loosen cookies from the pans while warm.
1 tablespoon soda	
1 tablespoon ginger	

NUT COOKIES

See variation of sugar cookies, page 173.

OATMEAL COOKIES

Yield: 100, 2-inch cookies

10 ounces (1½ cups) shortening	1. Cream the shortening and sugar thoroughly.
12 ounces (2 cups) sugar, brown	
4 eggs	2. Add the eggs and blend.
9 ounces (2¼ cups) flour, all-purpose	3. Sift the flour, baking powder, salt, and spices together. Add to the above mixture.
2 teaspoons baking powder	
1 teaspoon salt	
1½ teaspoons cinnamon	
½ teaspoon nutmeg	
¾ teaspoon cloves	
10 ounces (2 cups) raisins	4. Soak the raisins in hot water to cover or

177

11 ounces (1 quart) oatmeal, flaked
8 ounces (2 cups) nuts, chopped
¾ cup milk

steam them for a few minutes to soften. Drain.

5. Add the oatmeal, raisins, nuts, and milk, mixing thoroughly. Drop by the teaspoonful on lightly greased and floured baking sheet. Bake at 375° F. for from 12 to 15 minutes. Loosen the cookies from pan while still warm.

OATMEAL-DATE BARS

Yield: 5 dozen (medium size)

12 ounces (1½ cups) butter *or* fortified margarine
12 ounces (1¾ cups) sugar, brown packed
1 pound (1 quart) flour, all-purpose
4 teaspoons baking powder
½ teaspoon salt
12 ounces (1 quart) oatmeal, uncooked
1 cup milk

1. Cream the butter; add the sugar gradually, creaming these together until well blended.

2. Sift the flour, baking powder, and salt together; mix in the oatmeal. Add this to the creamed mixture alternately with the milk. Divide the dough and roll it out into thin sheets. Spread half with the date paste and fold the other half over. Press the edges together. Place this on a greased pan. Bake at 375° F. for about 30 minutes. Cut it into squares as soon as it is removed from the oven.

Date Paste

1½ pounds (4 cups) dates, chopped
1 cup water
¼ cup lemon juice
4 ounces (1 cup) nuts, coarsely chopped

1. Combine all the ingredients and cook the mixture until thick. Cool.

ORANGE COOKIES

Yield: 6 dozen (1-inch cookies)

1½ cups shortening
1 cup sugar

1. Cream the shortening and sugar together.

3 egg yolks
3 tablespoons grated orange and lemon rind

2. Add the egg yolks and grated orange and lemon rind.

12 ounces (3 cups) flour, all-purpose

3. Work the flour into the mixture using the fingers. Shape the dough into small balls.

3 eggs whites, unbeaten
Nuts, chopped fine (about 1½ cups)

4. Roll the balls in the unbeaten egg white, then in the nuts. Place them on greased baking sheets and flatten the balls. Bake at 350° F. for about 15 minutes until browned.

ORANGE REFRIGERATOR COOKIES

See variation of refrigerator cookies, page 176.

PEANUT BUTTER COOKIES

Yield: From 5 to 6 dozen (medium size)

8 ounces (1⅛ cups) vegetable fat

7½ ounces (1 cup) sugar, granulated

6 ounces (1 cup) sugar, brown, packed

1. Cream the fat; add the sugar gradually, creaming these together until well blended.

2 eggs, slightly beaten

1 cup peanut butter

2. Add the eggs, and beat the mixture; add the peanut butter.

12 ounces (3 cups) flour, all-purpose

2 teaspoons soda

½ teaspoon salt

3. Sift the flour, soda, and salt together and add these to the mixture; stir until all are well blended.

1 teaspoon vanilla

4. Stir in the vanilla. Shape the dough into small balls and place them on to greased baking sheets. Flatten with a fork until the cookies are ¼-inch thick. Bake at 375° F. for about 12 minutes. Loosen the cookies from the pan while still warm.

PINWHEEL REFRIGERATOR COOKIES

See variation of refrigerator cookies, page 176.

SALTED PEANUT COOKIES

Yield: 4 dozen (medium size)

2 eggs

14 ounces (2 cups) sugar, brown, packed

12 ounces (1½ cups) butter *or* fortified margarine, melted

6 ounces (1½ cups) salted peanuts (small with skins)

1. Beat the eggs, add the sugar and then the melted butter. Stir in the peanuts carefully.

10 ounces (2½ cups) flour, all-purpose

1 teaspoon soda

1 teaspoon baking powder

9 ounces (3 cups) oatmeal, dry

1 ounce (1 cup) cornflakes

2. Mix the flour, soda, and baking powder together; then mix these with the oatmeal and cornflakes. Add this mixture to the first and stir well. Drop it from a spoon onto greased baking pans. Bake the cookies at 400° F. Remove them from the pans as soon as they are taken from the oven.

TARTS

See variation of sugar cookies, page 174.

WALNUT SQUARES

Yield: 6½ dozen (1½-inch squares)

1 cup butter *or* fortified margarine
1 cup sugar, brown
2 cups flour, all-purpose

1. Combine the butter, sugar, and flour using the fingers to make a crumbly mixture. Place this mixture onto flat pans and pat it into layers over the bottoms of the pans. Bake at 350° F. for 10 minutes.

4 eggs, beaten
¼ cup flour, all-purpose
2 teaspoons baking powder
2 teaspoons vanilla
2 cups sugar, brown
3 cups coconut
2 cups nuts
1 teaspoon salt

2. Combine all the ingredients and stir thoroughly. Spread the mixture over the bottom layers. Bake at 350° F. until browned. Cool and cut into squares or bars.

FRUITS

Frozen Fruits

Frozen fruits to be used as a sauce should be partially defrosted in a refrigerator before they are served. Peaches and apricots should be left in their original packages (unopened) during defrosting to lessen discoloration.

Frozen fruits to be used for making pie fillings and other fruit desserts should first be completely defrosted. This will take several hours (overnight) at room temperature.

Frozen fruits usually contain added sugar. The amount of sugar for recipes using frozen fruit needs to be adjusted according to the proportion of sugar in the pack. Some fruits may be packed without sugar and are termed *dry pack*.

Cooking Dried Fruits

Dried fruit processed by more recently developed methods requires no soaking before cooking.

Dried fruit purees

Cook fruit according to above directions given in the chart but increase the cooking time. Force the soft fruits through a colander, sieve, or ricer. If a ricer is used first remove pits from prunes. One cup of uncooked dried fruit will yield about 1 cup of puree. In making whips and sauces, the cooked fruit may be beaten to a pulp instead of pureed.

Dried fruit cookery* chart

Fruit	Boiling time	Cups of sugar†	Approximate yield of cooked fruit‡	Notes
	Minutes	*Per pound of fruit*	*Cups*	
Apples	40 to 45	1¼ to 1½	8	Remove any particles of core
Apricots	30 to 40	1 to 1½	4½	
Figs	20 to 30	⅛ to ¼	4½	Add sugar during the last 15 minutes of cooking
Peaches	40 to 45	¾ to 1	4	Skins may be removed at the end of 5 minutes cooking
Pears	25 to 35	¾ to 1	5	
Prunes	45 to 60	¼ to ½	4	

*All fruit should be rinsed, covered with water, and boiled for the time given above or for the time given on the containers of specially processed fruits. If sugar is used it is best added in the last 5 minutes of cooking. A small pinch of salt improves the flavor.
†Sugar may be omitted entirely or less than the amounts suggested here may give the desired sweetness.
‡Yield of cooked fruit from 1 pound of dried fruit.

Recipes
BAKED APPLES

Yield: 50 servings

Size of serving: 1 apple

50 apples, large

Method 1
1. Core the apples and peel them about one-fourth of the way down.

2. Place the apples in large baking pans and fill the center of each apple with sugar. Add about 1 quart of water to to each pan, cover the pan and place in a moderate oven steaming the apples until slightly tender *or* cook the apples uncovered in a steamer.

3. Uncover the apples, sprinkle them generously with sugar and bake them at 475° F. basting them frequently.

Method 2

2. Bring to boiling 2 quarts of water and 4 pounds (8½ cups) of sugar. Drop the apples in this boiling sirup and let them simmer until slightly tender.

3. Remove the apples from the sirup, place them in baking pans and sprinkle them with sugar. Pour the sirup into the baking pan and bake the apples at 475° F., basting them frequently *or* place them under a hot broiler for from 10 to 15 minutes basting them frequently.

BAKED APPLE RINGS

See recipe, page 105.

ESCALLOPED APPLES

See recipe, page 105.

FROZEN FRUIT SAUCE
(for desserts)

Yield: 2 quarts

Size of serving: 2 tablespoons

3½ pounds frozen strawberries *or* raspberries

1. Thaw the frozen fruit over night. Strain the fruit, measure the juice, add the water, and heat.

2 cups water

Cornstarch (3 tablespoons per quart of liquid)

½ cup sugar

1 tablespoon butter *or* fortified margarine

3 tablespoons lemon juice

2. Figure the amount of cornstarch needed. Mix it with the sugar. Add this to the hot fruit and cook until thickened.

3. Add the butter and lemon juice and cool. Add the strained fruit.

NOTE: This sauce may be used for fruit shortcake. Prepare 4 to 5 quarts of the sauce for 50 servings of shortcake.

FRUIT CUP

Yield: 50 servings

Size of serving: ½ cup

2 quarts grapefruit sections

2½ quarts orange sections

2 quarts bananas, diced

1 quart fruit juice

1. Mix all the grapefruit and orange sections and fruit juice and chill. Add bananas before serving.

NOTE: Many other fruits may be used in making fruit cup: pineapple, pears, peaches, raw apples, grape halves, strawberries, raspberries, apricots, fresh blueberries, raspberries, cherries.

SPICED PRUNES

See recipe page 113.

BAKED RHUBARB SAUCE

See recipe page 113.

PIES

Pie crust should be short, tender, flaky, and delicately browned, with a rough blistered appearance.

Suitable shortenings for pie crust are all vegetable fat, half lard and half vegetable fat, or all lard; vegetable fats are best for crusts to contain cream and other bland-flavored fillings, but lard may be used for fruit pies and for meat pies. The fat should be soft but not liquid; usually it is in suitable condition if it is at room temperature.

In making crust, the ingredients need to be combined but not over-mixed. The fat should be in small particles and coated with flour; this mixture is gradually moistened with cold water. The crust should be lightly rolled out with as little added flour as possible. Crust may be made up in quantity, covered with waxed paper, and stored in the refrigerator for use as needed.

The type of crust produced is partially determined by the method of combining the fat and the flour:

A standard flaky crust: The fat and flour are mixed together until small lumps are formed throughout the mixture.

182

A short flaky crust: Half the fat and all the flour are mixed until the fat is well blended with the flour. The remainder of the fat is added and mixed lightly so that it is left in small lumps throughout the dough.

A short mealy crust: All the fat and half the flour are mixed thoroughly. The remainder of the flour is mixed in to break up the creamed mixture.

The top crust browns more readily if brushed with milk just to the edge, but not over it. The following ingredients beaten together produce an attractive glaze: 2 whole eggs, ½ cup of melted butter, and 1 cup of warm milk.

Fillings require less thickening if the pies are made in advance and

Photograph from General Foods

FIGURE 32.   CONCERNING PIES

Top: Pie rack that fits in a small space
Center: Pie top variations; uncooked meringue with coconut and fruit; criss-cross pastry
Bottom: Pie marker (upper left) for obtaining equalized portions, and cutting knife and pie server

183

are thoroughly cooled before cutting. Cream fillings are best when they are smooth and stiff enough to prevent their running when cut, but free from pastiness or rubberiness. Custard fillings are most desirable when they do not "weep" on standing, and when they are tender and quivery yet keep their angles when cut. Fruit fillings should be sufficiently juicy to run slightly. To keep fruit in whole pieces when making fillings, one should drain the fruit from canned packs or frosted packs that have been thawed, thicken the juice, and mix it carefully with the drained fruit before filling the crusts. Using a sufficient quantity of sugar and baking the crust at a high temperature are means of preventing the fruit sirup from boiling out.

Pie Crust

HAND-MIXED PIE CRUST

Yield: 8 8-inch pies *or*
      6 10-inch pies

Crust portions for 10-inch pies: 9 ounces for bottom
crusts; from 7 to 8 ounces for top crusts.

3 pounds (3 quarts) flour, all-purpose
4½ tablespoons salt

1. Sift the flour and weigh or measure it; add the salt.

2 pounds, 4 ounces (5¼ cups) shortening
1½ cups ice water
Flour for rolling

2. Work in the shortening carefully, handling the mixture as little as possible.

3. Add the ice water rather quickly, mixing very lightly. Chill the dough in the refrigerator before rolling it.

MACHINE-MIXED PIE CRUST

Yield: 8 8-inch pies *or*
      6 10-inch pies

1 pound, 2 ounces (4½ cups) flour, all-purpose
1 pound, 8 ounces (6 cups) flour, cake
2 pounds (4½ cups) lard*

1. Weigh all-purpose flour, cake flour, and lard into the bowl of the mixing machine. Using the pastry blender cut the lard into the flour using first speed. Mix only until the flour and lard appear in lumps. Do not mix to a pasty mass.

1½ cups cold water
2¼ ounces (4 tablespoons salt)
6 ounces (1½ cups) flour, all-purpose

2. Mix the water, salt, and flour until blended. Add this to the flour-fat mixture and mix on first speed until blended but *do not overmix*. Let the dough rest for 15 to 20 minutes before rolling or refrigerate until needed.

*Two pounds, 4 ounces (5¼ cups) of vegetable shortening may be used in place of the lard.

Directions for rolling

Pie crusts that have been rolled out and refrigerated for 12 to 18 hours before baking are likely to shrink less than if baked immediately after rolling. This is an especially good procedure in making one-crust pies. Place waxed paper between the unbaked crusts when storing.

Bottom crust

Weigh 9-ounce portions of pastry.

Roll the pastry into a circular sheet of uniform thickness about 2½ inches larger than the pie tin, using enough flour to prevent sticking.

Fit the crust into the pan so that there are no air spaces between the crust and the pan. Use care in trimming the edge of the crust; the rim of the tin should be entirely covered.

Upper crust

Roll 7- to 8-ounce portions of crust slightly larger than the pie to be covered, to allow for the rounded filling.

Moisten the edges of the pastry with milk or water. Make a few holes in the crust before placing it over the pie to allow the steam to escape.

Press the top crust firmly on the edges of the bottom crust. Trim off the surplus pastry, but keep the rim of the pan entirely covered.

Brush the top (not the edges) with milk or with the following mixture: two whole eggs, ½ cup melted butter, and 1 cup of warm milk.

Pie shells

Fit the crust over the inside or outside of a pie tin. Trim the edges.

Prick the bottom and side of the crust with a fork.

A second tin may be put over the crust for the first part of the baking; then removed and crust allowed to brown. The second tin helps to keep the crust in shape.

CRUMB CRUSTS

Popular and easily made are crusts containing graham-cracker or gingersnap crumbs, which may be filled with cream, chiffon, or thickened fruit fillings.

Yield: 8 8-inch pies *or*
      6 10-inch pies

2 pounds, 8 ounces (4 quarts) graham-cracker crumbs*
12 ounces (1½ cups) sugar
1 pound, 10 ounces (3¼ cups) butter *or* fortified margarine, melted

1. Roll or chop the crackers into fine crumbs. Add the sugar. Reserve 1 cup of this mixture for topping.

2. Work the melted butter into the mixture. Weigh 12 ounces of the mixture into each tin. To form the crusts, pack the mixture firmly into pie tins, building it well up on the sides. Set another pie tin in the shell so that the crust will hold its shape. Chill the shells in a refrigerator or bake them for 10 minutes at 350° F.

3. Place filling in the crusts and sprinkle the top with the crumb-sugar mixture. Whipped cream may be used for the topping.

*Gingersnaps, vanilla wafers, or chocolate wafers may be used in place of the graham crackers.

185

Individual pies or tarts (figure 33)

Small pie or tart tins, individual pyrex or oven-china casseroles, or muffin tins may be used to make individual pies or tarts.

For tart shells fit a crust either on the inner or outer surface of the tart tins, pricking the crust in several places; place a second tin over the crust and bake it for from 5 to 8 minutes; remove the extra tin and return the crust to the oven to brown. The second tin helps to keep the crust in shape.

Photograph from Wesson Oil and Snowdrift Sales Company

FIGURE 33.   TART SHELLS

Tart shells may be made by fitting rounds of pastry over bottoms of muffin tins

These shells may be filled with a cream filling and topped with whipped cream or with a meringue browned in the oven.

Deep-dish pies are made in casseroles with a top crust only. Individual meat pies may have the top crust cut in fancy shapes of the proper size for the casserole.

Meringue

Meringues should be slightly browned, light, and moist in appearance, and should adhere to the crust edge.

Topping for 8 8-inch pies *or* 6 10-inch pies

2¼ cups (from 18 to 22) egg whites

1½ teaspoons salt

1½ teaspoons vanilla

2¼ cups sugar, granulated

1. Have the egg whites at room temperature. Add the salt and flavoring to the egg whites and beat them until stiff but still shiny.

2. Add the sugar gradually; beat until the mixture piles up well in the bowl and the sugar is dissolved.

3. Swirl the meringue immediately over the warm pie filling, being careful to seal the meringue to the edge of the pie crust.

4. Bake it for about 5 minutes at 425° F. or 12 to 15 minutes at 375° F.

Pie Fillings

Cream pie fillings, thickened with cornstarch or flour, should be cooked thoroughly to get the maximum thickening and to prevent any raw starch taste. Heat the milk in the top of a double boiler, a hot water bath, or a steam-jacketed kettle. The flour or cornstarch are easy to add if they are blended with a part of the sugar and enough of the warm milk to make a smooth mixture. Add the slightly beaten egg yolks to the thickening or combine them with part of the sugar and add after the thickening. Beat the thickening into the scalded milk with a wire whip. Stir the mixture frequently but gently while it is thickening, but only occasionally during the remainder of the cooking period. Beating or vigorous stirring during the final stage of cooking or after cooling causes the filling to become thin. A 6-pie batch of filling takes about 20 to 25 minutes in a double boiler to thicken to the right consistency and to lose the raw starch taste. Larger amounts of filling, of course, take longer to cook.

Cream pie fillings should be creamy rather than rubbery or pasty and should be stiff enough so that the cut pieces of pie can be served easily. Flour gives a creamier consistency than cornstarch or a combination of flour and cornstarch. However, fillings in which some cornstarch is used thicken more rapidly and therefore require a shorter time for cooking. Cornstarch has about twice the thickening power of flour so, if flour is substituted for it, twice as much flour will be required.

Cream filling should be cooled slightly before it is put into crusts. If a meringue is to be used on the pies, bake the pies immediately. Refrigerate cream pies. If the cream filling must be held pour it into flat pans, cover the surface with waxed paper and refrigerate.

Fruit pie fillings made with frozen or canned fruit are usually thickened with cornstarch rather than flour; tapioca may be used. The fruit is drained and the juice brought to the boiling point over direct heat. The thickening is blended with the sugar and this dry mixture beaten into the hot liquid. If preferred, the cornstarch and sugar may be made into a paste with part of the liquid. The mixture should be stirred frequently while thickening. It is cooked until it is thickened and no longer tastes of raw starch. The fruit is added carefully at this point. The filling is usually partially cooled before it is put into the pie crusts. The filling should flow slightly when the pie is cut.

Pie filling recipes

AMBROSIA PIE

Yield: 8 8-inch pies *or* 6 10-inch pies   Size of serving: $1/_6$ or $1/_8$ of a pie

2¾ quarts hot water 2¾ cups cornstarch 4 cups sugar	1. Mix the cornstarch and the sugar thoroughly. Add about a quart of the hot water to this mixture and stir until smooth; add this to the remaining hot water and cook the mixture until thickened, stirring constantly with a wire whip.
2¼ cups (about 27) egg yolks, beaten	2. Combine the slightly beaten egg yolks and sugar. Add to the hot mixture and cook for

1 cup sugar

4¾ cups orange juice
1⅛ cups lemon juice
6 tablespoons grated orange rind
2 tablespoons grated lemon rind
2¼ teaspoons salt

Meringue (page 186)
6 to 9 oranges
3 cups coconut

about 5 minutes stirring frequently. Remove it from the heat.

3. Add the juice and rind from the oranges and lemons; add the salt. Cool the mixture slightly and put it into baked shells, about 1 quart in each 10-inch shell.

4. Cover the mixture with the meringue but do not brown it. Section the oranges and arrange the sections on top of the meringue and sprinkle ½ cup of coconut over each pie.

APPLE PIE

Yield: 8 8-inch pies *or* 6 10-inch pies Size of serving: ¹/₆ or ⅛ of a pie

9 quarts sliced apples* (15 to 20 pounds, fresh)

3½ teaspoons cinnamon
6 cups sugar†
¾ cup flour
¾ teaspoon salt
6 tablespoons butter *or* fortified margarine

1. Put 4 cups of apples in each 8-inch pie crust; 6 cups in each 10-inch crust.

2. Mix the cinnamon, sugar, flour, and salt together. Sprinkle the apples with this mixture, using ½ cup per pie. Add the remaining apples, using 3 cups more for each pie, and sprinkle ½ cup of the mixture over these; dot with the butter. Cover with a top crust. Bake at 375° F. for about 1 hour or until the apples are done.

*Canned apples may be used: 2 No. 10 cans and from 1 to 1½ cups of additional flour. Bake in a hot oven (425° F.) for about 30 minutes.
†If the apples are tart, increase the sugar by 2 cups.

Crust variations

Cheese crust: Add ⅓ cup of chopped cheese for each crust.

Spice crust: Add ¼ teaspoon of cinnamon and ¼ teaspoon of cloves for each crust; mix these in with the dry ingredients.

Streusel topping: see recipe page 196.

DUTCH APPLE PIE

Yield: 8 8-inch pies; 6 10-inch pies Size of serving: ¹/₆ or ⅛ of a pie

9 quarts sliced apples (15 to 20 pounds, fresh)

7½ cups sugar*
1½ cups flour
2½ teaspoons salt
1½ teaspoons cinnamon
2½ cups light cream *or* top milk (sweet *or* sour)
1¼ cups milk

1. Place 6 cups of apples in each 10-inch crust.

2. Mix the sugar, flour, salt, and cinnamon. Add the cream and milk and beat with a wire whip or in an electric mixer. Pour this mixture over the apples placed in the crusts, using 1¼ cups for each pie. Add a lattice top or plain top crust. Bake the pies at 425° F. for from 10 to 15 minutes; reduce the temperature to 350° F. and bake until done. If the crusts become brown before the apples are cooked, cover them with squares of brown paper.

*If the apples are tart, increase the sugar by 1 cup.

BERRY PIE
(Frozen fruit)

Yield: 8 8-inch pies *or* 6 10-inch pies   Size of serving: $^{1}/_{6}$ or $^{1}/_{8}$ of a pie

10 pounds berries, frozen
4½ cups water

1. Thaw and drain the fruit. Measure the juice and combine with the water. Heat to boiling.

9 tablespoons cornstarch (3 ounces) for 1 quart of liquid
4 to 6 cups of sugar

2. Figure the amount of cornstarch needed. Combine this with the sugar and add enough hot liquid to make a thin paste. Whip this into remaining hot liquid and cook until clear and thickened, stirring constantly but slowly with a wire whip. Remove the mixture from the heat.

⅓ teaspoon salt
⅓ cup lemon juice
¾ cup butter *or* fortified margarine (may be omitted)

3. Add the salt, lemon juice, and butter. Add the fruit to the mixture, stirring carefully. Cool. Use about 1 quart of filling for each 10-inch crust; cover with the top crusts. Bake the pies at 425° F. for from 30 to 40 minutes.

BUTTERSCOTCH PIE

Yield: 8 8-inch pies *or* 6 10-inch pies   Size of serving: $^{1}/_{6}$ or $^{1}/_{8}$ of a pie

3½ quarts milk (may use part evaporated milk)

1. Heat the milk in a double boiler.

2 pounds (4¼ cups) sugar, brown, packed
½ teaspoon soda
1 pound (1 quart) flour
1 cup cornstarch
1 quart milk

2. Combine the sugar, soda, flour, and cornstarch, using the fingertips to mix. Add the milk and stir until smooth. Whip this mixture into the hot milk and cook in the double boiler until thickened, stirring constantly but gently with a wire whip. Cook the mixture for from 15 to 20 minutes or until it no longer has any taste of raw starch.

1½ cups (about 18) egg yolks, beaten
2 cups sugar, brown

3. Combine the egg yolks and the remaining sugar; stir these into the hot mixture. Cook for from 5 to 10 minutes, stirring only occasionally. Remove it from the heat.

1 tablespoon salt
3 tablespoons vanilla
½ cup butter *or* fortified margarine*

4. Add the salt, vanilla, and butter. Cool slightly and pour the filling into baked shells, using 1 quart of filling for each 10-inch pie and ¾ quart for each 8-inch pie. Cover the mixture with a meringue and brown it at 425° F. for about 5 minutes or at 375° F. for from 12 to 15 minutes.

*The amount of butter or margarine may be increased to 1 cup to give a richer filling.

FROZEN CHERRY PIE

Yield: 8 8-inch pies *or* 6 10-inch pies   Size of serving: $^{1}/_{6}$ or $^{1}/_{8}$ of a pie

10 pounds cherries, frozen
4 cups water

1. Thaw the frozen cherries overnight. Drain.

2. Combine the cherry juice with the water and heat.

3 to 4 cups sugar
1¼ cups cornstarch

3. Mix the sugar and the cornstarch; whip the mixture slowly into the hot juice. Cook until thickened, stirring constantly with a wire whip. Remove the mixture from the heat.

¼ teaspoon salt
½ cup butter or fortified margarine
5 tablespoons lemon juice

4. Add the salt, butter, and lemon juice; then stir in the fruit carefully; cool. Pour about 1 quart of filling into each 10-inch crust; cover with the top crusts. Bake the pies at 425° F. for from 30 to 40 minutes.

CHOCOLATE PIE

Yield: 8 8-inch pies *or* 6 10-inch pies   Size of serving: ¹/₆ or ⅛ of a pie

3¾ quarts milk

1. Heat the milk in a double boiler.

5 cups sugar
2 cups cocoa
1½ cups cornstarch
1 cup flour
1 quart light cream *or* evaporated milk

2. Combine the sugar, cornstarch, flour, and cocoa and stir in the cream to make a smooth mixture. Beat this into the hot milk. Cook until thickened stirring frequently but gently.

1 cup (about 12) egg yolks
1 cup sugar

3. Beat the egg yolks slightly, add the sugar, and stir into the hot, thickened mixture. Cook 5 to 10 minutes longer stirring occasionally. Remove from the heat.

2 teaspoons salt
2 tablespoons vanilla

4. Add the salt and vanilla and cool slightly before filling baked shells. Use about 1 quart of filling for each shell. Cover the pie with meringue and brown it at 425° F. for 5 minutes or at 375° F. for from 12 to 15 minutes. Whipped cream may be used instead of meringue with shredded chocolate sprinkled over the top.

Variations

Charleston: Add 1 quart of chopped nuts to the filling.

Chocolate banana: Use 1 cup of sliced bananas for each pie. Spread a layer of the filling over the bottom of the pie, cover with the sliced bananas and then add the remainder of the filling.

CHOCOLATE CHIFFON PIE

Yield: 8 8-inch pies *or* 6 10-inch pies   Size of serving: ¹/₆ or ⅛ of a pie

4½ tablespoons (1½ ounces) gelatin, granulated
1½ cups cold water

1. Soak the gelatin in the cold water; place over hot water to dissolve.

2 cups (about 24) egg yolks, beaten
3 cups sugar
1½ teaspoons salt

2. Combine the beaten egg yolks, sugar, and salt and cook in the top of a double boiler until thickened, stirring frequently. Remove the mixture from the heat, add the dissolved gelatin and stir well.

190

3 cups boiling water
2¼ cups cocoa *or* 12 1-ounce squares chocolate
2½ tablespoons vanilla
3 cups (about 24) egg whites
3 cups sugar

3. Mix the cocoa or chocolate and the boiling water until smooth; add the vanilla. Add this to the custard mixture and chill until it begins to set.

4. Beat the egg whites until stiff but not dry; fold in the sugar. Fold beaten whites into the chocolate mixture. Pour the mixture into baked shells and chill.

1½ quarts cream, heavy
⅓ to ½ cup sugar, confectioners'
1½ teaspoons vanilla

5. Whip the cream, add the sugar and vanilla, and spread over the top of the filling. A pastry tube may be used to pipe the edge with some of the whipped cream. Additional chocolate may be grated over the top of the cream to garnish.

CREAM PIE

Yield: 8 8-inch pies *or* 6 10-inch pies   Size of serving: ¹/₆ or ⅛ of a pie

4½ quarts milk

1. Heat the milk in the top of a double boiler.

4 cups sugar
12 ounces (3 cups) flour
1 cup cornstarch

2. Mix the sugar, flour, and cornstarch. Add 1 quart of the warm milk and stir with a wire whip until perfectly smooth. Add mixture to the remaining hot milk and cook over hot water until thickened, stirring frequently but gently with a wire whip. Cover the mixture and cook for about 15 minutes or until it no longer tastes of raw starch.

1⅓ cups (about 16) egg yolks, beaten
2 cups sugar

3. Combine the egg yolks and sugar; stir into the hot mixture. Cook the mixture for from 5 to 10 minutes, stirring only occasionally. Remove it from the heat.

2 teaspoons salt
¼ cup vanilla
½ cup butter *or* fortified margarine*

4. Add the salt, vanilla, and butter. Cool slightly and pour the filling into baked shells, using 1 quart of filling for each 10-inch pie and ¾ quart for each 8-inch pie. Cover the pie with a meringue and brown it at 425° F. for about 5 minutes or at 375° F. for from 12 to 15 minutes. Whipped cream may be used instead of meringue. In this case the filling must be cold before it is covered with whipped cream.

*The amount of butter or fortified margarine may be increased to 1 cup to give a richer filling.

Variations

DIRECTIONS: Place 1½ cups of the cold filling in each pie shell. Add 1 cup of the drained fruit. Then add 1½ cups more of the cold filling. Yield: 8 10-inch pies

Apricot cream: Add 2 quarts canned drained apricots
Banana cream: Add 2 quarts sliced bananas
Date cream: Add 2 quarts diced, pitted dates

Orange cream: Add 2 quarts diced, drained oranges
Peach cream: Add 2 quarts diced, drained peaches
Pineapple cream: Add 2 quarts crushed or diced drained pineapple
Prune cream: Add 2 quarts cut-up, drained prunes
Raspberry cream: Add 2 quarts whole fresh berries
Strawberry cream: Add 2 quarts sliced fresh berries

DIRECTIONS: Mix the following ingredients into the cold filling. Place 1 quart of filling in each 10-inch pie shell.

Chocolate cream: Add 10 1-ounce squares of bitter chocolate and omit the butter
Chocolate bit cream: Add 1 quart semi-sweet chocolate bits
Coconut cream: Add 1 quart finely shredded coconut
Grapenut cream: Add 1 quart grapenuts
Macaroon cream: Add 1 quart macaroon crunch or coarse macaroon crumbs
Nut cream: Add 1 quart coarsely chopped nuts

CUSTARD PIE

Yield: 8 8-inch pies; 6 10-inch pies   Size of serving: $1/6$ or $1/8$ of a pie

32 (6¼ cups) eggs, beaten
5¼ quarts milk*
3¼ cups sugar
1½ teaspoons salt
1½ teaspoons nutmeg
3 tablespoons vanilla

1. Combine all the ingredients. Fill the crusts about two-thirds full and put the pies into the oven; finish filling the crusts and sprinkle the mixture with nutmeg. Bake at 450° F. for 15 minutes to set the crust. Reduce the temperature to 350° F. and bake until the custard is set. The blade of a knife, inserted in the center, will come out clean when the custard is done.

*Two cups of top milk or light cream may be substituted for an equal amount of the milk to give a richer and smoother custard.

Variations

Caramel custard: Caramelize one-half of the sugar. Add ¾ cup of hot water carefully. Add this to the custard mixture.

Coconut custard: Place ¼ cup of chopped shredded coconut in each crust before pouring in the custard mixture.

Macaroon custard: Put ¼ cup of macaroon crunch in each crust before pouring in the custard mixture.

DEEP-DISH FRUIT PIE

Yield: 50 servings   Size of serving: 1 square

Prepare the fruit filling as for berry, cherry, or peach pies.

Butter pudding pans or individual casseroles and put in the fruit to the desired depth.

Roll the crust ¼ inch thick and somewhat larger than the pan or casserole; arrange the crust loosely over the filling. Cut a few holes in the crust to allow steam to escape.

Bake the pie at 375° to 400° F.

Serve with whipped cream or hard sauce.

CANNED FRUIT PIE

Yield: 8 8-inch pies *or* 6 10-inch pies   Size of serving: $^1/_6$ or $^1/_8$ of a pie

4 quarts (1½ cans, No. 10) fruit*
7½ cups juice, heated

1. Drain the juice from the fruit. To the juice add enough water to make 7½ cups of liquid.

6 cups sugar
1 cup cornstarch

2. Mix the sugar and cornstarch; add this to the boiling juice slowly and cook until thickened, stirring constantly with a wire whip. Remove the mixture from the heat.

¼ teaspoon salt
3 tablespoons butter *or* fortified margarine
⅓ cup lemon juice

3. Add the salt, butter, and lemon juice, and then the fruit carefully; cool. Pour about 1 quart of the mixture into each 10-inch crust; add the top crusts. Bake the pies at 425° F. for from 30 to 40 minutes.

*Water pack (no sugar added).

NOTE: Black raspberries, red raspberries, blueberries, loganberries, cherries may be used for this pie.

LEMON CHIFFON PIE

Yield: 8 8-inch pies *or* 6 10-inch pies   Size of serving: $^1/_6$ or $^1/_8$ of a pie

4½ tablespoons (1½ ounces) gelatin, granulated
1½ cups cold water

1. Soak the gelatin in the cold water; place over hot water to dissolve.

24 (2 cups) egg yolks, beaten
3 cups sugar
¾ tablespoon salt

2. Cook the eggs, sugar, and salt in the top of a double boiler until thickened; remove the mixture from the heat; add the soaked gelatin and stir well.

3 cups lemon juice (about 12 lemons)
2½ tablespoons lemon rind, grated

3. Add the lemon juice and rind to the mixture and chill until the mixture begins to set.

24 (3 cups) egg whites
3 cups sugar

4. Beat the egg whites until stiff; add the sugar and continue beating until it is dissolved. Fold egg whites into the gelatin mixture carefully. Place 5 cups of the mixture into each 10-inch baked shell and chill.

1½ quarts cream, heavy
1½ cups confectioners' sugar
1½ teaspoons vanilla

5. Whip the cream; add the sugar and vanilla. Spread cream over the top of the filling. A pastry tube may be used to pipe the edge with some of the whipped cream.

Variation

Orange chiffon: In place of the lemon juice and rind use 3 cups orange juice, 2½ tablespoons orange rind, and ⅓ cup lemon juice.

193

LEMON PIE

Yield: 8 8-inch pies *or* 6 10-inch pies   Size of serving: $^1/_6$ or $^1/_8$ of a pie

4 quarts water	1. Heat the water to boiling.
7 cups sugar	2. Mix the sugar and cornstarch. Add 1 quart
2½ cups cornstarch	of the hot water and stir with a wire whip until perfectly smooth. Add mixture to the remaining hot water and cook until thickened, stirring constantly with a wire whip.
18 egg yolks (1½ cups), beaten	3. Combine the egg yolks and sugar; add to the
1½ cups sugar	hot mixture and stir until the eggs are well mixed. Cook the mixture for 5 minutes, stirring only occasionally. Remove from the heat.
2 tablespoons salt	4. Add the salt, butter, lemon rind, and juice.
½ cup butter *or* fortified margarine	Cool slightly. Place 1 quart of filling in each 10-inch baked shell. Spread meringue over the top
⅓ to ½ cup lemon rind (from 16 lemons)	and brown it at 425° F. for about 5 minutes.
1¾ cups lemon juice	

PRUNE-WHIP PIE

Yield: 8 8-inch pies *or* 6 10-inch pies   Size of serving: $^1/_6$ or $^1/_8$ of a pie

4½ tablespoons (1½ ounces) gelatin, granulated	1. Soak the gelatin in the cold water.
1½ cups cold water	
4½ cups prune pulp, strained	2. Combine the prune pulp, prune juice, sugar,
4½ cups prune juice	lemon juice, lemon rind, and salt; cook the mix-
1½ cups sugar	ture for about 2 minutes. Remove from the heat
6 tablespoons lemon juice	and add the soaked gelatin; stir unil the gelatin
2 tablespoons lemon rind	is dissolved. Chill until the mixture begins to
1½ teaspoons salt	congeal.
12 (1½ cups) egg whites	3. Beat the egg whites until stiff; add the sugar
1½ cups sugar	and continue beating until it is dissolved. Fold beaten egg whites into the prune mixture carefully. Place 5 cups of the mixture into each 10-inch baked shell; chill.
1½ quarts cream, heavy	4. Whip the cream and add the sugar. Spread
1½ cups confectioners' sugar	cream over the top of the filling. A pastry tube
1½ teaspoons vanilla	may be used to pipe the edge with some of the whipped cream.

NOTE: ¾ cup of orange marmalade may be whipped into the mixture before putting it in the shells.

PUMPKIN CHIFFON PIE

Yield: 8 8-inch pies *or* 6 10-inch pies   Size of serving: $^1/_6$ or $^1/_8$ of a pie

4½ tablespoons (1½ ounces) gelatin, granulated	1. Soak the gelatin in the cold water; heat over hot water until gelatin is dissolved.

194

1½ cups cold water

5 cups (2 pounds, 4 ounces) sugar, brown, packed

18 (1½ cups) egg yolks, slightly beaten

2 quarts (2 cans, No. 3, or 18 pounds fresh) pumpkin

4 tablespoons cinnamon

1 tablespoon ginger

1½ teaspoons allspice

1 tablespoon salt

2. Cook the sugar, egg yolks, pumpkin, and spices in the top of a double boiler until slightly thickened. Remove from the heat, add the dissolved gelatin and stir well. Chill until the mixture begins to set.

18 (2¼ cups) egg whites

3 cups sugar

3. Beat the egg whites until stiff; add the sugar and continue beating until the sugar is dissolved. Fold into the pumpkin mixture carefully. Place 5 cups of the mixture into each baked shell; chill.

1½ quarts cream, heavy

1½ cups sugar, confectioners'

1½ teaspoons vanilla

4. Whip the cream and add the sugar. Spread over the top of the filling. A pastry tube may be used to pipe the edge with some of the whipped cream.

Variations

In place of regular pastry, use gingersnap crusts (page 185).

One cup of molasses may be used to sweeten the whipped cream, in place of the sugar and vanilla.

Finely chopped crystallized ginger may be added to the whipped cream.

PUMPKIN *OR* SQUASH PIE

Yield: 8 8-inch pies *or* 6 10-inch pies   Size of serving: $^1/_6$ or $^1/_8$ of a pie

5½ cups sugar

1 teaspoon ginger

2¼ teaspoons cinnamon

½ teaspoon cloves

1 teaspoon nutmeg

1 teaspoon allspice

1 cup flour

2½ teaspoons salt

1. Mix the sugar, spices, flour, and salt.

3 cups (about 15) eggs, beaten

2½ quarts (3 cans, No. 2½, or 20 pounds fresh) pumpkin *or* squash

3½ quarts top milk, heated

2. Add the eggs, pumpkin and milk. Use 5 cups of the mixture in each 10-inch unbaked crust. Partially fill the crusts, place them in the oven, and then add the remaining filling. Bake them at 400° F. for from 45 to 60 minutes. The pie is done when a knife blade inserted in the center comes out clean.

195

RAISIN STREUSEL PIE

Yield: 8 8-inch pies *or* 6 10-inch pies   Size of serving: $^1/_6$ or $^1/_8$ of a pie

Filling:

4 pounds raisins

4 quarts water

1. Bring the raisins and water to boiling.

4 ounces (¾ cup) cornstarch

1½ cups water

2. Mix the cornstarch and water; add this mixture to the boiling raisins and cook until thickened and clear, stirring constantly.

1 tablespoon salt

2 cups sugar

1 lemon, ground

3. Add the salt, sugar, and ground lemon. Pour 1 quart of the mixture into each 10-inch unbaked crust.

Streusel topping:

3 cups flour

2½ cups sugar

6 tablespoons dry milk

¾ teaspoon salt

1 cup chopped pecans

8 ounces (1 cup) butter *or* fortified margarine

4. For the topping, mix together the flour, sugar, dry milk, and salt. Rub in the shortening; add the nuts. Sprinkle the mixture over the raisin filling. Bake the pies at 425° F. for from 30 to 40 minutes or until crust is baked and top is browned.

SOUR-CREAM—RAISIN PIE

Yield: 8 8-inch pies *or* 6 10-inch pies   Size of serving: $^1/_6$ or $^1/_8$ of a pie

3½ quarts sour cream (light or 20 per cent)

3¼ quarts (4 pounds, 8 ounces) raisins

8 cups (3 pounds, 8 ounces) sugar, brown, packed

2 teaspoons salt

14 eggs, beaten

¾ cup cornstarch

1½ teaspoons nutmeg

1½ teaspoons cinnamon

¾ teaspoon cloves

6 tablespoons lemon juice

1. Mix all the ingredients. Cook them over hot water until they are of a custard-like consistency. Cool. Place 1 quart of filling in each 10-inch unbaked crust. Place the top crust. Bake the pies at 375° F. for from 30 to 40 minutes until crust is browned.

OTHER DESSERTS

The dessert gives the finishing touch to the meal and, for many people, it determines whether or not that meal has been completely satisfying. Simple puddings, well prepared and attractively served, afford a pleasant change from ice cream, pie, and cake, (figure 34).

The sugar content in many of the desserts may be reduced one-fourth; honey or corn sirup may be substituted for all or part of the sugar.

FIGURE 34.   ATTRACTIVE CREAM DESSERTS

Different shapes of serving dishes and varied and colorful garnishes for cream desserts

CORNSTARCH PUDDINGS

Creamy puddings thickened with a starchy ingredient (cornstarch, flour, tapioca, or arrowroot) are similar to cream pie fillings, and the same directions and precautions apply (see page 186). If the liquid used is fruit juice or water, it may be brought to the boiling point over direct heat. Cooking may continue over direct heat if the product is stirred frequently to prevent sticking. Use of a double boiler or hot water bath, however, is safer.

Thickened puddings are better liked if they are creamy and just thick enough to remain piled up in a dish instead of flattening. Molded puddings are more acceptable when made from a recipe that includes some gelatin. There are countless variations. A few are given on the following pages.

VANILLA CREAM PUDDING

Yield: 50 servings
Size of serving: ½ cup

4½ quarts milk

1. Heat the milk in a double boiler.

1 cup (4 ounces) flour*
1¼ cups (7 ounces) cornstarch
2 cups sugar
2 cups cold milk

2. Mix the flour, cornstarch, and sugar; add the cold milk and stir the mixture with a wire whip until perfectly smooth. Add mixture to the hot milk and cook until thickened, stirring constantly with a wire whip. Cover and cook the mixture over hot water for 15 minutes.

20 (1⅔ cups) egg yolks, beaten
or
10 whole eggs
1¼ cups sugar

3. Combine the eggs and sugar; add them to the hot mixture and stir it until the eggs are well mixed. Cook the mixture for from 5 to 10 minutes, stirring only occasionally. Remove the mixture from the heat.

2¼ teaspoons salt
4 tablespoons vanilla
1¼ cups butter or fortified margarine, melted

4. Add the salt, vanilla, and melted butter. Stir the mixture only occasionally while it is cooling.

*In place of the flour and cornstarch, all cornstarch (1¾ cups) may be used.

Variations

Banana: Fold in carefully 12 to 15 sliced bananas.
Cherry: Omit vanilla. Add 2 cups chopped cherries, 2 tablespoons lemon juice, and 1 tablespoon almond extract.
Chocolate: Use 1½ cups of cocoa, combining it with the dry ingredients.
Coconut: Add from 2 to 2½ cups of moist coconut.
Date-nut: Add 3½ cups each of chopped dates and coarsely chopped nuts.
Marshmallow: Fold in 2 cups of cut-up marshmallows.
Orange cream: Add 5 tablespoons of grated orange rind; garnish the top of each serving with a section of orange.
Peanut brittle: Fold in 2 pounds of crushed peanut brittle.
Peppermint stick: Fold in 1 pound crushed peppermint sticks.
Fruit garnishes: Orange sections, banana slices, canned drained fruit, cut-up dried fruit, maraschino cherries.
Sauces: Fruit salad; chocolate, butterscotch, with nuts.

CUSTARDS, BAKED AND SOFT

Custards cooked just below the boiling point are less likely to curdle and become watery than if cooked at a higher temperature; therefore, it is advisable to bake them in a pan of hot water and to cook soft custards and custard sauce over hot water held just below the boiling point throughout the cooking. Baked custards are "done" when a knife blade inserted at the center comes out clean, and soft custards, when a thick layer clings to the spoon. Heating the milk before combining it with the other ingredients shortens the cooking time. Puddings with a custard base, such as bread or cake puddings, or rice combined with milk and eggs, should be cooked in the same way.

BAKED CUSTARD

Yield: 50 servings

Size of serving: ½ cup

6 quarts whole milk
3 cups sugar
2 teaspoons salt
2 tablespoons vanilla
24 eggs (5 cups), beaten
1 teaspoon nutmeg

1. Heat the milk.

2. Add the sugar, salt, vanilla, and eggs to the milk. Pour the mixture into greased baking pans or custard cups; sprinkle with nutmeg. Set these into pans of hot water. Bake the custards at 400° F. for from 20 to 25 minutes. Test for doneness by inserting a knife blade into the center of the custard; it will come out clean when the custard is done.

Variations

Caramel: Reduce the amount of milk to 5½ quarts. Caramelize 2 cups of the sugar, add 2 cups of boiling water to it, and add this to the scalded milk. Omit the nutmeg.
Chocolate: Add 12 1-ounce squares of melted chocolate to the scalded milk. Omit nutmeg.
Coconut: Add 1 quart of shredded coconut.
Grapenut: Add 1 cup of grapenuts.
Honey: Reduce the sugar to 1½ cups. Add ¾ pound of honey.
Maple: Omit the sugar. Use 2 cups of maple sirup and 2 tablespoons of maple flavoring.
Orange: Use orange extract in place of the vanilla. Add two orange sections to each cup of custard before baking.
Rice: Add 1 quart of cooked rice and grated rind of 4 lemons.

PUMPKIN CUSTARD

Yield: 50 servings

Size of serving: ½ cup

4 quarts top milk, scalded
20 eggs (4 cups), beaten
5 cups sugar
1 tablespoon ginger
4 tablespoons cinnamon
½ cup cornstarch
2 tablespoons salt

1. Mix the sugar, ginger, cinnamon, cornstarch, and salt; add to the pumpkin; then add the beaten eggs. Add this mixture to the hot milk and proceed as for baked custard.

199

2 quarts (2 cans, No. 3) pumpkin

2. Serve with whipped cream or soft custard sauce.

SOFT CUSTARD

Yield: From 16 to 20 servings as a dessert; 50 servings as a sauce (2 quarts)

Size of serving: ½ cup for dessert; 2 tablespoons for sauce

8 cups milk

1. Heat the milk.

½ cup (¼ cup for sauce) corn-starch
½ cup sugar

2. Combine the cornstarch and sugar; add 1 cup of the hot milk and stir with a wire whip until perfectly smooth. Add mixture to the hot milk and cook until thickened, stirring constantly with a wire whip. Cover the mixture and cook it over hot water for about 15 minutes.

8 egg yolks, (⅔ cup), beaten
½ cup sugar

3. Combine the egg yolks and sugar; add them to the hot mixture and stir until the eggs are well mixed. Cook the mixture for from 5 to 10 minutes, stirring only occasionally.

¼ teaspoon salt
1 tablespoon vanilla

4. Add the salt and the vanilla to the mixture; stir the mixture occasionally while cooling.

FRUIT MERINGUE

Yield: 50 servings

3½ quarts fruit,* cooked, drained and sweetened
5 quarts custard sauce, soft

1. Fill the custard cups or baking pans about one-third full with the fruit. Cover this with custard sauce.

12 (1½ cups) egg whites†
1 teaspoon salt
1½ cups sugar

2. Add the salt to the egg whites and beat them until stiff but still shiny. Add the sugar gradually and continue the beating until the mixture piles up. Cover the pudding. Bake it at 425° F. until brown. Serve the pudding cold.

*Prunes, apricots, peaches, berries, applesauce and others.
†More egg whites may be needed for the meringue if individual cups are used.

BAKED CAKE-FRUIT PUDDING

Yield: 50 servings

4 quarts cake, cut into cubes
2 quarts custard sauce, soft
2 quarts fruit (sliced bananas, crushed or cubed pineapple, sliced peaches)

1. Arrange the cake, custard sauce, and fruit in layers in baking pans.

12 (1½ cups) egg whites
1 teaspoon salt
1½ cups sugar

2. Make the meringue according to the above directions.

GELATIN DESSERTS

To shorten the time required for gelatin to set, add only enough hot liquid to dissolve it. The remaining liquid should be cold or iced.

Prepared gelatin, flavored and sweetened, is somewhat more expensive than are the gelatin products made with granulated gelatin and fruit juices, especially if juices left from canned fruits can be used. If some tart juices, such as lemon and orange are added, the dessert will be well flavored.

The proportion of gelatin to liquid varies. If the dish can chill for several hours, less gelatin will be required for the same amount of liquid; but gelatin becomes rubbery on standing and may be too stiff if left overnight. The gelatin dish made with acid liquids, such as lemon juice or a salad with part vinegar, needs somewhat more gelatin for the same amount of liquid than is required if all the liquid is bland. In warm weather, a slightly higher proportion of gelatin is required.

Making Gelatin Dishes

Prepared (flavored) Just enough hot liquid to dissolve the gelatin is used, then the remainder of the liquid is added cold.

Granulated (unflavored) The gelatin is soaked in a small amount of cold water, then dissolved in a small amount of hot liquid and the remaining cold liquid is added. Granulated gelatin, used as a stiffening agent in puddings such as bavarians, whips, and the like, may be incorporated in puddings by first soaking it in cold water and then placing it over boiling water long enough to dissolve the gelatin. This solution is then added to the mixture to be stiffened.

FRUITED GELATIN

Yield: 50 servings   Size of serving: ½ cup

For a base made with flavored gelatin

26 ounces (3¾ cups) prepared gelatin powder 1 gallon water and/or fruit juice 3 quarts fruit, cut and drained	1. Heat part of the liquid; add to the gelatin and stir until it is dissolved. Add the remaining cold liquid; chill. When the mixture begins to set, add the fruit. Chill the mixture.

For a base made with unflavored (granulated) gelatin

3 ounces (½ cup plus 1 tablespoon) gelatin, granulated 2 cups cold water 3½ quarts fruit juice 2½ cups sugar* 1 cup lemon juice 3 quarts fruit, cut and drained	1. Soak the gelatin in the cold water; heat 2 quarts of the fruit juice to the boiling point; add it and the sugar to the soaked gelatin and stir until all are dissolved. Add the remaining juice, cold, and the lemon juice; chill. When the mixture begins to set, add the fruit. Chill the mixture.

*Vary the amount of sugar according to the sweetness of the fruit juices used.

Variations

There are many combinations of fruits; some are:

Apricot halves or sliced bananas and pineapple cubes.
Chopped figs, dates or prunes, marshmallows and nuts.
Cut marshmallows.
Frozen strawberries or raspberries, drained.
Grapefruit sections and crushed pineapple.
Orange sections and coconut.

FRUIT AND RICE BAVARIAN

Yield: 50 servings | Size of serving: ½ cup

1½ cups (11 ounces) rice

1. Cook the rice in 3 quarts of boiling water with 1 tablespoon of salt; drain rice in a colander and rinse with cold water; chill.

5 tablespoons (1½ ounces) gelatin, granulated
½ cup cold water
5 cups pineapple juice, boiling
¾ cup sugar

2. Soak the gelatin in cold water; add the hot pineapple juice and the sugar and stir until all are dissolved; chill.

2½ cups pineapple, crushed, drained
2½ cups dates, chopped
2½ cups nuts, coarsely chopped

3. When the gelatin begins to set, add the pineapple, dates, nuts, and rice.

2 quarts cream, heavy, or evaporated milk
2½ tablespoons vanilla

4. Whip the cream or evaporated milk and add the vanilla; fold into the gelatin mixture; turn it into individual molds or flat pans. Chill.

JELLIED PRUNES*

Yield: 50 servings | Size of serving: ½ cup

6 cups prunes, cooked, pitted and drained

1. Prepare the prunes.

¾ cup plus 2 tablespoons (4½ ounces) gelatin, granulated
2 quarts pineapple juice, cold
4 quarts prune juice
2 cups sugar
¼ teaspoon salt
2 cups lemon juice (about 8 lemons)

2. Soak the gelatin in the cold pineapple juice. Heat half of the prune juice to the boiling point; add heated juice, the sugar, and the salt to the gelatin, and stir until all are dissolved. Add the remaining cold prune juice and the lemon juice; pour the mixture into molds or flat pans and let it chill.

1 cup nuts, coarsely chopped

3. When the mixture begins to set, add the prunes and sprinkle the nuts over the top.

2 quarts soft custard sauce

4. Serve the mixture with the sauce.

*This may be used for a salad.

Variation

Fig and date gelatin: In place of the prunes, use 3 cups of dates cut up and 3 cups of figs cut up.

PRUNE APPLE MOLD

Yield: 50 servings

Size of serving: ½ cup

¾ cup (4 ounces) gelatin, granulated
3 cups cold water
1½ quarts prune juice, heated

1. Soak the gelatin in the cold water; add the hot prune juice and stir until the gelatin is dissolved. Let the mixture cool.

4 quarts applesauce, sweetened
4 tablespoons grated lemon rind (about 12 lemons)
1 cup lemon juice (about 4 lemons)
4 cups sugar
¼ teaspoon cinnamon

2. Add the applesauce, lemon juice, grated lemon rind, sugar, and cinnamon. Mold the mixture in individual cups or in flat pans. Serve with sweetened whipped cream.

SPANISH CREAM* WITH MACAROONS OR GRAHAM CRACKERS

Yield: 50 servings

Size of serving: ½ cup

7 tablespoons (2½ ounces) gelatin, granulated
2 cups cold milk

1. Soak the gelatin in the cold milk.

3½ quarts milk
16 (1¼ cups) egg yolks, beaten
2 cups sugar
1¼ teaspoons salt
4 teaspoons vanilla

2. Heat the milk in the top of a double boiler. Mix the egg yolks, sugar, and salt together; add them to the hot milk and cook until thickened (for 3 or 4 minutes), stirring constantly with a wire whip. Remove the custard mixture from the heat and add the soaked gelatin and vanilla. Stir until the gelatin is dissolved. Cool.

16 (2 cups) egg whites, stiffly beaten
⅔ cups sugar
3 cups (7 to 9 ounces) macaroon or graham cracker crumbs

3. Fold the sugar into the beaten egg whites, and fold this mixture into the custard carefully; then fold in the crumbs and let custard chill. Garnish it with sweetened whipped cream and sprinkle crumbs over the top.

*For plain Spanish cream, omit the cracker crumbs.

VELVET CREAM

Yield: 50 servings

Size of serving: ½ cup

7½ tablespoons (2½ ounces) gelatin
2 cups cold water

1. Soak the gelatin for 5 minutes in the cold water.

2 quarts milk
3 cups sugar
1¼ teaspoons salt

2. Heat the milk in a double boiler. Add the soaked gelatin, sugar, and salt to the hot milk and stir until dissolved. Cool.

2 quarts cream, heavy
1½ tablespoons vanilla

3. Whip the cream and add the vanilla. When the mixture begins to thicken, fold in the whipped cream and vanilla. Place the mixture in custard cups or flat pans and chill. Remove

the mixture from the molds or cut it into squares.

Garnish with:

Fresh *or* canned fruit, chocolate *or* butterscotch sauce

OTHER DESSERT RECIPES

APPLE CRISP

Yield from 55 to 60 servings

Size of serving: from ½ to ⅔ cup

10 quarts apples, sliced

3 tablespoons cinnamon

5 cups water *or* fruit juice

1½ quarts sugar, granulated *or* brown

5 cups flour, all-purpose

2¼ cups butter *or* fortified margarine

1. Divide the apples into buttered baking pans.

2. Mix the cinnamon and water and pour the mixture over the apples.

3. Work the sugar, flour, and butter with the finger tips until crumbly; then sprinkle the mixture over the apples. Bake the mixture at 450° F. for 5 minutes; then lower the temperature to 400° F. and bake for from 25 to 35 minutes or until the apples are tender. Serve warm with top milk or sweetened whipped cream. Nutmeg may be added to the cream if desired.

APPLE REFRIGERATOR PUDDING

Yield: 50 servings

Size of serving: 2½-inch squares

5 quarts applesauce (16 pounds fresh apples)

9 cups (4 pounds) sugar, brown packed

4½ quarts (4 pounds) graham-cracker crumbs

1¾ cups butter *or* fortified margarine, melted

1. Make a thick sauce of the apples and sugar.

2. Mix the crumbs with the melted butter.

3. Using flat pans, place first a layer of the crumb mixture, then one of applesauce; continue the alternate layers, topping with the crumbs. Let stand in a refrigerator for several hours. Cut in servings; serve with sweetened whipped cream.

APPLE GOODIE

Yield: 60 servings

Size of serving: 1 2½-inch square (1 inch thick)

2 quarts sugar

½ cup flour

¾ teaspoon salt

4½ teaspoons cinnamon

9 quarts apples, chopped

1½ quarts dry oatmeal

1. Mix the sugar, flour, salt, and cinnamon; add this to the apples and mix together. Put the mixture into greased baking pans.

2. Mix the oatmeal, sugar, flour, baking powder,

1½ quarts (2½ pounds) sugar, brown, packed
1½ quarts (1½ pounds) flour, all-purpose
1½ teaspoons baking powder
1½ teaspoon soda
3½ cups butter *or* fortified margarine

and soda; add the butter and work it with the finger tips until the mixture is crumbly. Place the mixture over the top of the apples and pat it firmly. Bake at 350° F. until a crust is formed and the apples are tender. Serve hot or cold with top milk or whipped cream.

BAKED APPLES

See recipe, page 181.

APRICOT WHIP

See variation of prune whip, page 211.

BAKED FRUIT PUDDING

Yield: 50 servings

Size serving: ½ cup and ¼ cup sauce

2½ pounds leftover cake
6 pounds leftover fruit pies

1. Break the leftover cakes and pies into large pieces and place them in greased baking pans.

2½ quarts apples, thinly sliced
2½ cups prunes, cooked, pitted
1 cup raisins

2. Cover with the apples, prunes and raisins.

3 cups (1½ pounds) sugar, brown
1 quart fruit juice
1½ teaspoons cinnamon
1 cup butter *or* fortified margarine

3. Make a sirup of the sugar and fruit juices; add the cinnamon and butter. Pour sirup over the fruit. Bake at 350° F. for 1 hour.

Serve with:
2 quarts custard *or* lemon sauce

CHOCOLATE PUDDING

Yield: 50 servings

Size of serving: ½ cup

3½ quarts milk

1. Heat the milk in a double boiler.

3½ cups sugar
1⅓ cups (7½ ounces) cornstarch
1½ cups (6¼ ounces) cocoa
1½ quarts cold milk

2. Blend together the sugar, cornstarch, cocoa, and 1½ quarts cold milk. Add this mixture to the hot milk and cook until thickened stirring with a wire whip.

½ teaspoon salt
2½ tablespoons vanilla

3. Remove from the heat, add the salt and vanilla.

Variations

Chocolate-coconut: Add 2 to 2½ cups moist coconut.
Chocolate-marshmallow: Add 2 cups of marshmallows cut in quarters.
Chocolate-nut: Add 3 cups of coarsely chopped nuts.
Chocolate-mint: Add 1 pound of crushed peppermint sticks.

CHOCOLATE FUDGE PUDDING*

Yield: 50 servings

Size of serving: scant ½ cup

1¼ cups butter *or* fortified margarine

4 cups sugar

3 tablespoons vanilla

3 1-ounce squares chocolate, melted

1. Cream the butter and sugar together; add the vanilla and melted chocolate and continue to mix.

5 cups (1¼ pounds) flour

3 tablespoons plus 1 teaspoon baking powder

2 teaspoons salt

2½ cups milk

2. Sift the dry ingredients together; add all of them at one time to the first mixture, then add all the milk; stir them until well blended.

3 cups (12 ounces) walnuts, coarsely chopped

3. Fold in the nuts; pour the batter into baking pans.

Topping

4½ cups (2 pounds) sugar, brown, packed

5 cups sugar, granulated

¾ cup (3 ounces) cocoa

2 teaspoons salt

1. Mix the sugar, cocoa, and salt together. Sprinkle the mixture over the batter.

2½ quarts boiling water

2. Pour the boiling water over the mixture; *do not stir.* Bake it at 350° F. for about 1 hour. This will separate into two layers with the crust on top and the fudge on the bottom. Serve crust-side-down with the fudge sauce on top. Serve with sweetened whipped cream.

*Recipe from *Quantity Recipe File* by Lenore M. Sullivan. Collegiate Press Inc., Ames, Iowa. 1938.

FRUIT BROWN BETTY

Yield: 50 servings

Size of serving: ½ cup

10 pounds prepared fruit*

2 quarts crumbs

1. Prepare the fruit and the crumbs.

1 teaspoon cinnamon

½ teaspoon nutmeg

1½ pounds (3½ cups) sugar, brown

2 quarts fruit juice and/or water

¼ cup lemon juice

2. Combine the spices, sugar, fruit juice, and lemon juice. Arrange the crumbs and sliced fruit in layers in greased baking pans. Begin and end with crumbs. Over each layer pour some of the above mixture.

½ cup butter *or* fortified margarine

3. Place dots of butter over the top layer. Bake at 350° F. for one hour. Add more water or fruit juice if mixture seems too dry.

Garnish with:

Whipped cream *or* lemon *or* other fruit sauce *or* hard sauce

*Fresh, canned, frozen, or dried (stewed) apples, peaches, apricots, or plums may be used.

FRUIT COBBLERS

(canned and frozen fruit)

Yield: 60 servings Size of serving: 1 2½-inch square

Using canned fruit:

4 quarts fruit* canned (about 1⅓ cans, No. 10)
2 quarts fruit juice and water

1. Drain the fruit. Add enough water to the juice to make 2 quarts.

1¼ cups cornstarch
5 cups sugar†

2. Mix the cornstarch and sugar; add to the boiling juice and cook until thickened stirring constantly with a wire whip.

½ cup butter *or* fortified margarine
½ cup lemon juice
1 teaspoon salt

3. Add the butter, lemon juice, and salt, then the drained fruit. Divide the mixture into baking pans.

Crust

2 pounds (2 quarts) flour, all-purpose

1. Sift the dry ingredients together.

1¼ ounces (3 tablespoons) baking powder
1 tablespoon salt
8½ ounces (1⅓ cups) vegetable fat
2 to 3 cups milk

2. Rub the fat into the dry ingredients; add the milk and mix until just combined. Turn onto a lightly floured board and knead until dough is smooth. Divide the dough in equal portions for the pans; roll out each portion to fit the pan, and place it over the fruit. Brush the top with milk; the top may be sprinkled with sugar if desired. Bake at 400° F. for about 30 minutes.

*Strawberries, blueberries, boysenberries, raspberries, blackberries, peaches, plums, cherries.
†For water-packed fruit. Decrease this amount of sugar for sirup-packed fruit.

Using frozen fruit:

10 pounds frozen fruit
2 quarts fruit juice and water

1. Thaw the frozen fruit overnight. Drain the fruit. Add enough water to the juice to make 2 quarts.

1¼ cups cornstarch
2½ cups sugar (vary the amount of sugar according to the sweetness of the fruit)
½ cup butter *or* fortified margarine
½ cup lemon juice
¼ teaspoon salt

2. Proceed as above.

FRUIT CUP

See recipe page 182.

GINGERBREAD

Yield: 2 large pans (18 x 12 x 2 inches); from 56 to 64 squares

Size of serving: 3 x 2½ inches

1 pound (2½ cups) vegetable fat

1. Cream the fat; add the sugar, creaming together until well blended. Add the molasses and

14 ounces (2 cups) sugar
1 quart molasses
8 eggs
2½ tablespoons soda
4 teaspoons cinnamon
2 teaspoons ginger
2 pounds, 5 ounces (10½ cups)
flour, all-purpose
1½ teaspoons salt
1 quart hot water

eggs and beat thoroughly.

2. Sift the dry ingredients together, add them to the mixture, and beat them until smooth.

3. Add the hot water last. Bake the mixture at 350° F. for about 40 minutes.

Variations

Apple:
6 quarts apples, thinly sliced

7½ cups sugar
2 teaspoons cinnamon
¾ cup flour
¼ cup butter *or* fortified margarine
½ cup lemon juice

1. Arrange the apples in the bottom of greased baking pans.

2. Mix the sugar, cinnamon, and flour together and sprinkle the mixture over the apples.

3. Dot the butter over the mixture and pour the lemon juice over this. Spread the batter over the fruit. Bake at 350° F. Turn gingerbread out of the pans upside-down and cut into squares. Serve while warm.

Pear: In place of the apples, use 4 quarts (2 cans, No. 10) of pear halves; reduce the sugar to 5⅓ cups.

Tutti-frutti: Add 2 pounds (5 cups) of chopped raisins; frost with tutti-frutti icing (recipe, page 170).

Whipped cream garnish: Whip 1 pint of heavy cream; fold in ½ cup of molasses.

GRAHAM-CRACKER—DATE ROLL

Yield: 50 servings   Size of serving: 1 slice
3 pounds (6 quarts) marshmallows, cut in quarters
3 pounds (7½ cups) dates, cut up
3 pounds (13½ cups) graham cracker crumbs
3 cups nuts, chopped
2¼ cups water

1. Mix and knead together the marshmallows, dates, cracker crumbs, nuts, and water. Pack the mixture in loaf pans. Place in the refrigerator for 24 hours; turn out of pans and slice. Serve with sweetened whipped cream.

GRAPENUT PUFF PUDDING

Yield: 50 servings   Size of serving: ½ cup
1¼ cups butter *or* fortified margarine
10½ cups sugar
20 (1⅔ cups) egg yolks

1. Cream the butter; add the sugar, gradually creaming them together until well blended. Add the egg yolks and beat the mixture thoroughly.

1¼ cups (5 ounces) flour, all-purpose
2 cups grapenuts
2 teaspoons salt
2½ cups lemon juice
Grated rind of 10 lemons
2½ quarts milk
20 (2½ cups) egg whites, stiffly beaten

2. Mix the flour, grapenuts, and salt; add them, the milk, lemon juice, and rind to the mixture; beat until smooth.

3. Fold in the egg whites. Pour the mixture into greased baking pans; set these into pans of hot water. Bake at 375° F. until set, about 50 minutes.

LEMON SPONGE

Yield: 50 to 60 servings

Size of serving: ½ cup

10 ounces (1¼ cups) butter *or* fortified margarine
2 pounds, 8 ounces (5⅓ cups) sugar

1. Blend the butter and sugar together.

10 ounces (2½ cups) flour, cake
3⅓ cups lemon juice
Grated rind of 3 lemons

2. Add the flour, lemon juice and rind, and blend well.

2½ cups (about 30) egg yolks
3½ quarts milk

3. Beat the egg yolks and milk together. Add this gradually to the above ingredients.

3¾ cups (about 30) egg whites
½ teaspoon salt

4. Add the salt to the egg whites and beat them until stiff. Fold these into the above mixture. Pour the mixture into custard cups. Place the cups in pans of hot water and bake at 350° F. until set. A knife blade inserted in the center will come out clean when the pudding is done. Each cup will contain lemon custard at the bottom and sponge cake on the top.

MAPLE-NUT MOLD

Yield: 50 servings

Size of serving: ½ cup

2 quarts (3½ pounds) sugar, brown, packed
2 cups cornstarch
2¼ quarts boiling water
2 teaspoons maple flavoring
½ teaspoon salt

1. Mix the sugar and cornstarch; add mixture to the boiling water and stir until perfectly smooth. Cook until thickened, stirring constantly with a wire whip. Cover and cook over hot water for 15 minutes. Add the flavoring and the salt.

16 (2 cups) egg whites, stiffly beaten

2. Add the hot mixture to the beaten egg whites, beating with a wire whip until well combined*; cool the mixture.

3 cups nuts, coarsely chopped

3. Fold in the nuts; pour the mixture in molds or pans to set.

Serve with:

Custard sauce *or* whipped cream

*An electric beater may be used.

NORWEGIAN PRUNE PUDDING

Yield: 50 servings

Size of serving: ½ to ⅔ cup

3 quarts prunes, cooked, pitted, chopped and drained (use 6 pounds dried prunes)

1. Prepare the prunes.

4 quarts prune juice

2. Heat the prune juice to the boiling point.

4½ cups sugar
1½ tablespoons cinnamon
2 cups cornstarch
¾ tablespoon salt

3. Mix the sugar, cinnamon, cornstarch, and salt; add this mixture to the boiling prune juice and cook it until thickened, stirring constantly with a wire whip. Cover the mixture and cook it over hot water for 15 minutes. Remove from the heat.

¾ cup lemon juice

4. Add the lemon juice and chopped prunes. Serve the pudding cold with top milk or sweetened whipped cream.

PINEAPPLE DELIGHT*

Yield: From 45 to 50 servings

Size of serving: ½ cup

5 cups cream, heavy
⅓ cup sugar, confectioner's
2 pounds (120) marshmallows, quartered
1 can, No. 10 (2½ quarts), pineapple tidbits, drained
2 cups nuts, coarsely chopped

1. Whip the cream and sweeten it; add the marshmallows, pineapple, and nuts, and combine them carefully.

*This is an emergency dessert which may be prepared quickly.

PINEAPPLE–GRAHAM-CRACKER REFRIGERATOR PUDDING

Yield: 50 servings

Size of serving: 1 2½-inch square

2½ cups butter *or* fortified margarine
7½ cups sugar
15 (3 cups) eggs, beaten
5 cups pineapple, crushed, drained
5 teaspoons vanilla

1. Cream the butter and the sugar together and add the eggs. Then add the pineapple and vanilla.

4 quarts (3½ pounds) graham-cracker crumbs
2½ cups nuts

2. Using loaf or flat pans arrange the ingredients in layers; spread the crumbs on the bottom of the pans; then spread the pineapple mixture over the crumbs. Cover the pineapple mixture with the nuts. Chill the mixture in a refrigerator and cut into squares. Garnish with sweetened whipped cream.

PRUNE WHIP*

Yield: From 20 to 25 servings

Size of serving: ½ cup

1 quart prunes, sieved *or* chopped

1. Add the lemon juice to the prunes.

210

¼ cup lemon juice
1 cup (8) egg whites
⅛ teaspoon salt
1 cup sugar

2. Add the salt to the egg whites and beat them until stiff; add the sugar and continue beating as for a meringue; add the prunes and continue beating until the mixture piles up.† Chill.

Serve with:

1 quart soft custard sauce

*Whips are made more easily in a mixing machine; larger quantities may be made at one time.
†Gelatin may be added. Soak 1 tablespoon of granulated gelatin in ¼ cup of cold water and dissolve it over hot water. Add the dissolved gelatin at the same time prunes are added.

Variation

Dried apricots may be substituted for all or part of the prunes.

RICE-APPLE PUDDING

Yield: 50 servings
Size of serving: ½ cup

3¼ cups (1½ pounds) rice

1. Cook the rice in 1½ gallons of boiling water with 3 tablespoons of salt; drain in a colander and rinse with cold water.

3 cups raisins
3 quarts apples, diced

2. Pour hot water over the raisins and let them stand; drain and add them and the apples to the rice.

3¾ cups sugar
5 teaspoons cinnamon
3 teaspoons salt

3. Mix the sugar, cinnamon, and salt; add to the rice mixture.

10 (⅞ cup) egg yolks, beaten
1¼ cups butter *or* fortified margarine, melted

4. Add the egg yolks and butter to the rice mixture.

10 (1¼ cups) egg whites, stiffly beaten

5. Fold in the egg whites. If the mixture is too dry, add about 1 pint of fruit juice. Pour the mixture into greased baking pans; bake in a moderate oven (375° F.) for about 40 minutes. Serve the pudding hot or cold with top milk or whipped cream.

CREAMY RICE PUDDING

Yield: 50 servings
Size of serving: ½ cup

4¼ cups (2 pounds) rice
8 quarts milk
4 cups sugar
4 teaspoons salt
4 cups raisins
½ cup butter *or* fortified margarine

1. Heat the milk in the top of a double boiler; wash the rice and add it to the milk. Cook the mixture in the double boiler for about 45 minutes until the rice swells; stir it occasionally. Pour the rice-milk mixture into baking pans; add the remaining ingredients. Bake the pudding at 350° F. for about 30 minutes.

SHORTCAKE*

Yield: From 55 to 60 biscuits
Size of serving: 1 biscuit and ⅓ cup sauce

3 pounds (3 quarts) flour, all-purpose

1. Mix and sift the dry ingredients together.

3¾ ounces (½ cup) sugar
3 ounces (½ cup) baking powder
1 tablespoon salt

1 pound (2¼ cups) vegetable fat

2. Rub in the fat.

2 eggs
3½ to 4 cups milk

3. Combine the eggs and milk, beating slightly; add this mixture to the dry ingredients, handling lightly. Knead the dough on a lightly floured board until the dough is smooth. Roll it to ¾ inch thickness and cut into 2½-inch rounds or 2½-inch squares. Bake at 425° F.

Butter
4 to 5 quarts fruit sauce†

4. Split the shortcake, spread it with butter, and put fruit sauce over each half just before serving.

*Shortcakes may be placed on the pans close together or apart depending on the amount of crust desired.
†A recipe for preparing frozen strawberry or raspberry sauce is given on page 181.

CREAM TAPIOCA

Yield: 50 servings
Size of serving: ½ cup

6 quarts milk
14 ounces (2½ cups) tapioca, instant

1. Scald the milk in the top of a double boiler; add the tapioca and cook until the tapioca is clear, stirring occasionally.

3 cups sugar
1 cup (about 12) egg yolks, slightly beaten

2. Combine the sugar and egg yolks; add a little of the hot milk and stir; add to the hot milk-tapioca mixture and cook all for from 5 to 10 minutes until slightly thickened, stirring only occasionally. Remove the mixture from the heat.

¼ cup butter or fortified margarine, if desired
¾ teaspoon salt
1½ tablespoons vanilla

3. Add the butter, salt, and vanilla.

1½ cups (about 12) egg whites, stiffly beaten

4. Fold in the beaten egg whites.*

Serve with:

2 cups jelly or jam, 2 quarts fruit sauce, or sliced fresh or canned fruit

*Egg whites may be used as a meringue; beat them until stiff but not dry; add 1½ cups of sugar and spread meringue over the cold pudding. Bake at 425° F. for about 5 minutes until browned.

Variation

Peppermint-stick candy tapioca: Use only 1½ cups of sugar and when the pudding is partially cooled, fold in 1½ pounds of crushed peppermint-stick candy. Serve cold with a whipped cream garnish sprinkled with crushed peppermint-stick candy or with chocolate sauce.

UPSIDE-DOWN CAKE

Yield: 60 servings   Size of serving: 2½ x 3 inches

Cake

13 ounces (2 cups) vegetable fat

2 pounds, 2 ounces (4½ cups) sugar

12 eggs

1. Cream the fat; add the sugar, gradually creaming together until well blended. Add the eggs and beat them thoroughly.

2 pounds, 4 ounces (9 cups) flour, all-purpose

1¾ ounces (¼ cup) baking powder

1 teaspoon salt

3 cups milk

2. Sift the dry ingredients together; add them alternately to the sugar-fat mixture with the milk. Beat the mixture until smooth.

Glaze

¾ cup butter *or* fortified margarine

2 pounds (4½ cups) sugar, brown, packed

2 cups fruit juice

1. Cook the butter, sugar, and fruit juice until slightly sirupy. Divide this mixture into the baking pans. Arrange any of the following fruits over the mixture. Carefully pour the batter over the juice. Bake it at 350° F. Cover trays with waxed paper and turn the cakes out up-side-down, and cut. Serve them with a fruit sauce or sweetened whipped cream.

Fruits

Apricot and prune

¾ pound (60 halves) apricots, dried

1½ pounds (60) prunes, dried

1. Wash, soak, cook, and drain the apricots and prunes. Arrange them in the pans so that each cut will have an apricot and a prune.

Mincemeat

4 pounds (2 quarts) mincemeat

3 cups apples, chopped

1. Mix the mincemeat and apples; spread the mixture over the glaze.

Pineapple

60 half pieces pineapple rings

60 halves maraschino cherries

1. Arrange the pineapple rings over the glaze so that each cut will have half a ring; place a cherry in the hole of each ring.

Fresh cranberry

3 quarts raw cranberries

1. Spread the cranberries over the glaze.

Cherry

3 quarts frozen cherries, drained

1. Spread the cherries over the glaze.

Rhubarb

8 quarts rhubarb, diced

1. Spread the rhubarb over the glaze.

DESSERT SAUCES

BUTTERSCOTCH SAUCE

Yield: 2 quarts

Size of serving: 2 tablespoons

9 cups (4 pounds) sugar, brown, packed
5⅓ cups corn sirup
2⅔ cups butter *or* fortified margarine

1. Boil the sugar, corn sirup, and butter together to 230° F. (hard-ball stage).

½ teaspoon (scant) soda

2. Add the soda; remove the mixture from the heat.

5⅓ cups top milk or evaporated milk

3. Stir in the milk when the mixture has partially cooled.

CHOCOLATE ICE CREAM SAUCE

Yield: 2 quarts

Size of serving: 2 tablespoons

2 cups (14 ounces) sugar, brown, packed
2 cups sugar, white
2 cups corn sirup
2½ cups top milk or evaporated milk
2 cups cocoa
⅛ teaspoon soda
⅛ teaspoon salt
1 teaspoon vanilla

1. Combine all the ingredients; boil the mixture for a few minutes. Serve the sauce slightly warm but not hot.

CUSTARD SAUCE

See recipe, page 200.

FRUIT SAUCE

Yield: From 4½ to 5 quarts

Size of serving: ⅓ cup

4 quarts fruit juice

1. Boil the fruit juice.

2 cups sugar*
1 cup cornstarch

2. Mix the sugar and the cornstarch. Add these to the boiling fruit juice and cook the mixture until thickened and clear, stirring constantly with a wire whip. Remove the mixture from the heat.

½ cup lemon juice
¾ cup butter *or* fortified margarine
1 quart fruit, sliced or in chunks

3. Add the lemon juice, butter, and fruit to the mixture. Serve the sauce hot or cold.

*If fruit juices contain added sugar, omit or reduce the amount of sugar.

FROZEN FRUIT SAUCE

See recipe, page 181.

MARSHMALLOW SAUCE

Yield: 2½ quarts   Size of serving: 2½ tablespoons

1 quart (2 pounds) sugar, white 2 cups water	1. Boil the sugar and the water together to make a thin sirup (228° F.).
1 pound (60) marshmallows, quartered	2. Add the marshmallows to the sirup.
8 (1 cup) egg whites 1 tablespoon vanilla or other flavoring	3. Beat the egg whites until stiff and slowly add the sirup to them while continuing to beat. Add the flavoring.

DESSERT GARNISHES

Whipped cream may be put on with a spoon, or a pastry tube may be used for making rosettes; whip 1 pint of heavy cream and add from 3 to 4 tablespoons of confectioners' sugar for 50 servings of 1 tablespoon each, or for from 50 to 60 medium rosettes. Crushed fruit; crushed candy including peppermint stick, candied ginger, chopped nuts may be sprinkled over the whipped cream garnish.

Light or coffee cream or top milk may be used instead of whipped cream, and is especially good for desserts that have a dry texture. From 1 to 2 tablespoons per serving requires from 1¼ to 2½ quarts for 50 desserts.

Fresh fruit, as sliced bananas or peaches, sectioned oranges, whole or crushed berries, and frozen fruits that contain sugar ready for use, also fruit sauces as pineapple, cherry, berry, all add flavor and color to bland puddings. Allow approximately 2 quarts for 50 garnishes of 2 tablespoons each.

Soft custard sauce is a good addition for fruit puddings. Allow 2 quarts for 50 garnishes of 2 tablespoons each. (Recipe page 200).

Nuts, macaroon crumbs, dried-cookie crumbs, graham-cracker crumbs, and tasted coconut are garnishes that are crunchy. Use ½ teaspoon for each garnish; from 1 to 1½ cups are required for 50 servings.

Jelly, marmalade, and other preserves, a scant teaspoon for each serving, may be placed on top of each dessert; allow 2 cups for 50 servings.

Cinnamon candies, chocolate or other colored sprinkles, colored sugar crystals, crushed hard candy, grated or shredded, sweet or bitter chocolate add color. Allow from 1 to 1½ cups for 50 garnishes of ½ teaspoon each.

Marshmallow halves placed over baked puddings toward the end of the baking period and browned produce a meringue-like topping. Use 45 (¾ pound) marshmallows cut in halves for 50 servings.

BEVERAGES

COFFEE

Coffee should be freshly roasted, and ground to the correct fineness. Blends are varied to suit preferences; special blends for large-quantity service in which coffee must be held for some time may be purchased from wholesalers. Coffee made by the drip method is most satisfactory for production in quantity.

Coffee-making Equipment

Dripolator urn

FIGURE 35.   AN EASY-TO-USE
COFFEE MAKER

This 50-cup coffee maker is operated like a home-size drip coffee pot. An electric unit built into the bottom of the pot keeps the coffee hot

The dripolator urn (figure 35) is operated in the same manner as is a drip-type home coffee pot. Water is heated to the boiling point and poured over the ground coffee in the top compartment. The lower compartment contains an electric or gas element to keep the coffee hot (not boiling). Urns of this type on the market at present have a 2-gallon capacity which serves 48 cups. If a larger service is needed, two urns may be used to advantage.

Stock pot with draw-off faucet for drip or brewed coffee

For the drip method, ground coffee is placed in a coffee bag held in place over the top of the pot by a ring in the top of the bag. Boiling water is poured over the coffee, or ground coffee may be placed in the cheesecloth bags according to the directions given on page 217. The brew is kept hot (not boiling). The draw-off faucet is convenient for serving the coffee.

Coffee utensils should be used only for coffee. To keep the flavor of the coffee uncontaminated, the pot must be washed, dried, and aired well after each use, and kept absolutely free from stains and sediment. Coffee bags should be washed in clear cold water; soap or soap powder affects the flavor of coffee. If the bag is used daily, it may stand in clear cold water when not in use.

Directions for Making Coffee

The ground coffee must be carefully measured; in large-quantity preparation, weighing is most accurate. Water should be freshly drawn from the cold-water tap or freshly pumped; it, too, should be measured accurately and should be boiling when poured over the coffee.

Coffee made in quantity, tastes best if allowed to stand from 15 to 20 minutes to mellow. It should be held just below the boiling point. As soon as the flavor becomes undesirable, a fresh amount should be made. Coffee allowed to cool and then reheated has a stale flavor.

Proportions vary with the blend of coffee and the strength desired. Ordinarily, 1 pound of coffee and 2½ gallons of boiling water will give 50 cups.

For drip coffee made in a drip urn or stock pot

1. Place the coffee (drip grind) in a basket or a bag.
2. Pour the boiling water over it slowly. When all the water has been poured over, pour through again half the brew to give a little more strength and a fuller flavor; establish a repouring procedure suited to the kind and grind of coffee, to the equipment used, and to the strength desired.
3. Remove the grounds as soon as the water has dripped through.

For brewed coffee made in a large coffee pot, kettle, or stock pot

1. Mix the coarsely ground coffee with egg and shell (one egg for 1 pound of coffee); place the mixture in muslin or cheesecloth bags and tie them loosely enough to allow for the swelling of the coffee grounds.
2. Place the bags into the boiling water and cover the utensil; regulate the heat so that the coffee will be just below the boiling point and will simmer until the desired strength is obtained.
3. Remove the bags, cover the coffee, and keep it hot for serving.

Iced coffee

For iced coffee, use 1 pound of coffee to 1½ gallons of boiling water. Make the coffee according to one of the methods given and pour it over clean, chopped ice.

Instant coffee

For 50 cups of coffee use 2½ gallons of boiling water and 2½ cups of instant coffee. Dissolve the powdered coffee in a small amount of the boiling water and add to the remaining hot water. Keep hot just below the boiling point.

Cream for Coffee

Cream for coffee should be 20 per cent (light) cream. It may be more economical, however, to purchase heavy cream and milk and mix them in equal proportions than to buy light cream. Evaporated milk and top milk, combined in equal proportions, give a satisfactory product which is considerably cheaper than cream. A mixture of evaporated milk and homogenized milk gives a still richer product.

TEA

Tea in individual bags is not expensive, is easy to make, and gives a good product. It may be purchased in cartons of 100 or 500 bags; larger bags for making iced tea in as large quantities as 1 or 2 gallons may be purchased. Tea bags are easily made by placing the desired amount of tea in cheesecloth bags and tying them loosely to allow for the expansion of the tea leaves. Water for making tea should be actively boiling at the time it is poured over the tea.

For iced tea, the following proportions yield 50 large glasses:

3 ounces loose tea in cheesecloth bags *or* 3 1-ounce tea bags 1 gallon water, boiling 1½ gallons water, cold

Pour the boiling water over the tea; let the mixture stand for 10 minutes; remove the tea and add the cold water. Serve the tea over ⅓ glass of chopped ice.

Tea that is very strong becomes cloudy when ice is added; adding cold water makes the tea clear again.

FRUIT JUICE AND PUNCH

Fruit juices, in cans, may be purchased economically by the case; No. 10 cans cost less proportionately than do the smaller ones. Oranges or lemons purchased by the crate from a wholesaler cost less if the amount of juice needed warrants purchasing in such large quantities (1 crate of 216 oranges yields from 17 to 20 quarts of juice). Fruit juices served at the beginning of the meal should be served in 4- or 5-ounce glasses (½ cup) and should be chilled. Keeping the juice in a refrigerator long enough to chill it thoroughly is preferable to adding ice and thus diluting the product.

Bases in powder form or prepared gelatin powders may be used to make punch; some fresh-fruit juices should be added to obtain a satisfactory flavor. One gallon of weak tea may be used as a base for 5 gallons of punch. Punch should be made strong so that melting ice will not dilute it to the point of tasting flat.

A sugar sirup for sweetening punch is made by dissolving 2 quarts of sugar in 1 quart of water, heating to the boiling point, and cooling.

RECIPES FOR BEVERAGES MADE WITH MILK

BANANA MILK SHAKE

Yield: 2½ gallons (50 servings)

Size of serving: ¾ measuring cup (6 ounces)

28 (3½ quarts pulp) bananas, ripe
7 quarts milk*
3½ teaspoons salt
Sugar, if desired

1. Force the bananas through a sieve or mash them in an electric mixer. Add the milk and the salt and beat the mixture thoroughly. Add sugar if desired. Chill the mixture.

*Dry milk solids may be used in place of fresh milk; use 7 cups of the dry milk solids and 7 quarts of water.

COCOA

Yield: 2½ gallons (50 servings)

Size of serving: ¾ measuring cup (6 ounces)

2 cups cocoa
2 to 3 cups sugar
½ teaspoon salt
2 quarts hot water

1. Combine the cocoa, sugar, and salt. Mix with the hot water and boil the mixture for from 5 to 10 minutes.

8 quarts milk*
1 to 2 teaspoons vanilla, if desired

2. Heat the milk and cocoa sirup† in a double boiler. Beat it with a wire whip to prevent formation of a scum. Add the vanilla.

*In place of the fresh whole milk, the following may be used:
   6 quarts of whole milk and 2 quarts of water *or*
   6 quarts of skimmilk and 2 quarts of evaporated milk *or*
   8 cups (32 to 34 ounces) of dry milk solids and 7½ quarts of water.
†A sirup of the cocoa, sugar, salt, and water for use in making hot cocoa or a cold drink may be made up ahead and used as needed.

CAFÉ AU LAIT

(Coffee with hot milk)

Yield: 2½ gallons (50 servings)

Size of serving: ¾ measuring cup (6 ounces)

1 to 1½ pounds coffee
1½ gallons (6 quarts) boiling water
1¼ gallons (5 quarts) milk, hot

1. Make the coffee.

2. Combine the hot coffee and hot milk just before serving.

RECIPES FOR OTHER BEVERAGES

CHRISTMAS WASSAIL

Yield: 2 gallons (from 60 to 65 servings)

Size of serving: ½ cup (4 ounces)

4¼ cups sugar
2 quarts water
1 tablespoon cloves, whole

1. Combine the sugar and water and boil the mixture for 10 minutes. Add the cloves, cinnamon, and ginger; cover, and let the mixture

6 sticks cinnamon

3 tablespoons candied ginger, chopped

2 quarts orange juice

2 cups lemon juice

1 gallon cider

stand in a warm place for 1 hour. Strain the mixture.

2. Add the orange and lemon juice and cider; bring the drink to the boiling point and serve at once.

FRUIT PUNCH*

Yield: 3½ gallons (55 servings)　　Size of serving: 1 measuring cup (8 ounces)

4 quarts orange juice (20 to 30 oranges)

2 quarts lemon juice (30 to 35 lemons)

1 quart pineapple juice

1 quart raspberry, strawberry, or cranberry juice

1½ quarts tea infusion (6 tablespoons tea and 7 cups boiling water)

1. Combine the juices with the tea infusion.

5 cups sugar†

1⅓ cups water

2. Combine the sugar and the water and boil for 5 minutes.

4 quarts gingerale

Cracked ice

3. Add the gingerale and ice just before serving.

*Lime ice may be added to the punch just before it is served.
†Add sugar according to the fruit juices used, sweetening to taste.

FRUIT PUNCH WITH A PREPARED BASE

Yield. 3½ gallons (55 servings)　　Size of serving: 1 measuring cup (8 ounces)

2 gallons punch base

1. Make according to the directions on the package.

2 quarts tea infusion (½ cup tea and 9 cups boiling water)

2 quarts grapefruit or pineapple juice

1 cup lemon juice (4 lemons)

Sugar sirup* to sweeten

Cracked ice

2. Add the tea infusion, fruit juices, sugar sirup, and cracked ice to the punch base.

*The amount of sugar sirup needed will vary with the sweetness of the base.

NOTE: One quart of diced fruit improves this punch.

GRAPE JUICE PUNCH

Yield: 3½ gallons　　Size of serving: 1 measuring cup (8 ounces)

6 quarts grape juice

5 quarts cold water

1 quart lemon juice

Sugar or sugar sirup to sweeten

3 quarts crushed ice

1. Mix together all the ingredients, adding the crushed ice a short time before serving.

LIME-ICE GINGERALE PUNCH

Yield: 1 gallon (40 punch cups) Size of serving: 1 punch cup

2 quarts lime ice
2 quarts gingerale
⅔ cup lemon juice

1. Refrigerate all ingredients.

2. Place scoops of lime ice into punch bowl. Add the lemon juice. Pour the gingerale over this.

RHUBARB PUNCH

Yield: 3 gallons Size of serving: 1 measuring cup (8 ounces)

10 pounds (10 quarts) fresh rhubarb, diced
5 quarts water
5 pounds sugar (approximately)
5 teaspoons grated orange and lemon rind
2½ cups orange juice
1¼ cups lemon juice
5 quarts crushed ice

1. Simmer the rhubarb in the water and strain. There should be 6 quarts of juice.

2. Add the sugar to the warm juice. Chill the juice.

3. Add the grated rind, orange and lemon juice.

4. Add the crushed ice a short time before serving.

NOTE: One quart of gingerale may be added to this base.

Strawberry, raspberry, pineapple or cherry juice may be combined with rhubarb juice for making punch.

SPICED TEA

Yield: 7½ quarts (60 servings) Size of serving: ½ cup (4 ounces)

1½ ounces (½ cup) tea
1½ gallons boiling water
1 teaspoon cloves, ground
2¼ teaspoons cinnamon, ground
¾ cup lemon juice (3 lemons)
3 cups orange juice (6 oranges)
3 cups grape juice
3¼ cups sugar

1. Pour the boiling water onto the tea and let it stand for 10 minutes. Strain out the tea leaves.

2. Add the spices, fruit juices, and sugar to the tea. Serve the tea hot.

SPICED CIDER OR GRAPE JUICE

Yield: 2 gallons (from 60 to 65 servings) Size of serving: ½ cup (4 ounces)

1⅛ ounces (16 2-inch pieces) cinnamon sticks
2 tablespoons cloves, whole
2 tablespoons allspice, whole
1 teaspoon mace
1 teaspoon salt
Few grains cayenne pepper
1½ quarts (2¾ pounds) sugar, brown, packed
2 gallons cider or grape juice

1. Tie the spices loosely in a cheesecloth bag; add them and the mace, salt, cayenne, and sugar to the cider or grape juice. Heat slowly to the boiling point and simmer for 20 minutes. Remove the spice bag, and serve the drink hot.

HOT SPICED TOMATO JUICE

Yield: 2 gallons (60 to 65 servings)

Size of serving: ½ cup (4 ounces)

2 gallons tomato juice

4 bay leaves

4 sticks cinnamon

2 teaspoons cloves, whole

2 teaspoons peppercorns

⅓ cup sugar

2 teaspoons salt

1. Heat the tomato juice.

2. Tie the spices in a cheesecloth bag and heat them with the tomato juice.

3. Add the sugar and salt and simmer the juice for 10 minutes. Remove the spice bag. Serve hot.

REFERENCES

BOOKS

FOOD FOR FIFTY. S. F. Fowler and B. B. West. John Wiley and Sons, Inc., New York, N. Y. 1950.

FOOD SERVICE FOR RESTAURANT, COFFEE SHOP, HOTEL, CAFETERIA, HOME. Helen Livingstone. McKnight and McKnight Publishing Co., Bloomington, Ill. 1950.

FOOD SERVICE IN INSTITUTIONS. Bessie B. West and LeVelle Wood. John Wiley and Sons, Inc., New York, N. Y. 1945.

FOOD PREPARATION BOOK SET, LITTLE GOLD BUSINESS BOOKS. The Dahl Publishing Co., Haviland Road, Stamford, Conn.

HANDBOOK OF FOOD PREPARATION. American Home Economics Association, 700 Victor Building, Washington, D. C. 1950.

MANUAL FOR SCHOOL AND INSTITUTIONAL LUNCHROOMS. Ohio Dietetic Association, 1001 Huron Road, Cleveland, O. 1946.

NAVY COOK BOOK. United States Superintendent of Documents, Government Printing Office, Washington, D. C. 1944.

PUBLIC HEALTH ENGINEERING. VOLUME II. Earle B. Phelps with Walter D. Tiedeman. (Illustrates those principles of sanitation which, applied to the production, handling and distribution of food, have direct public health significance.) John Wiley and Sons Inc., New York, N. Y. 1950.

QUANTITY COOKERY. Lenore Richards and Nola Treat. Little, Brown, and Co., Boston, Mass. 1950.

QUANTITY RECIPE FILE. Lenore M. Sullivan. Collegiate Press, Inc., Ames, Iowa, 1944.

QUANTITY RECIPES FOR QUALITY FOODS. E. Evelyn Smith. Burgess Publishing Co., Minneapolis, Minn. 1950.

RECIPES AT MODERATE COST FOR SCHOOL, INSTITUTION AND COMMERCIAL FOOD SERVICE. Constance C. Hart. F. S. Crofts and Co., New York, N. Y. 1938.

SCHOOL MEALS. School Food Service Association. Available from Constance C. Hart, Board of Education, Rochester, N. Y. 1949.

BULLETINS

CAMP KITCHEN MANAGEMENT. Dorothy M. Proud. Department of Institution Management, New York State College of Home Economics, Cornell University, Ithaca, N. Y. 1948.

COMMUNITY MEALS. Katharine W. Harris and Marion A. Wood. Cornell Bulletin for Homemakers 743. New York State College of Home Economics, Cornell University. Ithaca, N. Y. 1948.

GUIDE TO SAFE FOOD SERVICE. John Andrews and Frances Champion. United States Public Health Service. Government Printing Office, Washington, D. C. 1946.

HOW TO PREPARE AND COOK POULTRY. Lillian Shaben and L. M. Hurd. Cornell Extension Bulletin 785, Cornell University, Ithaca, N. Y. 1950.

MEALS FOR PAYING GUESTS. Dorothy M. Proud. Cornell Extension Bulletin 783, Cornell University, Ithaca, N. Y. 1950.

ORDINANCE AND CODE REGULATING EATING AND DRINKING ESTABLISHMENTS. Public Health Bulletin No. 280. Government Printing Office, Washington, D. C. 1943.

PARTY SERVICE. Myrtle H. Ericson, Cornell Extension Bulletin 773, Cornell University, Ithaca, N. Y. 1949.

PRESERVING FOODS BY FREEZING. D. L. Mackintosh, G. E. Vail, G. A. Filinger. Circular 249. Agricultural Experiment Station, Kansas State College of Agriculture and Applied Science, Manhattan, Kan. 1949.

PURCHASING FOOD FOR FIFTY. Marion W. Crosby and Katharine W. Harris. Cornell Extension Bulletin 803, Cornell University, Ithaca, N. Y. 1950.

QUANTITY RECIPES TO EXTEND MEAT AND POULTRY. Marion A. Wood. Department of Institution Management, New York State College of Home Economics, Cornell University, Ithaca, N. Y. 1947.

SCHOOL LUNCH PUBLICATIONS. Production and Marketing Administration, United States Departement of Agriculture, Washington 25, D. C.
ESTIMATING THE COST OF FOOD FOR A SCHOOL LUNCH
QUANTITIES OF FOOD FOR SERVING SCHOOL LUNCH
RECIPES FOR QUANTITY SERVICE
SCHOOL LUNCH RECIPES FOR 25 AND 50
SCHOOL LUNCH RECIPES FOR 100
SCHOOL LUNCH RECIPES USING NONFAT DRY MILK
SCHOOL LUNCH RECIPES COOKING WITH DRIED WHOLE EGGS
SCHOOL LUNCH RECIPES USING FISH
SCHOOL LUNCH RECIPES USING TURKEY
SCHOOL LUNCH RECIPES USING DRIED FRUIT
SCHOOL LUNCH RECIPES USING TOMATO PASTE
SCHOOL LUNCH RECIPES USING POTATOES
SCHOOL LUNCH RECIPES USING HONEY
SCHOOL LUNCH RECIPES FOR SANDWICH FILLINGS
STORAGE FOR SCHOOL LUNCH FOOD AND SUPPLIES

SOME FACTS ABOUT BAKING. Mildred Dunn and Elizabeth Vollmer. Cornell 4-H Club Bulletin 91, Cornell University, Ithaca, N. Y. 1950.

TOOLS FOR FOOD PREPARATION AND DISHWASHING. Home and Garden Bulletin 3. United States Department of Agriculture, Washington 25, D. C. 1951.

TRADE ASSOCIATION BOOKLETS*

American Can Company, 230 Park Avenue, New York, N. Y.
SCHOOL LUNCH RECIPE CARDS

American Dry Milk Institute Inc., Chicago, Ill.
QUANTITY RECIPES USING NON-FAT DRY MILK SOLIDS

American Institute of Baking, Chicago, Ill.
QUANTITY RECIPES
RECIPE CARDS

California Fig Institute, Fresno, Calif.
QUANTITY RECIPES USING DRIED FIGS

Evaporated Milk Association, Chicago, Ill.
SCHOOL LUNCH RECIPES

Good Housekeeping Institute, New York, N. Y.
SANDWICH MANUAL

National Canners Association, Home Economics Division, Washington, D. C.
CANNED FOOD RECIPES FOR SERVING FIFTY
CANNED FOOD TABLES (servings per unit for various canned foods in common can sizes)
SCHOOL LUNCH RECIPES

National Fisheries Institute, Washington, D. C.
FISH COOKERY FOR ONE HUNDRED

National Livestock and Meat Board, Chicago, Ill.
COOKING MEAT IN QUANTITY
ECONOMY MEAT RECIPES FOR QUANTITY SERVICE
SIXTY-TWO LARGE QUANTITY RECIPES

National Turkey Federation, Mount Morris, Ill.
TURKEY HANDBOOK

Poultry and Egg National Board, Chicago, Ill.
CARVING AND SERVING POULTRY MEAT
FRYING CHICKEN

Washington State Apple Commission, Wenatches, Wash.
QUANTITY RECIPE SERVICE

Wheat Flour Institute, Chicago, Ill.
Monthly pamphlet: INSTITUTE IDEAS
LARGE QUANTITY BREAD RECIPES

*Many commercial food concerns have quantity recipes for distribution.

APPENDIX

Average Portion Size and Cost
of Portion, 1951

Foods	Size of portion	Cost of portion

APPETIZERS

Fruit juice . . . . ½ cup (4 ounces) . . . . $.03 –.035
Fruit juice with sherbet . . . . ⅓ cup (2⅔ ounces) and . . . . .04 –.05
    No. 30 scoop sherbet
Fruit cup (fresh) . . . . ½ cup (4 ounces) 045–.07
Tomato juice . . . . ½ cup (4 ounces) . . . . .02 –.025

SOUPS

Clear soups . . . . ¾ cup (6 ounces) 025–.03
Cream of tomato . . . . ¾ cup (6 ounces) . . . . .03 –.035
Cream of vegetable soups . . . . ¾ cup (6 ounces) 035–.05
Fish chowders . . . . ¾ cup (6 ounces) 055–.065
Vegetable soup . . . . ¾ cup (6 ounces) 035–.045

ENTREES

Poultry

Roast turkey (clear meat) . . . . 2¼–2½ ounces . . . . .28 –.30
Fried chicken . . . . 7–8 ounces . . . . .30 –.35
Chicken and vegetable pie . . . . ⅔ cup (5–6 ounces) . . . . .22 –.25
  (with biscuit)
Turkey and vegetable pie . . . . ⅔ cup (5–6 ounces) . . . . .18 –.22
Turkey a la king . . . . ⅔ cup (5–6 ounces) . . . . .25 –.28

Roasts

Ribs of beef . . . . 4–5 ounces . . . . .40 –.50
Pot roast of beef . . . . 3–3½ ounces . . . . .25 –.30
Roast veal (boneless shoulder) . . . . 3–3½ ounces . . . . .20 –.25
Roast pork (fresh ham) . . . . 3–3½ ounces . . . . .25 –.28
Roast loin of pork . . . . 3½–4 ounces . . . . .27 –.30
Baked ham . . . . 3–3½ ounces . . . . .22 –.28
Roast lamb . . . . 3–3½ ounces . . . . .30 –.35

Steaks and Chops

Baked round steak (beef) . . . . 4–4½ ounces . . . . .28 –.30
Breaded veal cutlet . . . . 4–4½ ounces . . . . .25 –.30
Pork chops . . . . 4–5 ounces . . . . .15 –.20
Ham steak . . . . 3½–4 ounces . . . . .22 –.25
Beef liver . . . . 3½–4 ounces . . . . .15 –.17
Lamb chops, shoulder . . . . 4½–5 ounces . . . . .20 –.25

Fish

Fillet (cod, haddock, mackerel, perch) . 4½–5 ounces . . . . .12 –.15
Salmon steak (halibut, swordfish) . . . . . 4½–5 ounces . . . . .23 –.25
Salmon loaf (pink) . . . . 4–5 ounces . . . . .12 –.14

Foods	Size of portion	Cost of portion

(Fish cont.)

Escalloped tunafish, mushrooms, and
noodles......................¾ cup (6–7 ounces).........$.15 −.18
Escalloped oysters................⅔ cup (5–6 ounces)..........18 −.22
Creole shrimp or shrimp Newburg...⅔ cup (5–6 ounces)..........20 −.25

Meat Extended

Meat and vegetable stews or pies......¾ cup (6–7 ounces)..........15 −.20
Meat loaf (ham, beef, veal)..........4½–5 ounces.................14 −.18
Meat patties (beef, veal, lamb).......3 ounces (raw meat)..........15 −.20
Hamburger on bun................2 ounces (raw meat)..........09 −.12
Spaghetti with meat balls...........⅔ cup (5–6 ounces) and 2 balls...15 −.18
Spaghetti with meat sauce...........¾ cup (6–7 ounces)...........135–.15
Chili con carne...................⅔ cup (5–6 ounces)...........105–.12
Chop suey on Chinese noodles.......⅔ cup (5–6 ounces)...........08 −.12
Escalloped potato and chipped beef....¾ cup (6–7 ounces)...........08 −.10

Meat Alternates

Baked omelet (souffle)..............2½ inches x 2½ inches........06 −.08
Cheese fondue....................2½ inches x 2½ inches........095–.11
Escalloped eggs and vegetables.......⅔ cup (5–6 ounces)..........10 −.12
Macaroni and cheese..............¾ cup (6–7 ounces)..........06 −.08
Welsh rabbit.....................½ cup (4½–5 ounces)........075–.09
Spanish rice with bacon strip........¾ cup (6–7 ounces)..........075–.09
Spaghetti with tomato-cheese sauce...¾ cup (6–7 ounces)..........06 −.08
Baked beans.....................¾ cup (6–7 ounces)..........045–.07

VEGETABLES

Asparagus, canned or frozen, buttered..½ cup (3–3½ ounces)........075–.10
Beets, fresh, buttered...............½ cup (3–3½ ounces)..........02 −.03
Broccoli, frozen, buttered..........3–3½ ounces.................055–.07
Brussels sprouts, frozen, buttered......3–3½ ounces.................075–.09
Cabbage, fresh, buttered............½ cup (2½–3 ounces)........015–.03
Carrots, fresh, buttered.............½ cup (2½–3 ounces)........02 −.03
Cauliflower, fresh, buttered..........3–3½ ounces.................045–.07
Corn, canned or frozen, buttered.....½ cup (2½–3 ounces)........045–.06
Green beans, canned or frozen, buttered.½ cup (2½–3 ounces)..........04 −.055
Lima beans, frozen, buttered.........½ cup (3–3½ ounces)..........055–.07
Onions, fresh, buttered.............3–3½ ounces.................025–.03
Peas, canned or frozen, buttered......½ cup (2½–3 ounces)........04 −.055
Potatoes
   Mashed......................4–4½ ounces (No. 10 scoop)....02 −.025
   Buttered.....................4½–5 ounces.................025–.03
   Escalloped....................4½–5 ounces.................045–.05
Spinach, fresh, buttered............½ cup (2½–3 ounces)........025–.05
Spinach, frozen, buttered...........½ cup (3½–4 ounces)........045–.05
Squash, summer, buttered...........½ cup (3–3½ ounces)........025–.04
Squash, winter, baked.............4–5 ounces.................03 −.045
Squash, winter, frozen.............3½–4 ounces (No. 12 scoop)....05 −.06
Tomatoes, stewed.................½ cup (3½–4 ounces)........04 −.055

SALADS

Foods	Size of portion	Cost of portion
Cabbage slaw	½ cup	$.02 –.03
Fresh fruit	½ cup	.06 –.08
Fruit gelatin	⅔ cup	.065–.08
Cottage cheese with canned fruit	No. 16 scoop and 3 pieces fruit	.07 –.10
Tossed vegetable	½ cup	.035–.05
Head lettuce with dressing	⅙ head	.03 –.05
Waldorf (apple)	½ cup	.03 –.05
Potato, macaroni or spaghetti	½ cup	.045–.05
Tunafish, salmon	⅓ cup	.125–.15
Deviled egg	1½ eggs	.07 –.09

SANDWICHES

Foods	Size of portion	Cost of portion
Sliced meat	1½ ounces	.08 –.12
Minced meat	2 ounces (No. 24 scoop)	.075–.10
Egg salad	2 ounces (No. 24 scoop)	.075–.10
Tunafish salad	2 ounces (No. 24 scoop)	.12 –.15
Sliced cheese	1 ounce	.035–.055
Minced chicken	2 ounces (No. 24 scoop)	.18 –.22

HOT BREADS

Foods	Size of portion	Cost of portion
Yeast rolls, plain	1½ ounces	.01 –.015
Baking powder biscuits	2 ounces	.015–.02
Plain muffins	No. 20 scoop	.02 –.025
Steamed brown bread	3 ounces	.01 –.015

CAKES

Foods	Size of portion	Cost of portion
Layer cake with frosting	16 cuts per 10 inch, 3 layer cake	.03 –.04
Angel food with butter cream frosting	12 cuts per cake	.02 –.03

PIES

Foods	Size of portion	Cost of portion
Canned fruit	8 cuts per 10 inch pie	.05 –.07
Frozen fruit (2 crusts)	8 cuts per 10 inch pie	.06 –.09
Apple	8 cuts per 10 inch pie	.035–.05
Cream pie with meringue	8 cuts per 10 inch pie	.055–.07
Chiffon pie with whipped cream	8 cuts per 10 inch pie	.075–.10
Pumpkin	8 cuts per 10 inch pie	.045–.06

OTHER DESSERTS

Foods	Size of portion	Cost of portion
Canned fruit (peaches, apricots, pineapple)	½ cup (4 ounces)	.05 –.09
Fruited gelatin with whipped cream	½ cup (4 ounces)	.055–.07
Cream pudding (chocolate, vanilla, butterscotch)	½ cup (4 ounces)	.025–.035
Baked custard	½ cup	.03 –.045
Upside down cake with whipped cream	3 inches x 3 inches	.045–.06
Frozen fruit cobbler (blueberry, cherry, etc.)	3 inches x 3 inches	.065–.075
Canned fruit cobbler (peaches, apples, etc.)	3 inches x 3 inches	.055–.065
Apple betty (apple crisp)	½ cup (4 ounces)	.03 –.04
Whipped cream garnish	1 teaspoon, rounded	.015–.02

INDEX*

*Numbers in italics indicate illustrations.

229

Published by the New York State College of Home Economics at Cornell
University, Ithaca, New York. L. R. Simons, Director of Extension.
This bulletin is published and distributed in furtherance of the purposes
provided for in the Acts of Congress of May 8 and June 30, 1914.